WRITING ON THE WALL

This book is due for return on or before the last date shown below.

WRITING ON THE WALL
SELECTED ESSAYS

PATRICIA DUNCKER

Pandora
LONDON, CHICAGO, SYDNEY

For S. J. D.

First published in 2002 by
Pandora Press
an imprint of
Rivers Oram Publishers Limited
144 Hemingford Road, London N1 1DE

Copyright © 2002 Patricia Duncker

Distributed in the United States of America by
The Independent Publishers' Group
814 North Franklin Street
Chicago, Illinois 60610

Set in Sabon by N-J Design,
and printed and bound in Great Britain by
TJ International Ltd, Padstow, Cornwall, UK

British Library Cataloguing in Publication Data
A catalogue record for this book is available from the British Library

ISBN 0 86358 431 4 (cloth)
ISBN 0 86358 432 2 (paperback)

CONTENTS

ACKNOWLEDGEMENTS   vii

KILLING DADDY   ix

I   CHALLENGING THE CLASSICS

   1. READING GENESIS   3

   2. THE SUGGESTIVE SPECTACLE   24
      QUEER PASSIONS IN CHARLOTTE BRONTË'S
      VILLETTE AND MURIEL SPARK'S *THE PRIME
      OF MISS JEAN BRODIE*

   3. FICTIONS AND HISTORIES   36
      ON HELLA HAASSE'S *EEN NIEUWER
      TESTAMENT* AND TOLSTOY'S *WAR AND
      PEACE*

   4. HOFFMANN'S UNCANNY   52
      REPLICANT
      FREUD, *FRANKENSTEIN* AND *THE SANDMAN*

II SEXUALITY AND CONTEMPORARY
    WOMEN'S WRITING

   5. REIMAGINING THE FAIRY TALES   67
      ANGELA CARTER'S BLOODY CHAMBERS

6. QUEER GOTHIC   84
   ANGELA CARTER AND THE LOST
   NARRATIVES OF SEXUAL SUBVERSION

7. HETEROSEXUALITY: FICTIONAL   101
   AGENDAS
   MARGARET ATWOOD *THE EDIBLE WOMAN*
   AND *LIFE BEFORE MAN* AND JENNY DISKI
   NOTHING NATURAL

8. 'THE LONG LINE OF BLOOD/AND   119
   FAMILY TIES'
   GRACE NICHOLS AND THE LONG-
   MEMORIED WOMEN

III MAKING WRITING

9. POST GENDER   143
   JURASSIC FEMINISM MEETS QUEER
   POLITICS

10. ON NARRATIVE STRUCTURES IN   157
    CONTEMPORARY FICTION
    J.M. COETZEE *DISGRACE* AND PAULINE
    MELVILLE *THE VENTRILOQUIST'S TALE*

11. ON THE IMPOSSIBILITY OF   172
    MAKING WRITING
    MRS ARBUTHNOT, MRS LEWES AND
    MRS WOOLF

12. WRITING ON THE WALL   187

NOTES & REFERENCES   202

INDEX   218

ACKNOWLEDGEMENTS

I wish to thank Dr Peter Lambert and Dr Jenny Newman for their thoughtful comments on drafts of these essays and all my students, past and present, with whom I discussed many of the ideas developed here. I would also like to thank my teachers, who have influenced me in immeasurable ways, especially John Batstone, George Bird, Sita Narasimhan, Jean Gooder, Hilda Brown and Marilyn Butler. No one mentioned above can be held responsible for what follows, and all the errors in this book are entirely my own. Earlier versions of some chapters have appeared in the following publications:

'Reading Genesis', *What Lesbians Do in Books*, ed. Elaine Hobby and Chris White (Women's Press: London, 1991).

'The Suggestive Spectacle: Charlotte Brontë's *Villette* and Muriel Spark's *The Prime of Miss Jean Brodie*', ed. Martin McQuillan, *Theorising Muriel Spark: Gender, Race Deconstruction* (Palgrave, 2002).

An earlier draft of the Hella Haasse material in chapter 3 was translated into Dutch and published as 'Een ander land' in the special issue of *Surplus*, Jahrgang 10, no.6 (November/December 1996).

'Reimagining the Fairy Tales: Angela Carter's Bloody Chambers' was first published in *Literature and History*, vol.10, no.1 (Spring 1984), and subsequently republished in *Popular Fictions*, ed. Peter Humm, Paul Stigant and Peter Widdowson (London: Methuen, 1986) and the Gale Literary Criticism Series, *Short Story Criticism*, vol.13, ed. David Segal (Gale Research Inc, Detroit, Washington, DC, London, 1993).

'Queer Gothic: Angela Carter and the Lost Narratives of Sexual Subversion', *Critical Survey*: Special Issue 'Diverse Communities', ed. Sharon Monteith, vol.8, no.1 (Spring 1996), pp.58–68.

'Heterosexuality: Fictional Agendas' was first published in *Feminism and Psychology*: Special Issue: Heterosexuality, ed. Celia Kitzinger and Sue Wilkinson, vol.2, no.3 (October, 1992), and republished in *Heterosexuality: A Feminism and Psychology Reader* (Sage, 1993).

In 'The Long Line of Blood/And Family Ties', chapter 8, thanks to Time Warner Books for permission to publish extracts from the work of Grace Nichols.

'Post-Gender: Jurassic Feminism Meets Queer Politics', *Post-Theory: New Directions in Criticism,* ed. Martin McQuillan, Graeme Macdonald, Robin Purves and Stephen Thomson (Edinburgh University Press, 1999).

A brief part of chapter 10 has been published in my article 'On Narrative Structures', *The Creative Writing Coursebook,* ed. Paul Magrs and Julia Bell (London: Macmillan, 2001).

I first delivered a version of chapter 11 at 'The Impossible Conference', University of Kent, in April 1998. I would like to thank David Sorfa and his colleagues, who organised the event. Another version was published that year: 'The Impossibility of Making Writing: Mrs Arbuthnot, Mrs Lewes and Mrs Woolf', *Women: A Cultural Review*, vol.9, no.3 (Autumn 1998).

KILLING DADDY

Desperate interviewers often roll out the following stock question when they are scraping the barrel for something to say to a contemporary writer whose work they have hardly read or cannot understand. Who are the writers who have influenced you? When Paul Théroux was asked to produce his list he mentioned Chekhov, Somerset Maugham, Graham Greene and Edward Lear.[1] Usually the list is left to speak for itself and very rarely includes Shakespeare. No one ever bothers to plumb the significance of the list or to tease out its hidden links and meanings. Men almost invariably mention other men. These are their Fathers. These are the writers who are the prime focus for their anxiety of influence, the intellectual flood mark on the wall, the oedipal standard at which to aim and eventually surpass. This is why Shakespeare is never on the list.

Women writers, when asked the fatal question, may mention other women. But they too are more likely to mention men. It is a good idea to put yourself inside the great tradition of The Fathers. You gain authority, respectability and security. You also sound like a safe bet. And if you do mention another woman writer it had better be Virginia Woolf rather than Anaïs Nin or, worse still, Radclyffe Hall.[2]

I don't think that it is possible to ignore The Fathers, who are the architects and advocates of our literary patriarchy, or The Great Tradition of Misogyny in western literature. The Fathers and all their works have formed the backbone of my literary education as well as my daily bread as a woman reader. It is easy to perform a chameleon reading role. I don't always read as a woman. There does, however, come a moment when a woman writer has to position herself in relation to The Fathers. And this will usually be the moment when she starts to write.

Here is the authorial voice of Marilyn French in her barnstorming 1970s roar of female rage, *The Women's Room* (1977). This book is not well written, but it articulates the anger of a generation. She too offers her list of The Fathers.

> You think I hate men. I guess I do...after all, look at what we read. I read Schopenhauer and Nietzsche and Wittengstein and Freud and Erikson; I read de Montherlant and Joyce and Lawrence and sillier people like Miller and Mailer and Roth and Philip Wylie. I read the Bible and Greek myths...I read or read about, without much question, the Hindus and the Jews, Pythagoras and Aristotle, Seneca, Cato, St Paul, Luther, Sam Johnson, Rousseau, Swift...well, you understand. For years I didn't take it personally...But the truth is that I am sick unto death of four thousand years of males telling me how rotten my sex is.[3]

Becoming a feminist is about taking it personally. And about reading hate literature, not from a detached position of desexed neutrality, but from the position of someone that has been personally insulted and abused. I remain suspicious of women who have never taken The Fathers' words personally, because it usually means that they are doing rather well out of the patriarchy and have made their peace with the system. This can be done by collaboration and compromise or by heroically refusing the victim position and severing yourself from your inconvenient female body in a flurry of post-modern queer theory. But making peace with The Fathers does also mean that you will have no sense of solidarity with women who are poor or uneducated, or trapped within a culture that denies them the right to be human, women who are silenced and savaged, simply because they are women.

There is nothing heroic about passing by on the other side of the road.

So how does a woman writer, self-conscious of her dangerous

sex, deal with The Fathers? How do I read The Fathers? Here's my advice. Read them as you would eat a bony, but delicious fish. Filet the thing carefully down the spine. Scrape the flesh and bin the bones. And here is an example of how I do this.

One of the first texts I consciously identified as belonging to The Fathers was the dramatic trilogy by Aeschylus, the *Oresteia*. I fell in love with the savage logic of the plays. I was bewitched by the poetry. I learnt Ancient Greek in order to decipher the Choruses. The *Oresteia* is about Killing Daddy and all the consequences thereof. I'll recap the murder trail through the House of Atreus for anyone who has forgotten the plot. Here's the back story. Agamemnon murders his daughter Iphigenia in return for a fair wind of good omen. He then sets sail for Troy. He comes back ten years later having won the war, accompanied by Cassandra, that original voice of doom, who shares his chariot and, we are led to assume, his bed. The first play begins here. Agamemnon's wife, Clytemnestra, is waiting for him. She and her lover Aegisthus hack him to death in his bath. Electra, who is Daddy's Girl, and who somehow hasn't taken Iphegenia's fate to heart, mopes about, plotting. She summons her brother Orestes and incites him to murder Clytemnestra. Helpfully, the oracle of Apollo has also suggested that Orestes should avenge his father and murder his mother. He does this offstage, but then he sees the Furies.

The Furies are very interesting. They are the vindictive female energy unleashed by the spirits of murdered women. They want blood for blood. They are horrifying to look at and have inspired many women's theatre groups. They are the glitch in the rhythm of patriarchy.

The conclusion of the *Oresteia* is a courtroom drama. Orestes seeks refuge at the feet of Apollo and passes the buck back to the Gods who sent him forth on his murderous mission in the first place. You told me to avenge my father and murder my mother. You get me out of this. The Furies writhe and seethe in a corner. Apollo accepts responsibility and sets up a court. The case is heard by Athene. If anyone is wronged they must not seek personal vengeance but bring their case to the court. The Furies are given their own altar and told that if they shut up they will be honoured and respected.

Greek women did not act. No real women were present on stage. Their parts were played by men. So the women were excluded, silenced, then represented. The Fathers did the talking. But the plots of these plays are suggestive. Kill a woman's daughter and she will wait ten years for the chance to kill you. Women beware women. Especially those loyal to The Fathers. She is all too likely to be your own daughter. The family is not a safe place. And beware Apollo and Athene, the lawgivers, who will buy you off with the bribe of respectability and an altar in the household. The counterpoint to The Fathers, and father-right, is not the power of the Mother but the Furies.

Writing is always about arguing a case, however oblique the method or the metaphors. As a woman writer I am in the business of luring the Furies back out of their hutch and into the field. The Furies are in opposition to The Fathers. Yet, I am very sensible of the fact that it is The Fathers who have first given the Furies breath and life. Patriarchy is not monolithic, but contains its own fissures and contradictions. And it is within these gaps that I live, breathe, write. Were anyone to ask me: who are the writers who have most deeply influenced you? I would list The Fathers, and I would begin with Aeschylus.

This is a book by a writer about writing. My themes and subjects are intensely idiosyncratic and autobiographical. There are two major agendas and preoccupations: the tense relationship between theory and experience, and the vital connection between writing fiction and reading literature, all kinds of literature, even or perhaps especially The Fathers. I began consciously reading as a feminist while I was still a student. I was then, and still am, interested in the ways in which women writers take on the canonical classics, transforming discourses from which women have always been excluded or within which we are interpreted or represented as something less than human. Re-reading, even rewriting those texts, their scaffolding and psychic structures, was part of the feminist project. This was our take-over bid. Contemporary women writers are still engaged in remaking myths and fictions. But, intriguingly, some of those myths are now of feminist origin. And they too, have been challenged and disturbingly re-drawn. The current emphasis on difference between women is not new. This was always a persistent theme. It was the masculine versions of women, that seemed to be astonishingly homogenous. Only men could have invented 'The Woman Question', as if there was only one point to interrogate, or referred to us as 'the sex'.

When I contemplate the misfortunes of feminism, especially the more radical varieties, and the erosion of the political connection between lesbianism and feminism in favour of the new sexual politics, queer sex, I see that this has had interesting implications for women's writing. The great flowering of the feminist presses and feminist political activism of the 1970s and early 1980s is now over. Early feminist writing has been associated with earnest, moralistic realism, now utterly discredited, while post-modernist writing has all the panache of radical chic.[4] As a generalization describing the literary facts of the matter this distinction won't hold; but it is a necessary political move to justify the dissolution of early feminist political insights, thus clearing the ground, for not so much a different kind of writing as a different kind of politics.

What I appreciated about the early feminist, and especially lesbian writing of the 1960s and early 1970s was its irreverence, and the writers' insistence on the virtues of insolence. What I came to loathe was the sanctimonious self-righteousness that characterized a certain strand of British and Anglo-American feminism and often baffled some of the European groups. Anyone who embraces the role of victim is in intellectual trouble, and so is anyone who thinks that they are in possession of The Truth. Happily, insolence and irreverence are also characteristic of queer politics and of many other contemporary kinds of active political engagement. That irreverence is reflected in this book, which takes on the ancient myths of power, the old wives' tales about heterosexuality and its crucial place in the gender system. Feminist literary theory has, of course, evolved in important and interesting ways over the past three decades. I have been deeply influenced by queer theory, whose practitioners—among the most interesting are Alan Sinfield and Eve Kosofsky Sedgwick[5]—still concentrate largely on male-authored texts. In this book that is not the case. But queer reading seems to me to offer a great deal to a woman reader, especially if we see ourselves, as I do, as gender transgressors.

The first section of this book, 'Challenging the Classics', is about past traditions: Milton's *Paradise Lost*, Tolstoy's *War and Peace*, Charlotte Brontë's *Villette*, E. T. A. Hoffmann's *The Sandman*, Mary Shelley and Sigmund Freud. What is their significance for a contemporary woman writer? What is the nature of the engagement when we read and re-read classic texts? How do writers read? How do we interpret the canon of women writers and what use can we make of their interventions in reinterpreting the work of other women writers? I chart the ways in which Muriel Spark made use of *Villette* in *The Prime of Miss Jean Brodie*. I compare Tolstoy's method of making historical fiction with that of one of my distinguished Dutch contemporaries, Hella Haase, a writer who is almost unknown among the monoglot English reading public. I argue for the centrality of reading in the making of a writer. Texts are born from other texts.

The second section on 'Sexuality and Contemporary Women's Writing' is the one that engages most closely with contemporary literary theory. The Carter Essays address the huge Angela Carter Industry within the academy. Her position there is unchallenged. Why? Is she simply a writer who can easily be read in creative and engaging ways by students armed with post-modern literary theory? The first essay on Angela Carter and the Fairy Tales has been frequently reprinted and has caused a good deal of controversy. The piece elicited so much energetic and paranoid aggression from women critics[6] that I returned to Carter's short fiction and her use of Gothic, to think further about her work and the reasons for her extraordinary cult status. This is the second essay: 'Queer Gothic'.

Sexuality in the context of writing is, for me, about clichés, borders, limits and scripts. Within a more general critique of the politics and structures of heterosexuality, I examine the unworkable pain of heterosexual experience in the fiction of Margaret Atwood and Jenny Diski. I see writing as a space where our sexual identities are interrogated, resolved and remade, or imposed and reinforced. Within writing we can create new borders and reconfigure our identities. We can, literally, attempt to rewrite the script.

One of my preoccupations, as a writer who has no native country and speaks three languages, is the relationship between writing and roots, nation and identity. I have been fascinated by the structures of nationalist discourse and the connection between nationalism and (hetero)sexuality, and I raise these questions in an essay on the work of Grace Nichols.

The last section is about the process of 'Making Writing'. Here, I am reflecting upon my own methods, obsessions and credos. A. S. Byatt has observed that 'many younger [writers]feel no relation at all to the world of academic criticism, which has moved far away from their concerns. This distance can be experienced as a space of freedom.'[7] Byatt is right. But there is now, I believe, a move back towards nurturing the necessary links between the study of rhetoric, the practice of making writing and the critical investigation of literary history. I still harbour an uneasy but passionate connection to the world where scholars (supposedly) still study literary works and the complexity of literary traditions. This was where I first learnt how to read difficult texts in rigorous and uncompromising ways. But I am not interested in the secret languages of exclusive knowledge. Nor in being one of the intellectual gate-keepers.

I have not assumed that my readers are literary scholars nor that they will, necessarily, be literary critics. I have tried to write in a way that addresses everyone who cares about writing as passionately as I do. Yet the Academy has remained the abrasive and uncomfortable place where I argue about writing, the place where serious writing still matters.

I
CHALLENGING
THE CLASSICS

1.
READING GENESIS

The grammar of heterosexuality is articulated in the myths of western culture. And the Bible is the text at the root, a vast encyclopaedia of stories, the book of patriarchy. It is a text that has been perpetually retranslated, reimagined, rewritten. But it is not, as many women may be tempted to think, a monolithic slab of sexist dogma. It is a checkerboard of contradictions, a text whose meaning has been fought over for centuries. What I have to say here, about Paradise, Eve, John Milton and the structures of heterosexuality, is part of that struggle for meaning. The Eden story in Genesis is crucial for any analysis of heterosexuality, because it is there that women's subordination to men within marriage as a sexual union, and the very fact of heterosexual pairing, are mystified and justified, with all the spurious authority of biblical myth. Myths are the incarnation of the unseen, 'the expression of unobservable realities in terms of observable phenomena'.[1] Usually the myths to which the greatest significance is attached are the least probable. But myths have a more sinister function. They are used to legitimate power relationships, to justify cruelty, injustice and an existing social order. Throughout history, Genesis has been used to do precisely these things.

Mythologies have a tendency to divide essences into opposites, and this is true of the creation myths in Genesis. The binary oppositions emerge: Heaven and Earth, Adam and Eve, male and female, good and evil, natural and supernatural, immortal and mortal, life and death. Heterosexuality, too, necessarily thrives upon the insistence that we exist within dualities, as opposites. The middle ground that exists between the two poles is always abnormal, non-natural, holy. It is a land full of monsters, virgin mothers and incarnate gods. Eden reflects this: here is a garden with speaking serpents and magical trees. The middle ground is also the land where our culture has chosen to locate homosexuality, the magic garden, the forbidden space.

There are of course two creation stories in the first chapter of Genesis. There is what Christian scholars describe as the Priestly Narrative, which shows God as The Author of All Things, the maker who creates not with his hands, but through his will. The passage is precise, repetitive, abstract. The narrative perspective is cosmic and remote. This is a myth about pure power, the power to call forth into being. 'And God said, Let there be light: and there was light' (Genesis 1: 3). The second story is what is known as the 'Jahwist' document, the narrative of Eden. This is the older story. The written form dates from the ninth or tenth century BC, but behind it there is likely to have been a more ancient oral tradition, or even several stories, woven together.[2] And here God becomes YHWH,[3] God incarnate, the speaking, breathing creator, walking in his garden. This God makes mistakes. He is arbitrary, cruel and despotic. He denies his creatures knowledge. He is envious, fearful, the jealous God. The association of the serpent with Satan is a later interpretation of the narrative. All that we have in the text is that the serpent was 'more subtil than any beast of the field' (Genesis 3: 1). There are malevolent reptiles in Semitic demonology, and the serpent in Genesis does tell lies. He promises Eve knowledge without the penalty of death, a promise that is not fulfilled. But Adam and Eve do not die from the fruit of the tree. They die because YHWH carries out his threat and condemns them to death. The final verses of Genesis 3 endorse the serpent. YHWH fears that they will eat of the tree of life, live for ever and become gods. The serpent's assessment of the fruit and the reasons why it was forbidden prove to be utterly accurate. His only miscalculation was of the unpleasantness of the Lord's temper.

The two creation stories in Genesis present a patchwork of intellectual problems. In the first story women and men are both created in the image of God, 'male and female created he them' (Genesis 1: 27), but in the Eden narrative Eve is an afterthought: 'an help meet' for Adam. The Eden narrative is a text full of gaps, like a ballad, a mesh of unspoken motives and circumstances, perplexing and peculiar. Each story is perfectly consistent within its own narrative perspective, but, taken together, we have two radically different versions of human being and different versions of God. We have two alternative accounts of creation, but only one of the Fall. And it is that version, the Garden of Eden and the Fall of Man which children illustrate at school, it is that version that has been painted again and again throughout Christian history, and it is that version that John Milton chose for the action of *Paradise Lost*.

Paradise Lost is a poem written by a revolutionary in defeat. It was first published in 1667 and Milton was paid five pounds for his poem by the bookseller. The poem is a rationalist epic, a search for a first cause, by a man trained in both logic and philosophy. Milton wrote his own treatise on logic, *Ars Logica* (1672);[4] for him logic was the handmaiden of theology. *Paradise Lost* is also the fruit of an enormous poetic ambition, to write a greater and more original epic than anyone else had ever done. It was to be original in both senses of the word, that is, unlike any other poem and dealing with the origins of all things. It was to embody a critique of classical epics and yet surpass them. Theodicy (Theos/Dikê) does not only mean the justice of God but also implies his justification. Milton knew that in order to justify the ways of God to men, he must gather up, include and explain all human history. He was writing within a tradition of Christian myth in which we cannot understand Eden without Golgotha. Nor can we justify God's creation without the ultimate Apocalypse and the image of *Paradise Regained*. No one part of God's plan can be seen to be just without the vision of Eternity, that perspective which can only be God's. *Paradise Lost* had therefore, of necessity, to commence with the back story, that is, the first creation, the fall of the rebel angels, and to carry the reader through the narrative of Eden, all the way to the Crucifixion, on to the end of all things, from Eden to Apocalypse.

> Of man's first disobedience, and the fruit
> Of that forbidden tree, whose mortal taste
> Brought death into the world, and all our woe,

> With loss of Eden, till one greater man
> Restore us, and regain the blissful seat,
> Sing heavenly Muse. (*PL* i. 1–6)

Notice that it is 'one greater man' who is to save us, not a god. But Milton is on God's side, one of the saints, God's soldiers. He says he is.

> What in me is dark
> Illumine, what is low raise and support;
> That to the height of this great argument
> I may assert eternal providence,
> And justify the ways of God to men. (*PL* i. 22–6)

But did Milton ever justify the ways of God to women? And who can presume to fathom the justice of God? I want to cast a fundamental doubt on the nature of the enterprise of *Paradise Lost*.

The key words in the poem are reason, justice, free will. Milton needed to believe in a God who is benevolent and intelligible, a God who can be grasped by human intellect and understanding. His concept of Providence and Divine Justice is legalistic. The law of God binds both parties, God and human beings, to a sequence of mutual obligations. For Milton, YHWH is desperately problematic. The God to whom the Hebrew Bible bears witness is passionate, unguessable, apparently irrational and capricious. He is consistent with the God described in The Book of Job and with the God of the Psalms who has to be wooed, implored, cajoled and begged like a lover. And it is in the nature of love that we are vulnerable and at risk, without security and at the mercy of another's pleasure. Milton could not be in love with the God he incarnated in *Paradise Lost*. The attempt is doomed precisely because it is anthropomorphic. If we limit our conception of God to the political metaphors by which we name Him, then we are left with a monster of theological sadism whose laughter, which echoes throughout *Paradise Lost*,[5] is savage, malicious and unjust. But the character portrait is based on the master text. Even God's laughter is Biblically based. 'He that sitteth in the heavens shall laugh: the Lord shall have them in derision' (Psalm 2: 4). I would suggest that the myth of Eden is too frail a thing to explain the experience of human history and the bitterness of human suffering. No amount of gratuitous theological exposition can ever match the eating of the apple to the misery of the world.

As women, we are burdened with this myth. It touches us whether we accept and believe in Christian myth or whether we don't. We are interpreted and harassed by the structures of heterosexuality articulated and mythologised in Genesis even if we don't want to live within them or define ourselves as celibate, homosexual or lesbian. It is therefore important to look the monster in the face and to question the ways in which this myth is used. Lesbians and homosexuals usually read both the margins and the gaps in the heterosexual text. We listen for silences, echoes, inconsistencies, contradictions. We listen for lies. Most lesbians and homosexuals have to live, speak and write lies.[6] Most lesbians and homosexuals have to lie about whom they love. Or even deny their love. When I read *Paradise Lost*, which is the most powerful, haunting poem I have ever read, I listen therefore for Milton's lies and contradictions. What is the engine that drives this poem? With whom is he settling his scores? If he didn't love God, and that didn't appear to be possible, who was it that he really loved? The answer to this is complex.

Poetry is the art of incarnation; the Flesh made into Word. Milton's imagination reveals that with which he was truly in love, the sensuality of the incarnate world, physical creation itself. Book vii of *Paradise Lost* is the story of God's Creating Word. It is the Son—Milton never refers to him as Christ or Jesus—who creates, the Father who condemns. In Book vii we watch the 'six days' work, a world' (*PL* vii. 568), the circle drawn with the golden compasses, God's cosmic geometry; creation rises out of chaos. The animals struggle into being from the earth.

> Now half appeared
> The tawny lion, pawing to get free
> His hinder parts, then springs as broke from bonds
> And rampant shakes his brinded mane. (*PL* vii, 463–6)

Man—and by that I mean the first man, Adam—is the crown of

creation. It is here that Milton's creation theology becomes dangerous. The Priestly Narrative in Genesis (Genesis 1:27) is explicit. 'So
God created man in his own image, in the image of God created he
him; male and female created he them.' I would have thought that
this simple statement of equality in the hands of God was unambiguous. But Milton is equally unambiguous. Man is created in the
image of God, but woman is *created inferior*. She is God's second
thought, a sexual necessity. She does not reflect her male creator.
And yet she is part of the adored and sensual world. This is one of
the central contradictions in Milton's thought, which is also one of
the paradoxes of heterosexuality. Adam is sexually entranced by a
thing that is less than himself, an inferior being whom he is ordered
to govern and to patronise. He is disempowered by his desire.

We first see Eve and Adam in Book iv, through Satan's voyeuris-
tic eyes. Here is Milton's famous statement of eternal inequality.
The subjection of women is primordial, unchanging, and ordained
by God (*PL* iv. 292–9).

> The image of their glorious maker shone,
> Truth, wisdom, sanctitude severe and pure,
> Severe but in true filial freedom placed;
> Whence true authority in men; though both
> Not equal, as their sex not equal seemed;
> For contemplation he and valour formed,
> For softness she and sweet attractive grace,
> He for God only, she for God in him.

The marriage of Adam and Eve and their relationship of power and
subordination exactly mirrors the hierarchy of power between God
the Father and his hapless creation. For this too there is ample
scriptural support. 'The head of every man is Christ, and the head
of the woman is the man; and the head of Christ is God.' (1
Corinthians xi: 3).[7] But Milton did not take the doctrine of natural
inequality for granted. He insists upon it with neurotic intensity,
as if this assumption was unproven, challenged and in doubt. As
indeed it was during his lifetime.

The creation of Eve, described in Book vii, is an extraordinary
piece of male pornographic fantasy. And it is here that the contra-

dictions, for which I was listening, begin to splinter the text. Adam begs God, explicitly, for a companion who is his true equal.

> Hast thou not made me here thy substitute,
> And these inferior far beneath me set?
> Among *unequals* what society
> Can sort, what harmony and true delight?
> Which must be mutual, in proportion due
> Given and received.
> (*PL* viii. 381–6. [*my emphasis*])

But God promises 'Thy wish exactly to thy heart's desire' (*PL* viii. 451), and produces the inferior sex, Eve.

God's injustice is not in question here, because Adam's dream is of woman as 'the spirit of love and amorous delight' (PL viii. 477), and how can women and men ever be equals if woman is the erotic dream made flesh as the object of men's pleasure? The Fall takes place in Book ix; so here, at Eve's creation, long before she stands in front of us with the apple of her undoing in her hand, Milton takes care to point out Adam's vulnerable heel—sex.

> Here passion first I felt,
> Commotion strange, in all enjoyments else
> Superior and unmoved, here only weak
> Against the charm of beauty's powerful glance.
> (*PL* viii. 530–3)

Note that it is 'superior' to be unfeeling. Sexual desire so unhinges Adam that he is in danger of forgetting Eve's subservient status. And in case we too become so bewitched that we forget, Milton says it all again.

> For well I understand in the prime end
> Of nature her the inferior, in the mind
> And inward faculties, which most excel,
> In outward also her resembling less
> His image who made both, and less expressing
> The character of that dominion given

O'er other creatures. (*PL* viii. 540–6)

Here, neatly articulated, is one of the foundation myths of hetero-sexuality. To pursue that obscure object of desire, woman and her sex, is to desire something less than perfect, less than man and less than God. The reverse side of male heterosexual desire is contempt.[8]

Milton was a revolutionary. He supported a republican govern-ment, the execution of the king, the freedom of the press, the separation of Church and State. Yet he could not unthink the most fundamental political oppression of all, the subjection and exploita-tion of women by men. He was married to Mary Powell in June 1642. Within a month she abandoned him and went back to her mother. She could not be persuaded to return. During the next three years Milton published a series of books urging that the law be reformed so as to permit divorce not only for gross breaches of matrimony on the woman's part, such as adultery or frigidity, but also for personal incompatibility. Divorce was, however, to be for men only. Milton even argued for legally and socially sanctioned polygamy. Here again, he found ample scriptural justification in the 'Old Testament'. It has been suggested that Milton's first marriage was unconsummated during the brief weeks that Mary Powell was with him in London. This speculation is based on a passage in *The Doctrine and Discipline of Divorce* (1643).

> Whereas the sober man honouring the appearance of modesty, and hoping well of every social virtue under that veil, may easily chance to meet, if not with a body impenetrable, yet often with a mind to all other due conversation inaccessible.[9]

It is disturbing, but not surprising that Milton's idea of marriage in this passage is coercive. Women's bodies are there to be pene-trated, preferably with their consent, their minds to be influenced and controlled. 'Conversation' could also mean 'intercourse'. So minds were presumably there to be penetrated too. In his common-place book, Milton wrote: 'Marriage: see Of Divorce'. These entries are not without wit, and I laughed out loud at another entry, which reads: 'Official Robbery or Extortion: see Pope'. Yet the last laugh is on me for it is clear from these entries that Milton could question an existing ecclesiastical hierarchy, but not a sexual one. He had firm ideas about what men could expect from marriage and what women deserved. What women wanted or needed was not his concern and, in any case, he never asked them.

Mary Powell eventually returned to Milton three years later, in the summer of 1645. Her reasons were very clearly economic and political. Her family had royalist allegiances. They needed a Puritan ally in the Civil War. Eventually they all moved into Milton's London house. Mary bore Milton four children and died giving birth to the last one in May 1652. Milton's second wife, Katherine Woodcock, 'the late espoused saint' of his sonnet, 'Methought I saw my late espoused saint/Brought to me', also died in childbirth after 15 months of marriage. The child, another daughter, Katherine, died six weeks later. Milton's third wife, Elizabeth Minshull, cleverly avoided bearing any of his children—we don't know how—and survived him. She lived to be 90. For the women who have gone before us and for many other women in the world today, marriage and heterosexual sex was and remains, very often, a sentence to ill health, sexual subjection and early death.

It is not true to say that Protestantism is necessarily liberating for women. Certainly the reformers, women among them, did attack the old Catholic ideology of regarding women, if they didn't happen to be virgin mothers, as carnal temptresses and vessels of sin incarnate. Instead, however, they created the image of woman as the good wife, the symbol of domestic purity, spirituality, helpfulness and loyalty. This is Eve's image cleaned up. Neither Catholic nor Protestant priests or theologians denied that woman was created inferior. She was naturally suited to a life of submission and obedience. Prelapsarian Eden was not a paradise of equality. Eve's transgression made the burden of her sex more painful, but the yoke was already there. The Protestant notion of the priesthood of all believers did, however, mean that religion was not safely confined in a spiritual space. The Christian life, all aspects thereof, had to be lived in godly, righteous and sober ways. This made family life a critical area in the struggle for godliness. The family becomes 'a little church...a little state'. William Gouge, a prominent Puritan preacher, celebrated marriage in the following terms: 'Marriage is the Preservative of Chastity, the seminary of the

Commonwealth, seed plot of the Church, pillar (under God) of the world, right-hand of providence, a supporter of laws, states, orders offices, gilts and services.'[10]

Gouge also argued that the husband's adultery was as bad as that of the wife. Chastity was to be preserved by men as well as by women.[11] But Puritan marriage was built upon an intractable contradiction. As Milton's Adam supposedly desired, husband and wife should enjoy the close and loving mutual companionship of working partners, yet the marriage relation should nevertheless be based on the inexorable subordination of the woman to the man. This is the contradiction at the heart of heterosexuality and of marriage. John Milton and I pose the same question. 'Among unequals what society/Can sort, what harmony or true delight?' (*PL* viii. 383–4) Yet the Protestants turned to St Paul for his most unequivocal statements on the necessary subordination of women, and so did Milton. Man is the image and glory of God, God's substitute on earth, woman is the glory of the man. 'He for God only, she for God in him' (*PL* iv. 299). Here is William Whateley, another Puritan.

> Every good woman must suffer herselfe to be convinced in judgement that she is not her husband's equall. 'Out of place, out of peace'; and woe to those miserable aspiring shoulders, which will not content themselves to take their room below the head.[12]

So the first law of patriarchy was not challenged. The Puritans merely shifted the terms of the argument. The Catholics relied on priests to shepherd their flocks. The Puritans saw this duty of discipline and authority passing to fathers and husbands. One person's authority necessarily means another's submission, and the dethroning of female images of divine power, the Virgin and her sisters, all the martyred heroines of the Catholic Church, left only the ruling male Gods, God the Father, God the Son. The disbanding of women's religious houses, which had at least given women some small measure of power and control as brides of Christ, the conveniently absent husband, left women with the paradigm of natural rather than spiritual marriage, and husbands who were all too physically present. We were to define ourselves in relation to men, as maids, wives, widows, mothers. And marriage was to be a sweet friendship within a coercive structure of power. The subversive contradiction within all this was of course The Holy Spirit. The Holy Spirit, which feminist theologians have assiduously attempted to reclaim as the feminine principle, played too masculine a role in the Annunciation to be entirely convincing as a female deity. But if The Spirit had descended upon Mary—'Behold the handmaiden of the Lord'—women were at least spiritually equal and worthy to be God's messengers. Might a wife not, in all conscience, be forced to disobey her husband if the Higher Authority so demanded? Some women claimed that they were following divine orders. And no one could prove that they were not.

The most insidious threat to family life was adultery. Even the more moderate Puritans prescribed a single standard of sexual behaviour. More radical libertarian groups even advocated free love. But the problem with libertarian sexuality as well as simple straightforward adultery is that women always have the worst of it. Gerrard Winstanley warned women against the groups he regarded as extremists. 'Therefore you women beware, for this ranting practice is not the restoring but the destroying power of the creation …by seeking their own freedom they embondage others.'[13] The seventeenth-century radicals were warm advocates of hetero-sexual sex, marital love patterned on devotion to God and stable, life-long, non-adulterous marriages. They were deeply suspicious of lust, which was possible even between husband and wife. This is an important point in *Paradise Lost*, where it actually happens, and is the first consequence of the Fall, the first fruit of sin.

> Carnal desire inflaming, he on Eve
> Began to cast lascivious eyes, she him
> As wantonly repaid; in lust they burn. (*PL* ix. 1013–15)

Post-lapsarian sex, no longer honourable and innocent, becomes carnal lust. The problem here is that the language that Milton and the radicals used to describe lust is the same language used by the Anglican Church to describe sex. In Milton's fallen Paradise post-coital tristesse ensues. One would have thought that this was punishment enough.

Milton's misogyny is most clearly stated in Book iv, where, long before the Fall, heterosexuality is hymned as the source of all joy.

> Hail wedded love, mysterious law, true source
> Of human offspring, sole propriety
> In Paradise of all things common else.
> By thee adulterous lust was driven from men
> Among the bestial herds to range, by thee
> Founded in reason, loyal, just, and pure,
> Relations dear, and all the charities
> Of father, son and brother first were known.
> (*PL* iv. 750–7)

There are some remarkable assertions here. Married love is the only aspect of Eden that includes property rights. Eve is Adam's property. Lust is brute desire and confined to the animals, in whom, presumably, it is made perfect as befits their unfallen state. If mutual desire is impossible between unequals—and Milton himself begged that question—then surely, given that Eve is property within marriage, heterosexuality in Paradise is, at best, coercive sex. Eve cannot bargain. She can only submit. The language of heterosexual eroticism is pitched in terms of conquest and surrender, in Paradise just as it is everywhere else: 'he in delight/Both of her beauty and submissive charms/Smiled with superior love' (*PL* iv. 497–9). And the only charities (affections) that can exist within the family institution, according to Milton, are those appertaining to relationships between men: fathers, sons, brothers. The exclusion of mothers, daughters, sisters is pointed, and, I suspect, deliberate.

The most usual and insidious device male writers and some of their female collaborators use to belittle women is to place the expression of delight at our own oppression in women's mouths. Thus Eve:

> O thou for whom
> And from whom I was formed flesh of thy flesh,
> And without whom am to no end, my guide
> And head.
> (*PL* iv. 440–3)

Throughout all literary history women sing hymns to the phallus, praise obedience to men, advocate utter submission, worship male gods. Eve sounds like the abject sexual robot of pornography, infinitely pliable, infinitely desiring whatever the gentlemen desire.

> Unargued I obey; so God ordains,
> God is thy law, thou mine: to know no more
> Is woman's happiest knowledge and her praise.
> (*PL* iv. 635–8)

For us then, there would obviously be no point whatever in reading Milton if he were simply one more massive block on that pyramid of misogyny otherwise known as Theology and Literature. But Eve doesn't simply wander through Genesis and *Paradise Lost*, swathed in tendrils of erotic hair, muttering, 'Unargued I obey'. Milton's reading of Genesis is most interesting at those moments where he interprets the gaps in the biblical narrative, the moments where he invents. It is here that the poem begins to explode, it is here that he becomes subversive and contradictory. The margins invade the page. The unthinkable actually happens. Homosexual desire enters the text.

The first person Eve sees is not Adam but herself, reflected in the 'liquid plain'. And the face she sees returns 'answering looks/Of sympathy and love' (*PL* iv. 465). Eve's first desire is for a female image, for another woman. Milton is being imaginatively honest here. The first body we know is a woman's, that of our mother. Eve is of no woman born, yet her first love is for a woman. God's voice pursues her, pointing out that her great role as mother of the race awaits and that her destiny is Adam, 'whose image thou art'. But Eve, upon seeing Adam, knows at once that she is not made in his image. Amazingly, Milton says so. Eve is speaking.

> Till I espied thee, fair indeed and tall,
> Under a platan, yet methought less fair,
> Less winning soft, less amiably mild,
> Than that smooth watery image; back I turned.
> (*PL* iv. 477–80)

There is a structural echo here with Adam's assertion in Book viii that he perceives Eve 'resembling less/His image who made both' (*PL* viii. 543–4). But we hear Eve first—refusing to acknowledge that they are one bone, one flesh. Eve's response to Adam is unequivocal. She runs. And she takes considerable persuading before she will have anything to do with him.

Milton's first love was a man, Charles Diodati, whom he knew from his schooldays at St Paul's. Diodati's family were originally Italian Protestants from Lucca who abandoned Italy during the Counter-Reformation.[14] The main branch of the family settled in Geneva, where Giovanni Diodati became a professor of Hebrew, an internationally famous theologian, who translated the Bible into Italian. Milton adored Charles. His early death in 1638, while Milton was in Italy, was a terrible blow. The Latin elegy for Charles, the *Epitaphium Damonis* (1640), was the first poem Milton published separately. In the poem he not only suggests that he saw himself married to Charles (line 65: 'innuba'), but also imagines his dead friend admitted to erotic Bacchic orgies in Paradise. The heterosexism of Genesis may indeed have troubled Milton; the politics of heterosexuality certainly did. Marriage as a sacrament, a symbol, a mystery, interestingly and thoroughly confused with compulsory heterosexuality as a coercive institution for the policing of women, is deeply bound into the mythology of the Christian religion. The metaphor of marriage stretches from Genesis to Apocalypse, where it is used as a primal image of union between God and Jerusalem, Christ and the Church.

'For this cause shall a man leave his father and mother and shall bejoined unto his wife, and they two shall be one flesh. This is a great mystery: but I speak concerning Christ and the Church' (Ephesians v: 31–2). This great mystery of perfect union remains satisfyingly invisible; the dispute of power and authority between women and men, disturbingly close to the bone of daily existence. Milton married three times. He had three daughters. He abused his first wife in his divorce pamphlets. Although he did teach his daughters to read, his pamphlet *Of Education* (1644) has nothing whatever to say on the education of women. And this is a stark omission because most other education reformers of the period did discuss the issue.[15] We do have some independent comments from

Milton's daughters. Deborah, who eventually became a school-mistress, tells us that her father was a tyrant and that he forced them to read to him in languages they did not understand. His first mother-in-law described him as a harsh and choleric man. His daughter Mary, aged 15, said that 'her father's death would be better news than his third marriage'.[16]

Milton neither liked nor respected women. But his unrelenting contempt did not bring him complacency or peace. If we really were all one in Christ Jesus then he was faced with an irresolvable problem. And he had the intelligence and sense to acknowledge this.

He saw in Genesis what every woman sees, a myth that legitimates male power and ensures male access to women, to our bodies, our labour, our energy and our strength. Even Satan becomes sexually involved with Eve in Milton's version, as he approaches her to tempt her and bring about her 'ruin' (*PL* ix. 493). She is 'pleasure not for him ordained' (*PL* ix. 470), but by implication a pleasure created for someone else.[17] The slave is unconditionally accessible to the master, in whatever way he pleases. Total power is unconditional access, sexual and otherwise. Milton knew this. And I think that this insight is at the root of one of the finest, most extraordinary passages in the poem. I don't read Milton for his intellectual consistency but for his immense intelligence and his capacity to articulate his imaginative fears. We are both preoccupied with the same questions, the same troubling issues of sexual politics, and Milton does us the honour of taking these questions seriously. He is desperately serious. He knows what is at stake. We are simply on different sides.

Eve confronts the serpent alone. This is a crucial incident in the theology of the Fall. Why was she alone? Where was Adam? Once again, Milton, without guidance from the Scriptures, for there is none to be had, invents. Eve decides to do some gardening alone. She proposes a sensible division of labour on the grounds of efficiency. In Book ix it emerges that Eve had heard the Angel Raphael's warning about Satan's presence. She was listening in the bushes. She knows that God's enemy may try to assault or seduce them. But she insists that this does not justify Adam's initial prohibition on her departure. If, as he argues, it is best that

> The wife, where danger or dishonour lurks,
> Safest and seemliest by her husband stays,
> Who guards her, or with her the worst endures
> (*PL* ix. 267–9)

is she then less able to withstand temptation? Ironically, and unknown to her, Eve's temptation has already begun, for Satan, upon his first incursion into Eden—'Squat like a toad' (*PL* iv. 800), the toad is a traditional image of male sexuality—had hovered close at her sleeping ear, filling her mind with phantasms and dreams, vain hopes, vain aims, 'high conceits engendering pride', dreams of power. But, as Eve insists, with irrefutable logic,

> And what is faith, love, virtue, unassayed
> Alone, without exterior help sustained?
> (*PL* ix. 335–6)

Milton envisaged human virtue as developing and dynamic. In *Areopagitica* (1644) he rejected 'cloistered virtue': 'for thou art sufficient both to judge aright, and to examine each matter'.[18] Reason, his other God, is on Eve's side. Adam is caught in his own logic. If God has made them free, able to judge and choose for themselves, then it would be blasphemy to doubt the creator's capacities and purposes.

> his creating hand
> Nothing imperfect or deficient left
> Of all that he created, much less man,
> Or aught that might his happy state secure,
> Secure from outward force; within himself
> The danger lies, yet lies within his power.
> (*PL* ix. 344–9)

And thus, Adam's relation to Eve, one of supposed authority and love, exactly mirrors his own relationship to God. And his dismissal follows the pattern of God's insistence on human free will in Book iii: 'of freedom both despoiled, / Made passive both, had served necessity/ Not me' (*PL* iii. 109–11). Quite so. Adam, reluctantly, against his better judgement, and not underestimating the risk, lets her go. 'Go; for thy stay, not free, absents thee more' (*PL* ix. 372). We all know what happened. And we know what happened in this crucial moment before it happens. So that our privileged position, as fallen readers, enables us to read the scene with full knowledge, the knowledge of good and evil. Is this moment of separation in fact the Fall from innocence? The Separation Scene shows Adam's refusal to exert the power he undoubtedly has over Eve, and within the inevitable outcome of the story, and the story stands irrefutably, unchangeably, according to the Scriptures, this failure to enforce his will is disastrous. Adam is the stronger partner. The Fall is Adam's fault. Or we could argue on the other side. Milton is using that story, the story of Genesis, to lay the sin even more firmly at the woman's door. She may have had the more convincing arguments at that moment. But she should never have left her husband. The original sin is Eve's and that sin is separatism.

Genesis is about power, authority, obedience, domination, submission and rebellion. So is *Paradise Lost*. Women's powerlessness ends when separation begins; for the moment of' 'conscious and deliberate exclusion of men, from anything', even as in this case from a bower of myrtle and roses in Paradise, is blatant insubordination.[19] It is also the moment of self-definition. It is the moment when Eve refuses to acquiesce submissively, and mouth her given formula, 'Unargued I obey'. She argues, and she wins the argument. There are two rebellions in *Paradise Lost*: Satan's and Eve's. Both are regarded by Christian theology, and by Milton, as falls from perfection and grace. Both are defiant assertions of self against an authority that has not been chosen, but arbitrarily imposed. Both Satan and Eve are on the receiving end of the realities of power. Their rebellions are moments of separation, separation from God and separation from man. Satan and Eve are natural allies.

Milton's accusation against Eve, and against her individualism, which was as uncompromising as his own, was this savage retelling of Genesis. You, woman, my wife, turned away from me and betrayed the whole world for all time and in all eternity. For a woman's duty is submission to men. It says so in the Bible. And, just in case I have given the impression that the seventeenth century was a place full of light and that John Milton was the last misogynist in England, see also John Dod and Robert Cleaver, *A Godley Form of Household Government* (1630),

> So then the principal duty of the wife is, first to be subject to her husband (Ephesians 5: 22, Colossians 3: 18, Peter 3: 1–2). To be chaste and shamefast, modest and silent, godley and discreet. To keep herself at home for the good government of her family and not to stay abroad without good cause.[20]

My reply to Milton's accusation is simple: I am one of the women who make it my just cause 'to stay abroad', to leave home. Separation from men and from the institutions that give men access to our bodies and our minds is the barrier reef surrounding any woman's independent identity. Heterosexuality, marriage, motherhood: these are the institutions which most obviously maintain the power structures of patriarchy. They form the core triad of all anti-feminist and anti-lesbian ideologies, in the seventeenth century and in our own.

Men have always used the Bible against women. And we have always answered back. Across hundreds of years we have argued against Genesis and against Milton. Mary Wollstonecraft picks out Milton's contradictions in *A Vindication of the Rights of Woman* (1792). Why, she demands, when Adam asked for an equal partner, was he given an Eve? Why was Eve created subject to man's will? Why should sexual difference necessarily entail injustice and subordination? My own generation of feminists has also struggled with Genesis. Angela Carter's futuristic sci-fi dystopia, *The Passion of New Eve* (1977), ironically recreates women as transsexuals. Women made in the image of men will always be transsexuals. Playing the feminine game turns us into transsexuals. Contemporary writers have only just begun to explore the ways in which this is interesting and useful. Michelene Wandor's *Gardens of Eden: Poems for Eve and Lilith* (1984)[21] is a game for women's voices, arguing, challenging, questioning—God, men, each other, other women. The poems score off the aggression of the individual voice, which dares to answer God back. These poems take Genesis and the Hebrew Bible seriously. They work within the terms of the old stories. But the shadows of Milton's anthropomorphism still encircle the text and circumscribe the limits of Wandor's thinking. Here, in 'Lilith takes tea with the Lord', the conventional metaphors used in the Bible to invoke the power of God become Hollywood special effects.

> you fly upon the wings of the wind
> you hail stones and coals of fire
> you shoot arrows of lightning
> and the breath from your nostrils
> burns
>
> you have all the good bits
> and I scare easy.[22]

The theological sadist, Milton's version of God, still lurks on the edge of the page. These poems make good polemical points for women. But they offer no new thinking of God. At the end of her sequence Wandor unites the two women, Lilith and Eve, appropriating the marriage metaphor of the *Song of Songs*, 'Eve to Lilith',

> Your mouth is a pomegranate
> ripening in smile
>
> I can see into the garden
> my sister, my love.[23]

The lesbian implications of the last poems are not spelt out. Elsewhere in the sequence Wandor capitulates to the coerciveness of the old stories. These are the wives talking to each other, God's bad girls, Adam's wives. Monique Wittig and Sande Zeig have neither Wandor's scruples nor her inhibitions. They bind Lilith and Eve to one another in their exuberant dictionary text, *Lesbian Peoples* (1976).

Eve and Lilith
Two famous companion lovers who lived in Palestine during the Bronze Age. Their love was so strong, it is said, that it survived a long, forced sojourn in the desert. There they developed their legendary endurance.[24]

But, humorously, Wittig and Zeig dispense with God, creation and all the rest of the myth. Genesis rises, only to be finally dismissed. Here is their entry for Fall.

Fall

If it is a question of falling, better to do it into the arms of one's companion lover, forward or backward, with eyes open or closed. If this is not possible, one would be best to fall upon piles of leaves, sand, hay, snow.[25]

Wittig and Zeig, like myself, are the inheritors of Genesis. For us this myth recounts the beginning of the spiritual history of patriarchy; which is the beginning of division, the original division into opposites and hierarchies: Heaven and Earth, Adam and Eve, male and female, good and evil, natural and supernatural, immortal and mortal, life and death. The myth of Eden is of no use in the enterprise that we have undertaken, the imagining and the creation of a different world, a world in which women are free.

John Milton did not believe that it was necessary to belong to any Christian community or congregation. He was in himself a temple of the Holy Spirit, a solitary pillar of righteousness. Early on in his career he had planned to become an Anglican priest, but his disillusionment with the state church became complete. He supported the sectarian Protestants, the visionary Utopians, the religious radicals. From the 1640s onwards he was working on his *De Doctrina Christiana*. This heterodox theological tract was never published in his lifetime. He called it his 'dearest and best possession'. It is the theological basis for *Paradise Lost*. In the Preface to *De Doctrina Christiana* he denounces 'those two repulsive afflictions, tyranny and superstition'.[26] It is not only the right, but also the duty of the oppressed to fight for their freedom. On this point Milton never recanted. I agree with him—fervently. And I believe that we should take this insight from him if we take nothing else.

Milton created a monstrous God, who in his turn could only fashion a man in his own monstrous image, the image of injustice and tyranny. Within Milton's unconventional theology Adam's sin is neither rebellion nor disobedience, but sexual weakness. His eventual capitulation is pitched in terms that have been described by one of my colleagues, Zachary Leader, as 'heroic matrimony'.

> I feel
> The bond of nature draw me to my own,
> My own is in thee, for what thou art is mine;
> Our state cannot be severed, we are one,
> One flesh; to lose thee were to lose my self.
> (*PL* ix. 955–9)

But, being a resisting reader and a woman impervious to 'heroic matrimony', in whatever form it takes, I want you to read this passage cynically. Adam's love is based on property and possession. Eve is 'my own'—'what thou art is mine'. And Milton is articulating one of his deepest terrors: that women do not in fact need men and, if not properly disciplined, might choose each other or, worse still, serpents, first.

The original sin is Eve's, mine, yours, if you choose to exercise your freedom, and ours—whether as radical feminists, dissident homosexuals, unrepentant queers, transgressively transgendered persons of all sexes, lesbians or lovers of serpents: separation. Our insistence on our own difference and integrity as separate beings, on the possession of our own bodies, on our own freedom, places us outside patriarchal male rule. It is our necessary heresy. It is not negotiable. And there, my Lord God, John Milton and Ladies of the Jury, my case rests.

2.
THE SUGGESTIVE SPECTACLE
QUEER PASSIONS IN CHARLOTTE BRONTË'S *VILLETTE* AND MURIEL SPARK'S *THE PRIME OF MISS JEAN BRODIE*

'The spectacle was somehow suggestive.'
'The Fete', *Villette,* chapter xiv

The spectacle that Lucy Snowe, the schoolmistress in *Villette* (1853), Charlotte Brontë's haunted novel of thwarted sexual desire, is describing as suggestive is the moment in the text where Lucy, dressed as a man from the waist up, but as a woman from the waist down, takes a part in the school play. She sets out to win the flirtatious Ginevra Fanshawe away from not only the male lead role on stage but also the man in the audience with whom Lucy is infatuated, but who is in love with Ginevra. This suggestive combination of transvestism, sexual substitution and genderbending performance is echoed in Spark's novel, *The Prime of Miss Jean Brodie* (1961). The girls of her set become objects of sexual exchange for the ambitious, manipulative Brodie. She chooses the one who should fill her place with the art master Teddy Lloyd, but her sexual game collapses when the pupil she has not chosen betrays her. Spark, like Brontë, is interested in the ambiguous sexual electricity of single-sex classrooms.

Spark has compiled a volume of the Brontës' letters, which is still in print.[1] She first encountered Charlotte Brontë when she was under the spell of 'Miss Kay', the source of Miss Jean Brodie. 'It was when I was in Miss Kay's class that I read *Jane Eyre*, and Mrs Gaskell's *Life of Charlotte Brontë*' (CV, p.64). In *The Prime of Miss Jean Brodie*, Spark picks up the central themes of *Villette*: women's communities, spinsters, spying and female sexuality. The subject of *Villette* and of *The Prime of Miss Jean Brodie* is repression and excess, set within the claustrophobic and sexually charged environment of an all-girls school. Neither writer is sentimental about women's solidarity or sisterhood. If anything the emphasis suggests women, beware women. The lesbian text in Brontë's novel is more subtle, but no less present than the lesbian theme in *The Prime of Miss Jean Brodie*.

Schoolgirl stories set in women-only institutions lend themselves to lesbian ambiguities and to the extension of conventional gender roles for girls. Enid Blyton's Malory Towers series of novels[2] are filled with girls whose names do not immediately signal femininity: the heroine, Darrell, and even the more contentiously named Bill, short for Wilhelmina. In women-only narratives the usual men's roles of explorer, adventurer, rescuer, are shared out among the girls. Women are permitted to have adventures and ask nasty questions. They are also permitted to know things. The Brodie set in Spark's novel are 'vastly informed on a lot of subjects irrelevant to the authorised curriculum' (*MJB*, p.5), and among these figure 'the love lives of Charlotte Brontë and of Miss Brodie herself' (ibid.). The authors of *Villette* and of *The Prime of Miss Jean Brodie* were both intrigued by sexual knowledge of an unauthorised nature. Lucy Snowe and Miss Jean Brodie are arrogant, opinionated and passionately obsessed with power. They are both schoolteachers, and they are both spinsters. They have the limited authority permitted to women as teachers, and because neither of them is married or lives in her father's house they are both outside male control. Both are frequently referred to as 'Miss', underlining their unmarried state: Miss Lucy Snowe and Miss Jean Brodie. Both women are travellers, adventurers. They are women on the loose, free and independent women. And therefore dangerous.

The widow who endows the Marcia Blaine School for Girls favoured Garibaldi, the champion of liberty. Miss Brodie prefers Mussolini. She wishes to exert power over her pupils rather than empower them. Miss Brodie and Lucy Snowe are both women who take risks. As Miss Brodie persuasively argues, 'But Safety does not come first' (*MJB*, p.10). For the Brodie set, their years with Miss Brodie are the years of living dangerously. Lucy Snowe never lives in any other way. She leaves home, travels across the Channel, wanders the city streets at night, insists on her own opinions, looks closely and critically at pictures of naked ladies, desires men, two different men, all without scruples or hesitation. In Victorian terms she is exceedingly unwomanly and a bad example.

Spark's Miss Brodie was based on the teacher into whose hands she fell at the age of eleven during the last two years at junior school in 1929 and 1930: Miss Christina Kay. Spark herself, in her autobiography, *Curriculum Vitae*, (1992) describes Kay as 'that character in search of an author' (*CV*, p.56). Outside the gossip pages of literary biography it is now peculiarly unfashionable to identify literary characters in fiction with their sources in the writer's lives. This strikes me as odd. Spark at once puts her finger on the ambiguity of this relationship between fiction and its sources. Who is the fiction and who is the character? Miss Jean Brodie is larger than life. Her force and imagination explode beyond the boundary of her classroom, Marcia Blaine's School for Girls and even her pupil's lives. Christina Kay was already a character, waiting to be written. Writers never use random elements in their lives as sources. They pick on something—or someone—who is already becoming fiction.

Teaching has a great deal in common with theatre, as do all professions, that require public performances, from television journalists, to politicians and high-court judges. Spark makes the link between teaching and one-woman performances. 'I had always enjoyed watching teachers. We had a large class of about forty girls. A full classroom that size, with a sole performer on stage before an audience sitting in rows and listening, is essentially theatre' (*CV*, p.57). Miss Kay was already performing a role. To perform Miss Jean Brodie all she has to do is take on an adopted character. It is Spark who unleashes Miss Brodie. As she says (*CV*, p.57),

> children are quick to perceive possibilities, potentialities in a remark, perhaps in some remote context; in a glance, a smile. No. Miss Kay was not literally Miss Brodie, but I think Miss Kay had it in her, unrealized, to be the character I invented.

It is not only children but also writers who are quick to seize upon possibilities and potentialities. Making fiction is a process of building on the suggestively possible. Miss Kay has the potential to become Miss Brodie. She is already partly fiction. Her making is a process of enlargement. She grows into Miss Brodie. Only those readers of Spark's novel who already knew Miss Kay personally recognised her 'with joy and great nostalgia, in the shape of Miss Jean Brodie in her prime' (CV, p.57). The relationship of a successful fictional character to her source in flesh and blood is parasitic. If the fiction thrives and grows strong the host is consumed and ceases to exist. Spark knew this and in *Curriculum Vitae*, she devotes at least a dozen pages to Miss Kay, pointing out her teacher's influence on her own life, as if by way of apologia for her own power over her teacher. 'Miss Kay predicted my future as a writer in the most emphatic terms. I felt I had hardly much choice in the matter' (CV, p.66). Miss Kay encouraged her own re-creator. The character who has achieved an after-life is not Miss Kay, but Miss Jean Brodie.

A teacher is always searching for the pupil who will surpass her, the pupil whose intelligence will subsume and challenge hers, the pupil who will grow beyond her. The good teacher should be looking for the intellect that will bring about the dissolution of her own power and influence. This is, of course, a tall order. M. Paul Emmanuel believes he has seen that mind in Lucy Snowe and, consequently, he is furious. Miss Jean Brodie doesn't even attempt to do it. She never lets her pupils go. And takes the consequences. The only way that Sandy can escape her is by destroying her.

Classrooms are incipient sites of revolution, the stage where power struggles are the name of the daily game. Power is a volatile element. It can pass from teacher to pupil in an instant. The potential dramatic situation in the classroom is that of the dictator, confronting the mob. Lucy Snowe's trial by fire comes when she is asked to give a dictation to the second class. 'They always throw over timid teachers' (*Villette*, p.76), as headmistress Madame Beck points out. The girls of Labassecour are in a state of perpetual rebellion, ready to rise up and persecute a teacher who is too weak to control them. Teaching is an exercise in authority, domination and command. Lucy Snowe triumphs by establishing her superior power and sharper wits. She jeers at one rebel's ignorance and locks another in the closet. This entire scene is of course enacted between women. But the conflict is given the status of men's conflicts. When Madame Beck challenges Lucy to take the class 'At that instant she did not wear a woman's aspect, but rather, a man's' (*Villette*, p.76). Lucy takes up the gage, fights, wins. Teaching is still, largely, a women's profession. Classrooms in girls' schools are the fields of conflict and battle, which turn women into heroes.

And into spies. Madame Beck spies on her staff and her pupils as a matter of course. Miss Mackay, Brodie's headteacher, never gives up pumping the Brodie set, hoping to be able to pin some colourful iniquity upon Miss Brodie. Brontë and Spark represent the mechanisms of power and rebellion inside closed systems. Both girls' schools operate with elaborate systems of surveillance and control. Information is attained by the most underhand methods. Lucy catches Madame Beck going through her private drawers. And, significantly, decides to say nothing. The schools are institutions regulated to work in the interests of those who run them. They are designed to keep order and control among young women. The watchwords are discipline and punish. Women are not represented in either novel as innocent, obedient and docile. The girls of Labassecour are sexual predators: knowing, callous, lazy, hardened, unscrupulous and dishonest. Brodie's girls know far too much and have all the arrogance of the chosen 'crème de la crème'. They are made in their teacher's image.

In Brontë's *Villette* her heroine follows the author's own biographical trajectory: the pensionnat in Brussels/Villette to the encounter with her teacher, Monsieur Paul/Constantin Héger. The final outcome of this voyage of sexual discovery was no different either in life or in fiction. Love ends in loss, absence, grief. There was only one critical difference. M. Paul sought and returned Lucy Snowe's love, unambiguously, in a way that Constantin Héger never answered Charlotte Brontë. Silence was his stern reply to her passionate letters. And her fictional hero, while in many ways otherwise engaged, is not married.

Both novels are about sex and the single girl. The triangle patterning is the same. Lucy Snowe has two men to choose between: Dr John, aka Graham Bretton, and M. Paul. Miss Brodie is courted by Gordon Lowther and Teddy Lloyd. Two other elements are crucial to the themes and patterning of both books: the paintings, that form a crucial part of the iconography of both texts, and play a critical role in the discussion and delineation of female sexuality. The second figure to be found in the common textual carpet is the Nun.

Sandy Stranger, Miss Brodie's unrecognized antagonist, eventually becomes Sister Helena of the Transfiguration, living out her days behind the bars of another women's community. Her famous psychology book is entitled *The Transfiguration of the Commonplace*, a title that reflects exactly what Miss Brodie did for her set. She made the ordinary extraordinary and turned dailiness into fairy tales. Sandy never escapes Miss Brodie, neither her memory nor her influence. She continues to live at second hand. The Nun in *Villette* has a Gothic pedigree that goes back to Ann Radcliffe's novels of the 1790s.[3] The Nun has a remarkable consistency of cultural meaning in fiction that uses the machinery of the Gothic. The Nun is both eroticised and taboo. She signifies death, repression, madness and either warped excessive desire or the fatal denial of sexual knowledge. Lucy's Nun serves two purposes. She is a warning against the repression of desire. She is also Ginevra's cross-dressed lover, stalking round the school, male sexual desire achieving its own ends by any means available. Neither nun in either novel is quite what she seems.

Sister Helena, aka Sandy Stranger, has always been a writer, an inventor of fictions. Spark interweaves Sandy's fantastic imaginative text—*The Mountain Eyrie* by Sandy Stranger and Jenny Gray—which contains all their secret sexual speculation on the love life of Miss Jean Brodie. Sandy's own bisexual fantasies include Mr Rochester, John Buchan's heroes, episodes from *Kidnapped* and an upmarket policewoman whom she christens Anne Gray. The name itself is significant and has a link to the Brontës: Anne Brontë's first novel was *Agnes Grey*. The imagined narratives are not textually distinguished from Spark's main narrative. What is the effect of this? Both narratives become unstable and insecure. Neither narrative, one dominated by Miss Jean Brodie's meanings and the other by Sandy's revisions, has complete authority. Both narratives are therefore unreliable. Miss Jean Brodie's sexual clues to forbidden knowledge are planted in the texts she reads or recites to the girls of her set. Tennyson's '*The Lady of Shalott*' tells the tale of the prisoner of art, condemned to watch the world through the mirror and never to seize experience directly. The Lady's moment of sexual daring, having a direct look at bold Sir Lancelot's brazen greaves, is also the moment of her downfall. Charlotte Brontë's love life, also a subject of Miss Brodie's lessons, can only have been her illicit passion for a married man, her master and her teacher, Constantin Héger. Miss Brodie has been seen kissing another married teacher, Mr Teddy Lloyd. Miss Brodie's narratives generate other narratives in Sandy's imagination, each one more explicit and more daring than any offered by Miss Brodie. Sandy therefore perpetually displaces Miss Jean Brodie's version with her own. Her rebellion and betrayal is silent, but constant throughout the novel until the moment when she finally betrays Miss Brodie to Miss Mackay.

Lucy Snowe and Sandy Stranger are observers, dissenters and rebels. Both of them have names that signify their outsider status. Brontë hesitated between the names Frost and Snowe for Lucy, insisting to her publishers that she must have a 'cold name'. Lucy was to be the chilly observer of life, the woman who gives nothing away. Brontë's Lucy Snowe is a classic unreliable narrator, not because she is obtuse, but because she is secretive and has no confidence in the reader. Lucy's high-handedness in withholding information creates a radical insecurity in the reader. What else does she know, but is not telling? There are two other women within the structure of Brontë's fiction whose fates offer alternative narratives: Paulina de Bassompierre and Ginevra Fanshawe. Paulina is the tiny, doll-like happy-ending heroine, the Victorian woman whose sole desire is to service men. She transfers her affection from father to lover to husband without ever interrogating her need to adore rather than criticize. This is the selfless devotion that is always rewarded with happiness in fairy tales, as it is in *Villette*. It is, however, ironised. Lucy Snowe is destined for a more interesting fate and higher things. The other woman, Ginevra Fanshawe, is a flirt, fickle, light and egotistical: 'Ginevra lived her full life in a ballroom, elsewhere she drooped, dispirited' (*Villette*, p.143). But Ginevra has the intelligence to notice Lucy Snowe, to court her attention and approval and to realise that Lucy is not all she seems. 'Who are you, Miss Snowe?' (*Villette*, p.315). Lucy's answer is intriguing. She calls attention to her own role in her own story: 'I am a rising character' (*Villette*, p.317). All Brontë's heroines—Jane Eyre, Caroline Helstone, Lucy Snowe—are ambitious, rising characters. They want money and power. They want to marry above themselves. Their uncompro-

mising desire is for sexual satisfaction and financial independence. Lucy is never humble. She trusts her own judgement and
keeps her own counsel, even from her readers, which is very
disconcerting. We may well demand, alongside Ginevra Fanshawe,
'Who are you, Miss Snowe?'

The presentation of ambitious, powerful women in the work of
women writers is always problematic. A fixed plot already exists.
Nemesis follows hubris and often takes the form of sexual punishment. It would take an uncompromisingly daring writer to overturn
this particular coercive structure. Often the women who get away
with it are relegated to the sub-plot. Spark and Brontë both settle
for ironic compromise. We know what happens to the heroines and
it is a mixture of mastery and defeat. In both texts the writers play
narrative games with present and past tenses so that the future fates
of the characters are present before us throughout the main action.
This is a clever device, because it enables the writer to overstep the
limits, to go further in her presentation of her heroine, the opposition and her own speculations. Brodie gets her comeuppance; we
always know she will. Part of the interest of the fiction is finding
out why Sandy betrays her. But Miss Brodie retains her power. None
of Brodie's girls escapes her influence, and their subsequent fates can
all be traced back to her dominance in their early lives. Brontë never
allows Lucy Snowe to experience heterosexual union, but the young
women who seek her, Paulina and Ginevra, pass on into what is
presented as the less charged and less interesting state: marriage. Lucy
is still there at the end of the book, white-haired, independent, alone,
passing judgement on other people.

Lucy waits three years for the return of Monsieur Paul. She says,
'Reader, they were the three happiest years of my life' (*Villette*,
pp.504–5). They are not only the years of sexual anticipation but
also the years of economic independence and the freedom to make
her own decisions.

Lucy Snowe was a radically unconventional heroine for a
Victorian novel. Brontë's contemporaries were perfectly aware of
the writer's deliberate gender transgressions and criticized her for
her boldness. Thackeray wrote in a letter to Mrs Carmichael Smyth
(28 March 1853), 'I don't make my good women ready to fall in
love with two men at once,' and continued to Mrs Procter (4 April

1853): 'That's a plaguey book that *Villette*…How clever it is! And how I don't like the heroine.'[4] Lucy Snowe is clearly not a good woman. Anne Mozley in the *Christian Remembrancer* went further still. She was writing anonymously, but as a man.

> We want a woman at our hearth; and (Currer Bell's) imper-sonations are without the feminine element, infringers of all modest restraints, despisers of bashful fears, self-reliant, contemptuous of prescriptive decorum; their own unaided reason, their individual opinion of right and wrong, discreet or imprudent, sole guides of conduct and rules of manners— the whole hedge of immemorial scruple and habit broken down and trampled upon.[5]

This all sounds uncannily like Miss Mackay's views on Miss Jean Brodie. Both *Villette* and *The Prime of Miss Jean Brodie* are texts about women breaking the rules, knowingly, deliberately and without fear. Remember that 'Safety does not come first' (*MJB*, p.10). Anne Mozley does not consider her own impersonation as a male reviewer, but accuses Currer Bell of presenting 'impersonations' of women. The fight for femininity, what it is, of what it should consist, and how it should be represented, is thus being carried on between two women in literary drag. This is what gives the debate authority in the nineteenth century and, for us, over a century later, a peculiarly piquant humour.

The key scene in *Villette*, the school play, to which I have referred as 'the suggestive spectacle', foreshadows the events of the book. Ginevra, the heroine of the piece, acts nothing but herself when she flirts with Lucy. She does just that all the way through the novel. Ginevra will reject Dr John and marry the fop, De Hamal, played by Lucy, cross-dressed as a man in the farce. Neither Ginevra nor Lucy chooses Dr John, the conventional hero. Lucy falls in love with the despotic Monsieur Paul, and Ginevra elopes with the cross-dressed visiting Nun. De Hamal is extravagantly feminine in appearance. "His lineaments were small, and so were his hands and feet; and he was pretty and smooth, and as trim as a doll; so nicely dressed, so nicely curled… he was charming indeed' (*Villette*, p.148). Women, it seems, fancy men who resemble women and who dress up as women. In the disruption of gender roles with which the novel plays, Lucy lays claim to a man's intellect and a man's authority, but keeps her woman's sex. In the play she substitutes herself for de Hamal, and wins the girl.

Spark takes up the theme of sexual substitution in *The Prime of Miss Jean Brodie* and plays with its implications. The girls of the Brodie set become substitutes for their teacher in the paintings of Teddy Lloyd. He cannot paint her. So he paints them. All the images of the girls look like Miss Brodie. What the text does not make clear is whether this is simply a function of Teddy Lloyd's obsession with the teacher or whether it is the girls themselves who have begun to take on the likeness of Miss Brodie.

The scene in the gallery in Brontë's *Villette* (chapter xix 'The Cleopatra') involves Lucy's judgement of womanhood and femininity. She rejects the naked Cleopatra, the conventional pornographic object of male desire, but she also spurns 'La Vie d'une Femme', the roles of maiden, wife, mother, widow represented in the genre pictures. The role of spinster is not represented. The paintings present conventional versions of women. Lucy chooses none of them. For the Brodie set there is no other convincing, dynamic, desirable image of what a woman is other than their vivid mistress—therefore all Teddy Lloyd's images of the girls look like Miss Jean Brodie.

In all her imagined narratives Sandy Stranger perpetually displaces Miss Jean Brodie as the heroine and takes her place. Finally she displaces Miss Jean Brodie's chosen substitute as a lover for Teddy Lloyd and becomes the art master's mistress. The sexual substitution works both ways of course. It is unthinkable for Miss Jean Brodie to sleep with the art master, so she sends her girls. It is also unthinkable that she should sleep with her girls. So she hands them over to the art master. Then asks them to tell her all about it in detail. But somewhere or other she does think the unthinkable: 'Sandy thought, too, the woman is an unconscious Lesbian' (*MJB*, p.120). Sandy thought so, and Sandy is one of Miss Jean Brodie's creations. Sandy Stranger is a familiar figure in Spark's fictions. She is the calculating observer. She wears the mask of Lucy Snowe, the 'looker-on at life' (*Villette*, p.142). Lucy and Sandy both have the Brodie virtues, instinct and insight. Both women finally withdraw from the world. Sandy is a far less sympathetic figure than Lucy because she is always framed by Spark's ironic third-person narrative. And because, in the economy of Spark's method, she is characterized as the spy. Sandy, with her tiny piggy eyes, is the woman who refuses to comply with what she recognizes as Brodie's unconscious lesbianism. What she refuses to acknowledge is her own lesbianism. She wanted to be chosen by Miss Jean Brodie as her sexual substitute, and therefore, by proxy, as her lover. So she steals the place that is not chosen for her and betrays Miss Brodie.

The discourse that signals the heroine's intellectual rebellion and absolute difference in *Villette* is her Protestantism; the violent anti-Catholic propaganda expressed in the novel equates Rome with a philosophy of discipline and control that is little short of Fascist. Englishness is associated with Protestantism. Yet Lucy is saved from terminal hysteria by telling all in the Catholic confessional. Miss Brodie's dedication to Fascism is at the heart of her educational philosophy, where she plays the role of Führerin. Spark finally links Catholicism and Fascism when she comments on Sandy's decision to become a Catholic nun: 'By now she had entered the Catholic Church, in whose ranks she had found quite a number of Fascists much less agreeable than Miss Brodie' (*MJB*, p.125). The sharpness of this comment cuts both ways. Miss Brodie is an elitist to her fingertips, a woman who sees Hitler as a 'prophet-figure like Thomas Carlyle, and more reliable than Mussolini' (*MJB*, p.97). But Sandy is mean, egotistical, manipulative, with none of the colour and panache of Miss Jean Brodie in her prime. No one comes out of this conflict with the reader's sympathy for his or her fate still intact. And so indeed the moral seems to be: women beware women.

Passions between women, when they are unacknowledged yet acted out, through substitution and impersonation, become twisted dangerous things. Like Lucy Snowe, Jean Brodie is a gender transgressor, in love with power, sexual and otherwise. Spark's ironic register and the careful distance she keeps between her characters and her reader ensures that we never care too deeply about any of her characters. They are fictions. Persuasive, charismatic, vivid, but still fictions. She is a writer who punishes her characters. Everyone gets what they deserve. The narrative voices of both texts reflect the spirit of their respective heroines, Miss Lucy Snowe and Miss Jean Brodie: acid, dogmatic, eccentric, independent. The versions of womanhood on the fictional stage deliberately transgress the limits of convention. Men have key sexual roles to play, but these are essentially walk-on and lie-back parts. They are all shamelessly manipulated. The main tension, conflict, the suggestive spectacle itself, is acted out between the women.

3 .

FICTIONS AND HISTORIES

ON HELLA HAASSE'S *EEN NIEUWER TESTAMENT* AND TOLSTOY'S *WAR AND PEACE*

Why should any writer choose to write historical fiction? Nearly every classic fiction writer has written at least one solid period piece. George Eliot wrote *Romola* describing Florence in the 1490s and the rise and fall of Savanorola. Dickens wrote *A Tale of Two Cities*, remaking the French Revolution to terrifying effect. Tolstoy's *War and Peace* is in fact a historical novel, although it does fall into that intriguing genre of period writing, like Sir Walter Scott's *Waverley*, Charlotte Brontë's *Shirley* and George Eliot's *Middlemarch*: the recreation of the remembered past. When a writer chooses to set a novel fifty or sixty years back from the time of writing the contemporary reader is always made to reflect upon recent shifts and changes. We contemplate what we have become by looking at the choices made by the previous generation. This can be a frightening business.

But it takes effort, industry, research and a giant leap of the imagination to create another fictional space in a remote time. Flaubert wanted to write nothing but fiction dealing with classical antiquity and when he had murdered Madame Bovary he produced *Salammbô*, a novel set in Carthage during the Punic Wars. His classical heroine, however, like the hapless nineteenth-century doctor's wife, also ends up dead. And of course, in the end, all novels take on the mask of the historical novel as they step back from us into the past. So why do we write self-consciously historical fiction? And why do we want to read these fictions that play games with recreating history? What, indeed, is history, so far as historical fiction is concerned? For every writer who attempts the project of remaking history must have, whether they are aware of it or not, a quite concrete notion of what history is, what it means, and what its ultimate significance must be to us, the past's inheritors. It is not only professional historians who write history, and, as some recent historiographical debates bear witness, it is not only novelists who invent fiction.[1] The common term for a novelist in the nineteenth century was 'an historian'. George Eliot describes Fielding as an historian. The French word for 'story' is *histoire*. I cannot, and do not want to avoid the connections.

I think that there are several reasons why fiction writers should busy themselves with an imaginative historical reconstruction of the past. Some writers use historical fiction for a very serious purpose: to avoid the consequences of speaking openly on taboo subjects. Wrap it up in period exotica and the reading public will not feel threatened or uncomfortable. The most obvious examples of this are to be found in homosexual historical fiction, usually, but not always, set in classical antiquity. If homosexual passion was socially accept- able in Ancient Greece, and if clever men like Socrates or heroic ones like the Emperor Hadrian carried on with gorgeous boys, then it can be described as if it were an admirable and natural state of affairs. And if it were then, why not now? This is the Progressive Past School of History. One way or another, homosexual passions between men have always been more socially acceptable than passions of any kind between women. But, if the reader is in a state of denial the whole thing can be viewed as a very peculiar practice that went on in remote times and only concerned chaps who were keen on gladiators, actors and pretty athletes. Interestingly, several women have used classical antiquity to write about homosexual love, keeping themselves safe at two removes: by writing historical rather than contemporary fiction and about homosexual men rather than lesbians. Marguerite Yourcenar's *Memoirs of Hadrian* and Mary Renault's many novels (*The Bull from the Sea, The King Must Die, The Praise Singer* among others) are obvious examples. Both women were writing in the 1940s and 1950s before the advent of the women's movement and militant lesbian writing of the 1970s and 1980s. So their work might be described as an historical closet.

History looks temptingly seasonal. The broad outlines can appear to repeat themselves. The rise of a city or an empire will always be the prelude to its fall. Revolutions always consume their own children. The inevitable decadence sets in. This is the Cycles of Eternal Return School of historical fiction. A cyclical version of history is always conservative. Fiction writers are often beset by the awful urge to use history as a moral basket full of metaphors for change, decay and rebirth, all disappointingly predictable. Novelists rarely present this kind of history as teleological or progressive, but it is usually seen as deterministic. Mutability is inexorable. Indeed change, rather than development, is that which constitutes history. Inevitable Change and its equally inevitable return to recognizable original structures or points of origin is akin to the *longue durée* of the *Annales* school—that which changes so slowly it has the stealth of geological time, the grand continuities of history. Build all this into the structure of a novel and it is easy to think that you are mouthing a Great Truth. Your pronouncements will all sound deeply significant, with no effort on your part. Thus it was, is now, and shall be evermore.

The writers of historical fiction that I find most suspect is the History Enables Us to See Essential Truths More Clearly school. One trick often used here is to extract a contemporary problem—religious conflict, drugs or terrorism—and then write an historical novel about the Reformation, Elizabeth Barrett Browning's opium addiction or Guy Fawkes. The trap here becomes clear when we ask what remains unchanged, however far we venture into the past. The answer is always the same: human nature and the most fundamental passions of the human heart. This is the most conservative political conclusion of all and perhaps the most mendacious. If we do not change now, then we are looking at nothing but tragedy and general catastrophe. To argue that we, as human beings, have not changed our behaviour, customs and practices, at the very least, is to misread the facts.

The Essential Truths school is also the version of the historical novel that is most vulnerable to the 'God wottery, thou saucy knave' style of writing, that is, the Jolly Heritage version of history. Usually, in these worlds, whatever the period, although in the English pulp historical novel it tends to be Regency, Napoleonic or sub-Jane Austen, the heroines are prettier, with ever more slender waists, and the men are nobler, braver and hairier, with bigger balls. No one ever farts or fucks, although they may occasionally—daringly—vomit and faint. These fictions are always remorselessly heterosexual, tediously predictable and best sellers. These books usually embody the prejudices of the readers who consume them.

The pleasure of historical fiction, for both the writer and the reader, is simple. The novel is an ideal form for conveying information, the sense of landscapes, customs, objects, interiors, carrying us into the other country of imagined worlds. Fiction is the original form of virtual reality. We want to live for a while in another world and to forget our own.

I want to consider two novels, as case studies if you like, which represent two different methods of making historical fiction. These novels are written 100 years apart, one in the 1860s and the other in the 1960s, one is written by a man and one by a woman. One deals with the remembered past, the other with a remote period, that has left little upon the historical record. These two novels demonstrate two different methods of constructing the illusion of history, two different practices of historical fiction. I want to speak about Hella Haasse's classic of fifth-century Rome, *Een Nieuwer Testament* (literally, a more recent testament: the novel is translated under the title *Threshold of Fire*), and Tolstoy's *War and Peace*. Both novels have been in print ever since they were published.

Tolstoy was born in 1828 and the gigantic historical fresco, which made his name in Russia, is set in his parents' lifetimes. Indeed, his father makes a brief appearance in the novel. The book opens in Anna Pavlovna's salon in July 1805, and the epilogue, describing Pierre Bezuhov's marriage to Natasha, and Tolstoy's theory of history, ends the book in 1824. When Tolstoy was writing there were survivors from that generation still living. One of Tolstoy's critics, who bemoaned his lack of respect for great men and generals, had fought in the battle of Borodino. He did, however, praise Tolstoy's description of the battle.

War and Peace was first published in instalments over four years. He began writing in 1863; the first instalment was published in 1865 and the last in 1869. This method of publication meant that like many other nineteenth-century novels, their first audience would have experienced the story as part of their own personal histories, an unfolding through time, rather than the concentrated, somewhat devastating experience of reading one and a half thousand pages, which we have now. Tolstoy's theory of history is elaborated at length, and very repetitiously, throughout the book. Again, the first audience would have encountered his diatribes in small doses. Thus the first experience of reading this novel, alongside the process of its making, is unique and can never be repeated.

The narrator of *War and Peace* remains very close to the author. At one point he tells us that his 'father's house' in Moscow was not burned. The history of Russia that he is describing is his history, the national history to which he lays claim. He has a tale to tell and an axe to grind. His argument is with his primary sources. His enemies are the professional historians. His fiction is mobilized to convince us of his version of history. And his version of history is as follows.

History is a mighty engine, made up of a mass of apparently random, unpredictable events. No human being knows and none can therefore determine the course of history. Least of all those who imagine that they are in command. In fact, it is especially interesting to look at the lives of great men, and I do mean men here, women appear to belong to the unconscious of history, for, as Tolstoy (p.718) argues,

> A king is the slave of history...The higher a man stands in the social scale, the more connections he has with others and the more power he has over them, the more conspicuous is the predestination and inevitability of every act he commits.

The random, unpredictable nature of history is an illusion. It may appear like that to us, but that is not how it appears to God. Every act is preordained and was so throughout all eternity. History cannot be altered and cannot be stopped. It is a living process of organic nature whose only purpose is to fulfil itself. Tolstoy's version of history is chiliastic, pessimistic and magnificent. Human lives are neither unnecessary, nor without meaning. Our whole happiness depends upon understanding this gigantic force, that has us in its claws, and following the destiny that is already ours, preordained from the beginning of time itself, with joyous hearts.

Kutuzov, the commander-in-chief of the Russian armies, is the

real hero of *War and Peace*, because he understands that the invad-
ing armies of Napoleon will inevitably be destroyed. They will fling
themselves against the passive, stoic refusal of Russia to be
possessed, and be broken in the attempt. This passive stoic refusal
manifests itself in every aspect of the Russian retreat: the victory
at Borodino, which no one but Kutuzov described as a victory, the
peasants setting fire to their grain stores, the departure of the
Moscow society ladies to their country estates, rather than receive
the self-styled Emperor, the looting of the shops and the firing of
Moscow, even the appalling weather, everything resists Napoleon,
because it is in the nature of Russia to resist. Kutuzov both comprehends and embodies the most powerful force in Russia's history:
'the unconscious, universal swarm-life of mankind' which 'uses
every moment of the life of kings for its own purposes'. This 'unconscious, universal, swarm-life' is, by a curious fictional affiliation,
linked to the will of Providence. The will of the people incarnates
the desire of God. Kutuzov, is 'one of those rare and always solitary individuals who, divining the will of Providence, subordinate
their personal will to it' (Tolstoy, p.1285).

Kutuzov achieves this mystical union with history by struggling
to do nothing whatsoever. He turns procrastination into high politics. He spends most of the novel asleep, or reading novels, or
sobbing, whenever he is confronted by a sentimental and moving
expression of the Slavic Soul. He orders the armies to retreat, retreat,
and retreat again. He avoids battles at all costs. He is so fat that he
has to be assisted on to his pony. All his generals are plotting against
him. He does not, in short, act the part of a hero. We see Petya
Rostov doing just that and getting a bullet in his brains for his
idiocy. It is not courage, but cunning, that is vindicated in Tolstoy's
theory of history. Kutuzov, and he alone, is listening to the music
of history. He understands its significance because he understands
the people. 'This extraordinary power of insight into the significance
of contemporary events sprang from the purity and fervour of his
identification with the people' (Tolstoy, p.1287). And this, according to Tolstoy, is real Russian patriotism, this passionate bond with
ordinary people. And Kutuzov's passion is reciprocated. In one
telling scene (part three, chapter 4) a peasant's small daughter,
Malasha, hidden on the top of the stove in the front room that

becomes the army council chamber, listens to the disputing generals. Tolstoy describes the scene from her point of view. We see Kutuzov from the outside. Without understanding the arguments she hears, the child instinctively sides with the old man, whom she nicknames 'Granddad'. She registers his homely simplicity, his passive resistance to his warmongering colleagues, his 'sly glance', his cunning.

It is the peasant in Kutuzov who resists. But Tolstoy goes further. The central characters of *War and Peace*, Prince Andrei Bolkonsky, who dies as much from superciliousness as war wounds, and the slightly dotty Pierre Bezuhov, are both searching for meanings, answers, the key to the moral life. They are both aristocrats with more money than sense. The secret of goodness and happiness, however, is effortlessly understood by an illiterate peasant, Platon Karatayev, whom Pierre encounters among the prisoners hustled out of Moscow. Karatayev is a Christ figure. He talks in proverbs and foretells the story of his own martyrdom in a tale of the merchant and the murderer, both of whom are saved by God's goodness. The secret of his happiness is in love, the love of his fellow men and of all living things, and in his contentment with his inevitable destiny. Karatayev never struggles against fate. He accepts and teaches others to do likewise. Not surprisingly, this insistence on the part of Tolstoy, as novelist and alternative historian, that it is the peasant and the ordinary soldier who are the agents of history, and that the upper classes have everything to learn from them, went down exceedingly well with the Bolsheviks. One of the most acute critics of Tolstoy is Vladimir Ilyich Ulyanov, otherwise known as Lenin.

Lenin realized that the period of Tolstoy's writing life, 1862–1904, was the crucial element, that shaped his interpretation of the earlier period in history. Kutuzov's passive pessimism was inevitably attractive to Tolstoy. It was his own response to the upheaval in his own times. Commenting on Tolstoy's work in 1911, Lenin wrote,

> Tolstoyism, in its real historical content, is an ideology of an Oriental, an Asiatic order...Pessimism, non-resistance, appeals to the 'Spirit', constitutes an ideology inevitable in an epoch when the whole of the old order 'has been turned upside

down', and when the masses...do not and cannot see *what kind* of a new order is 'taking shape'.[2]

The charge of reactionary pessimism was among the early attacks delivered against the novel. Tolstoy's philosophy destroyed all hope of progress and improvement. Shelgunov, in the progressive paper, *The Affair*, declared that *War and Peace* set 'Eastern fatalism against Western reason' (Troyat, p.317). What Tolstoy's first critics could not forgive was the fact that he not only glorified vulgar peasants but was also rude about great men. An article in the conservative journal, *The Russian*, made the following comment:

> What the novelist absolutely cannot be forgiven is his offhand treatment of figures such as Bagration, Speransky, Rostopchin and Ermolov, who belong to history. To study their lives and then judge them on the basis of evidence is all well and good; but to present them, without any reason, as ignoble or even as repellent...is in my opinion an act of unpardonable irresponsibility and provocation, even in an author of great talent.[3]

Nobody *belongs* to history. The past does not take out a copyright on our lives. Anyone can be remade or reinterpreted in fiction. But, in fact, the problem here is not only Tolstoy's politics but also his method of making writing: realism. Realism gives the illusion of truth through the intensity of detail. Detail is intimate, but it is also merciless. In one famous passage in the novel Tolstoy takes on Thiers, one of Napoleon's historians, and routs him utterly, with a wicked flourish. Thiers recounts an incident in which Napoleon interrogates a captured Cossack. Tolstoy gives Thiers's version inside his own, so that the fictional text becomes a commentary on the supposedly historical anecdote. Tolstoy gives the Cossack a context, a history and a name. And then retells the incident, not from Napoleon's point of view, but from that of the cunning Cossack. The positioning of the reader is crucial in this passage. We too know who Lavrushka is, and where he comes from. We are inside the novel's discourse. Our view of Napoleon and his hagiographers is ironic, because we already know the Emperor and his generals too intimately to be overawed. We have become as insolent as Lavrushka.

The very detail with which Tolstoy describes the self-serving Cossack stakes a claim for the novelist's omniscient authority. Thiers makes assumptions about the unsophisticated 'Oriental mind'. Tolstoy undermines his racism. The balance of power played out in the Frenchman's text is reversed. It is Napoleon who is left looking like a pompous fool. It is the French who have been duped. Lavrushka is given the hindsight of history. He warns the Emperor, 'it's likely to be a long job,' and he is proved right. But, above all, the Cossack has the same sly look as the old man, Kutuzov.

Women have decorative rather than significant roles in Tolstoy's epic. I am tempted to retitle the novel *War and Women*, given that courtship is the central occupation of the principals when the battles recede. Women become historically significant once they are married. Tolstoy's Natasha, poetically radiant, but fatally naïve for most of the book, spends her time singing and dancing or leaning enchantingly out of windows. At the end of the novel she fulfils history's purpose for her and marries Pierre.

> Natasha needed a husband. A husband was given her. And her husband gave her a family. And she not only saw no need of any other or better husband but as all her spiritual energies were devoted to serving that husband and family, she could not imagine, and found no interest in imagining, how it would be if things were different. (Tolstoy, p.1372)

In all fairness to Tolstoy, he did not remain wedded to these reactionary views on women's destiny. Indeed, *The Kreutzer Sonata*, written over twenty years after *War and Peace*, the book that caused a scandal in Russia and was widely debated throughout society, proposes a trenchant case against heterosexuality. Tolstoy argued that husband and wife should live together like brother and sister, apart from the odd bid to conceive children, on the grounds that heterosexual intercourse, being an act that takes place between unequals, is degrading, humiliating, even disgusting for both parties. Not surprisingly, *The Kreutzer Sonata* has proved something of a discovery among some circles of radical and revolutionary feminists.[4]

Do women write a different kind of historical fiction from men? Do they construct history in a different image? Not necessarily, I would argue, although the accent may well fall rather differently. Everything will depend upon the mode of making writing, that the novelist chooses to use. Tolstoy's method of making history was shaped by his method of making writing. He is persuasive because the minute, domestic detail of his realism gives the illusion of the camera. His history is not narrated at second hand from a great distance, it is visualized by the characters in action, it is experienced, overheard. Napoleon and Alexander the First are presented in exactly the same terms as Pierre, Andrei Bolkonsky, Lavrushka, Natasha, Denisov. There are no textual markers to distinguish them. If you believe in one, you will believe in the other. The boundaries between fiction and history are deliberately blurred.

Hella Haasse's novel *Threshold of Fire* is set during the fifth century, *circa* AD380 to 414, an obscure but key period in the later Roman empire when Christianity, now the official state religion, began to stamp out all the old pagan rites by force. Haasse chooses a moment of transition when the old order changes and gives way to the new. Writers are the scribes who register these changes, so it is entirely appropriate that the action of the novel should centre on a writer, Claudian, the last great Latin poet. Claudian's work has been crucial to historians attempting to reconstruct the first decade of the rule of the Emperor Honorius, beginning in AD395. This was also a period when the successful writer had a public role to play, access to power and the ears of the great. Claudian was a flatterer and a satirist. He put his art at the service of the factions who fed him. But his writing could still be a direct influence on public events. A good epigram gets him into trouble. Fiction and poetry are now consumed and produced largely as private entertainment but still can and do have a public role as commentary and critique on contemporary, public events. In rare, but significant instances, books cause riots.

The book is about loss, waste, endings. Haasse's cast of characters presents a list of displaced persons, poised at the moment of accepting their dissolution. The book is an oblique, but telling attack upon state Christianity. This is the religion that preaches intolerance and sanctimoniousness. 'Pride, pride, but dressed in deceptively humble garments.... The Nazarene did not act wisely when he preached a doctrine that most people would misunderstand' (Haasse, p.71). Narrow, authoritarian Christianity is the motive force for the Prefect Hadrian. His opinions are not described. The reader hears what he thinks, watches what he does.

What kills an historical fiction most thoroughly and rapidly is a too obvious overdependence on sources. This happens to the best of us. George Eliot tells her readers far more about Renaissance hats in the opening chapters of *Romola* than we could ever wish to know. Walter Scott gets lost in anecdotes told by voluble yokels with authentically and unintelligibly represented Scottish accents. But on this point Haasse is deft, subtle, atmospheric and downright clever. The design of *Threshold of Fire* actually aids her in conveying a sense of place and her particular period of history. Most of the novel is created through memory. One single incident, the fatal dinner party at the house of Marcus Anicius Rufus, with an impending live sex act and animal sacrifice, is interrupted by Hadrian's soldiers and then investigated by the Prefect himself. The dinner party brings together all the main players and the themes of the book. Hadrian, as judge of the affair, interrogates each character in turn and finds that he too is forced to reconstruct his own past, his personal links with the people before him and to interrogate himself.

Memory, in fiction, is closely tied up with description. Thus Haasse is able to solve the problem of recreating her sources. As Hadrian remembers, so she describes. Memory is always selective; details stand out, a smell, a texture dominates. Memory, unreliable, wavering, unstable, is nevertheless the most potent tool we have to uncover our past. For the historian, memory survives in sources, archives, ledgers, bills, buildings, clothes, physical objects and written documents, in the texture of the earth. Oral traditions, oral histories, however dubious, are the closest we can approach to historical memory in societies, that do not preserve written documents. A novelist uses all those things, but even stranger ones besides: the scent of a woman's dress, a dream, a family resemblance, a china cup, the smell of crushed hay, or in the case of the Prefect Hadrian, his own raised hand, as he speaks the words of his office in the ritual oath: 'I swear that I shall pass judgement in the spirit of the law' (Haasse: p.86). The words 'I swear.' are first uttered by the prisoner, the disguised poet Claudian. They cause Hadrian to remember his promise to his dying mentor, Eliezar: 'Under the spell

of those lacklustre eyes, Hadrian raises his right hand: I swear'
(Haasse, p.85).

The novelist observes, creates and manipulates patterns, repetitions. Plots, which are causal, cannot operate without them. These
are the ironic methods fiction uses to teach its meanings. Random,
unconnected events may be the stuff of life, but they are not and
cannot be the stuff of fiction. Nor of history. We desire meaning
and significance. We look for connections and causes. We look for
a pattern, and when it is not to be found in the evidence, we find
it anyway, so great is our desire for the reassurance that our lives
are not senseless and beyond our understanding. Memory supplies
the key. When Claudian says, 'But I swear that I have never sacrificed a cock unless it was in your presence' (Haasse, p.43), Hadrian
remembers (pp.53–4),

An image rises from the depths of time... A walled villa and
outbuildings, a small settlement set among fields, olive groves,
fishponds...Memory focuses on a flimsy lean-to of woven reeds
standing on one of the countless marshy islands; a raft, tied to
poles thrust in the mud... Statues move, come to life: half-naked
youths, surprised in their hiding place, leap away from a fire-
blackened stone used since time immemorial by the farm
workers for secret sacrifices to the ancient fertility gods.

The descriptions are built from fragmented perceptions, sharp,
imagistic and always closely tied to the consciousness of the character that remembers. Here Hadrian is remembering his first
encounter with Claudian. He sees the figures as statues, moving,
coming back to life in his memory. But this is how the reader will
also imagine the figures in classical antiquity. And historical fiction
set in this period will also try to do precisely what Hadrian does:
make the statues live.

The descriptions of the monuments in Rome demonstrate the
cleverness of Haasse's method. The temples are ruined, abandoned,
desolate. These are, in fact, the first days of their ruin, but, in an
even greater stage of decay, this is how the visitor would see them
now. She is placing us in history, but also reaching to touch our
own consciousness of Roman Rome, as a city ruined. Haasse

(p.153) chooses the metaphor of the fresco.

> I see images from that former life as though they appear on
> a mural partially obliterated by age: a face, a gesture, the
> outline of a figure, a group of faded colours, suggesting what
> it was when it was fresh, but now eaten by decay, cracked,
> slowly peeling.

Her themes and the metaphors she is using are superimposed upon
each other; they also echo the reader's only possible experience of
the period she is describing.

One of the things that would strike us most forcibly as different in the ancient world would be the furniture and the interiors.
Haasse never labours these details; instead she works very carefully
with the character's point of view. Description in fiction, if it is to
be effective, always develops a particular character's point of view.
Description, like memory, is always partial and selective. It therefore needs to be located in a particular consciousness. Otherwise
the description floats free of its context. Description gives the text
eyes and a mind. Why are we watching this rather than that? If
description is tied to a particular point of view you know why—
and the text then pushes outwards, into the world, making the
world, and inwards, into the mind of the person seeing what is
described. Claudian, in the house of Marcus Anicius Rufus, gazes
at the traditional decorations, the mythological paintings, and interrogates their power: 'Was it the glow of the lamps...was it the
painted figures on the walls...Through the open door, I could see,
directly before me in the reception room, the dark form of Pluto'
(Haasse, p.163). The effect of this interior will lead to Claudian's
sudden resurgence, his acknowledgement of the man he was. Thus,
the character registers things he would normally take for granted
with an intensity that justifies their representation in the narrative.
We are not being given a gratuitous fifth century stage set. Claudian
sits reading the past off the walls, and so do we. Thus, the interiors are both objectively described and psychologically experienced
by the character himself.

There are only two female characters in *Threshold of Fire*, and
both of them have minor parts. The first is Serena, wife of Flavius

Stilicho. She is a powerful, calculating bitch whose head ends up on a stake, nailed to the Aurelian wall. A clear case of hubris and nemesis for, out of vanity and the lust for power, she had stolen the goddess's necklace. Thus, subversively, the justice of the old pagan gods is still suggestively present. Offend them, and they strike. The patterns of the fiction give back to the gods their ancient respect. The other woman is Urbanilla the whore, streetwise, unthinking, animal. There is a perpetual problem with women in historical fiction, especially fiction that deals with public events. We, the women, did not, could not, act directly within the public sphere. We were excluded from power. What we could do was influence individual men, often in the most underhand way. For many of us, dishonesty, cunning and sex were all the weapons we had.

It is no coincidence that feminist writers have tended to exploit the territory of science fiction, speculative fiction and Utopian fantasy rather than history in our quest to imagine other, different roles for women. In fact, I don't think that women writing historical fiction about men need be any less illuminating than women writing about women if we do it from a critical, feminist consciousness. And Haasse does. But the point is of general importance. Reinterpreting masculinity in history is a fascinating, subversive thing to do. It may even be a backhanded method of revenging ourselves upon the histories from which we have been so zealously excluded. History is, by and large, the possession of the masters. Our own history is often lost for ever. So? Rewrite theirs.

Haasse's Hadrian is an obsessive, jealous man who has 'ever but slenderly known himself'. The search for someone to persecute, the villain he can punish, leads remorselessly back to himself. One of the most haunting, elegiac motifs Haasse uses is Hadrian's dream. The dream is the key to his betrayals. Memory and conscience are intertwined in Hadrian's dream. When he understands its meaning, he will understand himself. In both pagan and Christian traditions, dreams are significant sources of meaning, prophecy, revelation. Hadrian's dream gives a sinister shape to his doubts and presages his destruction. Fiction is always filled with the satisfying echoes of superstitions justified. Brutal state Christianity may have triumphed in history, but in her fiction Haasse evens up the stakes.

What does not change in Haasse's novel? What do we find instantly recognizable? Well, human nature may not alter, but human behaviour does. Absolutely. Claudian reflects how 'Over two decades I have seen a world perish, and the birth of something new that is completely alien to me' (Haasse, pp.120–1). But what have stayed the same are the tenements of the poor where he now lives, the squalid hovels where people struggle to survive. Poverty and destitution look the same in every age. This is one of the great continuities of history. And as the new prophet predicted: 'The poor you will have with you always.' This is an interesting point to make about historical shifts. High politics usually only affects the highly placed. I would be a passionate advocate of the postmodernist theory of discontinuities if I believed that the dispiriting evidence to the contrary could be ignored. As the Marxist critic Terry Eagleton points out, 'What strikes a socialist most forcibly about history to date is that it has displayed a most remarkable consistency—namely, the stubbornly persisting realities of wretchedness and exploitation'.[5]

Tolstoy argued that 'History has for its subject the life of nations and of humanity' (p.1400). But we all write through the filter of our own nation as the didactic patriotism of *War and Peace* makes abundantly clear. Kutuzov is the hero of *War and Peace* because he alone has grasped the significance of the Russian will, the Russian people and the Russian soul. Tolstoy comprehends this because he too is Russian. We make our fictional nations out of the nation that is written within us. What then makes Haasse's antiquity especially Dutch? Ah, well, that I can't say, as I have so little experience of Dutch writing. But I am quite certain that there will be, within the novel's discourses, elements that signal its engagement with Dutch concerns, Dutch desires and fears, Dutch histories and Dutch dreams. I can say what makes it a great novel, a classic in every language.

Historical-fiction writers often try to explain the gaps in our knowledge of the past. Claudian mysteriously disappeared after AD404, and, rumours and speculation aside, we don't know what happened to him. Haasse imagines the end of his story. This work is like restoring the fresco, repainting the gaps. The completed picture is transformed; given other, different meanings. Haasse completes the design, suggesting rather than laboriously reconstructing the rest of the image. The economy of her method—the trial scene, which is intrinsically dramatic, generating questions which unleash memory, her use of flashback, first-person confessional narrative and the shifting point of view between Claudian and Hadrian—none of these techniques has ever been associated with the great sagas of classical antiquity, not with *Quo Vadis*, *Ben Hur*, or even Gore Vidal's *Julian*. The grand historical narrative is usually an action narrative, that makes no attempt to present a particularly complex inner psychology of character or to investigate its own discourses. Haasse's novel, in its method and condensed intensity, is a modernist work. Her story is specific to her literary historical moment, as was Tolstoy's great epic.

And my own views on the relationship of the novelist to history? I think I should probably come clean and say that I do not think that history in the sense that Tolstoy argues for History, that indifferent, unfurling force, eerie, inscrutable and irresistible, actually exists. The past is a quilt of traces and texts, ambiguous and often incoherent fragments out of which we make stories. We make up history as story, and until we do, it does not exist. But the past existed, and we are the proof of its passage. The past is written into us.

Novelists are not often professional historians. So it is rare that a novelist, approaching a particular period, will be aware of the recent, significant debates in the historiographical scholarship. But historians, apart from those on the madder fringes of psychohistory, seldom describe the inner psychic lives of the people they address. This is the novelist's territory. We both read the past, play it like a score, but in different registers. Haasse's fiction and Tolstoy's epic enter the psychic interiors of their characters, inhabiting a moment of inexorable and terrifying change. These books are republished, reread and remembered, because their versions of history are not stage sets, canvas backdrops of painted exotica, but another country.

4.

HOFFMANN'S UNCANNY REPLICANT

FREUD, *FRANKENSTEIN* AND *THE SANDMAN*

Beware the waking dream. It is the psychological state, that begets monsters. E. T. A. Hoffmann's hero of *The Sandman*, Nathanael, is beset by dreams and premonitions out of which he constructs his literary compositions, which are 'gloomy, unintelligible and formless' (Hoffmann, p.101). Nathanael's writings, which are described in some detail, sound unpleasant and unreadable. Mary Shelley claims to have conceived the genesis of *Frankenstein* in a state between sleep and wake.

> When I placed my head on my pillow I did not sleep, nor could I be said to think. My imagination, unbidden, possessed and guided me, gifting the successive images that arose in my mind with a vividness far beyond the usual bounds of reverie.[1]

'Reverie' is that state of wise passiveness[2] in which the ego relinquishes control to the unconscious, the state that allows ideas to surface and be remembered without censorship or restraint. It is also a way of describing creative invention as an involuntary process over which the writer does not have complete control and cannot therefore be held to be entirely responsible. Shelley describes the origins of *Frankenstein* as a 'waking dream'. Her account of the 'dream' was written some fifteen years after the event. And the entire narrative is carefully structured to draw attention to the importance of Mary's entourage. *Frankenstein* was the result of a ghost-story writing competition. She would never, she insists, have written the story without the presence of Byron, her husband and the bored literati of that wet summer in 1816.

The Sandman, composed in November 1815, and Shelley's *Frankenstein*, begun in 1816, and first published in 1818, were both written within a year of each other. While there can be no question of any direct influence, the shared themes and the proximity of their respective dates of composition are remarkable. Both tales are horror stories, still fashionable in the period, which deal with a fabricated being, the doll Olimpia and the unnamed Monster. Both tales call attention to their own indirect narrative structures, using letters and multiple narrators, and both employ all the classic devices of the uncanny: doubling, repetition, the return to places already visited and the lifeless being that comes to life. Both tales are meditations on the process of creation and on the relationship between creation and creator. The psychic structures of both narratives hinge upon oedipal fantasies of paternity.

Both these texts have complex afterlives. The afterlife of a text is contained not just in its re-reading and reinterpretation by subsequent generations, but in its continued and extended existence, reimagined, reinterpreted or remade by many different hands, across genres, across time. *Frankenstein* became a stage play in Shelley's own lifetime and, in the last century, one of our most enduring cinematic cultural myths. *The Sandman* became part of an opera—Offenbach's *Tales of Hoffmann* and a ballet, *Coppelia*. In every case the aspect of both tales that has most fervently agitated our imaginations is the figure of the lifeless being who comes to life, the Monster and the Doll. Why are these figures so important to us?

There are many reasons for their enduring uncanny fascination, not least being that they are both myths of creation, and we are now in a position to make human beings, beings that are potentially perfect, whatever that may mean. But one of the most fundamental reasons that these creatures continue to intrigue us is, I believe, because their very lack of humanity forces us to reflect upon what it is that makes us human.

The words and concepts that derive from 'human' are peculiar and merit a moment's reflection. Humane, humanist, humanitarian are all words that have highly charged and by and large positive moral meanings. When we speak of a person's 'humanity' we mean their tolerance, generosity, compassion. But none of these things is a quality that I would instantly associate with 'humanity' as a species.

It is immaterial whether or not Mary Shelley ever had the waking dream of the Monster's creation. What is significant is that she chooses to locate her inspiration in the connections made by the unconscious mind, because that is one of the central preoccupations of her tale. And of Hoffmann's *Sandman*. Nathanael's dreams and premonitions lead him to imagine his own death and damnation at the hands of the advocate Coppelius in 'a circle of flames which is rotating with the speed of a whirlwind' (Hoffmann, p.102). And his dream comes true. The patterning of the tale endorses the insights of the fatal reverie. Premonition becomes prophecy. Nathanael dies precisely as he had imagined that he would. He has written his own death.

Letters and documents play a key role in both tales. Both narratives begin with a series of letters whose significance for the overall meaning of the tale only gradually becomes apparent. In Shelley's *Frankenstein* the explorer Walton is on his way to the North Pole, which, he is persuaded, is a region of 'beauty and delight'. He is actually in the grip of the 'waking dream'. Its glamour is upon him. As he writes, 'Inspirited by this wind of promise, my daydreams become more fervent and more vivid' (Shelley, p.15). In both texts clear links are made with dream, premonition and delusion. Nathanael and Frankenstein fall into the hands of academic quacks and charlatans. Nathanael attends lectures by the infamous Spalanzani, professor of physical sciences, at the university town of G** and believes everything he hears. Frankenstein's head is full of magic and alchemy rather than science even before he departs for Ingolstadt and becomes inspired by Monsieur Waldmann 'to penetrate into the recesses of nature and show how she works in her hiding-places' (Shelley, p.47). Note the sexual metaphor and the fact that Nature is inevitably feminine. Spalanzani's creation is female, the daughter-doll, Olimpia.

Both Shelley and Hoffmann argue for a suspicious, rational scepticism, especially in relation to the waking dream. In both tales the writers present a critical counterpoint between a daylight world and a nightworld in which their protagonists make monsters—and art. The tension between reason and hysterical delusion, a common trope of the Gothic and used to thrilling effect by Ann Radcliffe, is in fact undermined by the uncanny. Coppelius does murder Nathanael and the Monster has a textual reality outside the mind of his creator. Clara, a key figure in *The Sandman*, represents good sense and rationality. She resists the dream. But she is not safe from the machinations of the uncanny. When Coppola, the alter ego of Coppelius, invades her imagination, she admits, 'I'm almost ashamed to confess that he disturbed even my usually sound and healthy sleep with all manner of strange dreams' (Hoffmann, p.98). However, within a day everything is back to normal. And Clara denies the narratives of horror, the nightworld of writing itself.

The voice of reason is associated with women in both tales: the shadowy Elizabeth in Shelley's Frankenstein and the discriminating Clara. Yet however firmly she dismisses the patterns of the uncanny, Clara almost becomes its victim. Elizabeth, cast in the unfortunate role of the bride of Frankenstein, is sacrificed to his uncanny double on her wedding night. She is murdered by the Monster. In Shelley's tale the waking dream became substance. She fused the novel and the Monster in her mind when she described the text as 'my hideous progeny' and bid the creature to go forth and prosper. It has certainly done so. It is not the daylight world of reason that has been vindicated by the afterlives of either text, but the premises of the uncanny and the hideous progeny of the waking dream.

In his essay on *Creative Writers and Day-Dreaming* (1923) Freud argues that a writer's material represents their fantasies, usually their repressed fantasies, of wish-fulfilment. I would argue that the fantasy life of an imagined character is one of the most crucial areas of critical investigation in the work of many writers: pre- and post Freud. And so are memories, the place where we generate our fantasies. It is of immense significance to me that both Nathanael and Frankenstein present themselves to other characters and to the reader by recounting events in their childhoods and explaining their present obsessions in relation to these childhood memories. Even the Monster begins with his birth, childhood and essential reading. It is these early experiences that have shaped his psyche and desires and made him what he is. In Frankenstein's case it is his reading of Cornelius Agrippa and Paracelsus, that give rise to his obsessions. This is dismissed as 'sad trash' by his father, which results in an ever more passionate investigation of the works of the false fathers. Frankenstein is quite literally in search of the Facts of Life. Philosophy, he says 'had partially unveiled the face of

Nature, but her immortal lineaments were still a wonder and a mystery' (Shelley, p.40). As a student Frankenstein is still asking the infantile question—'Where do babies come from?'—until he can make his own child out of resurrected body parts. In Nathanael's case the formative childhood experience is the primal scene. Nathanael hides behind the curtains to spy on his father and the Sandman. He wants to see what it is that they actually do together when everyone else is sent away or to bed. Coppelius, the figure of the Sandman, is introduced as satanic, the ogre in the fairy tale.

> Imagine a big, broad-shouldered man with a massive, misshapen head, a pair of piercing, greenish cat-like eyes sparkling from under bushy grey eyebrows, and a large beaky nose hanging over his upper lip. His crooked mouth was often distorted in a malicious smile, and then a couple of dark red spots appeared on his cheeks, and a strange hissing sound proceeded from between his clenched teeth. (Hoffmann, pp.88–9)

Nathanael quite specifically identifies Coppelius as Satan:'He was a hateful, spectral monster, bringing misery, hardship and perdition, both temporal and eternal, wherever he went' (Hoffmann, p.89). The mother has been banished from the father's study. The feared satanic figure and the gentle father combine together to forge human beings out of gleaming lumps of fire and flame. The hysterical memory of childhood is of 'human faces (were) visible from all sides, but without eyes, and with ghastly, deep black cavities instead' (Hoffmann, p.90). There is a crucial detail in the description, that links the father and Coppelius: 'As my old father bent down to the fire he looked quite different. A horrible, agonising convulsion seemed to have contorted his gentle, honest face into the hideous repulsive mask of a fiend. He looked like Coppelius' (Hoffmann, p.90). The father and the satanic visitor, engaged upon their sinister task of making babies without recourse to women's bodies, have become one in the child's mind.

The Sandman is a key text for Freud. In his essay on The Uncanny (Das Unheimliche, 1919), Freud uses the tale to define what he means by 'unheimlich'. He develops his theory of the uncanny in relation to elements of Hoffmann's narrative technique: the phenomenon of doubling, repetition, the return to places visited earlier in the text and above all the figure of the automaton, which appears to be human, but is not, the living doll. Freud concentrates on the oedipal theme in his reading of *The Sandman*—and I want to come back to this—but first I would like to call your attention to another very relevant study by Freud, *A Seventeenth Century Demonological Neurosis (Eine Teufelsneurose im siebzehnten Jahrhundert*, 1923).

Freud became fascinated by the Faustian fate of Christoph Haizmann, a seventeenth-century Austrian painter. Haizmann was brought to the shrine of Mariazell, a pilgrimage shrine some 80 miles south-west of Vienna. He was convinced that only the direct intervention of the Virgin Mary could save him from the satanic pact he had made with the Devil nine years before. Haizmann doubted his artistic ability and his capacity to earn his living as a painter after his father's death and had signed a pact with the Devil. Oddly enough two pacts existed. One was written in ink and the second was written in Haizmann's own blood.

> Anno 1669
> Christoph Haizmann. Ich verschreibe mich diesen Satan, ich sein leibeigner Sohn zu sein, und in 9. Jahr ihm mein Leib und Seel zuzugeheren.
> (I sign a bond with this Satan, to be his bounden son, and in the ninth year to belong to him body and soul). (Freud, vol. 14, p.395)

Haizmann had lost his own father. Satan became his father substitute.

Freud's explanation of Haizmann's satanic obsession was simple. Our relations with our fathers will often contain

> two sets of emotional impulses that (are) opposed to each other...impulses of an affectionate and submissive nature, but also hostile and defiant ones. It is our view that the same ambivalence governs the relations of mankind to its Deity. (Freud, vol.14, p.400)

Freud maintains that God and the Devil were once the same person, and, in the later history of religion, they were 'split into two figures with opposite attributes' (ibid.). The good father and the satanic father are in fact, the same.

Hoffmann's tale is littered with deceased or absent fathers and satanic father substitutes. All the sinister, uncanny figures—Coppelius, Spalanzani—Coppola, are linked to each other and to the first father in the story. The element of doubling contributes to the uncanny effect. Spalanzani, who is perceived as a benevolent figure by Nathanael, explicitly associates the evil Coppola, the double of Coppelius, with Satan in the moment when they are pulling the doll Olimpia apart in their struggle to possess her. He shouts, 'get out-Satan-stop-you tinker-you devilish creature-stop-get out- let go!' (Hoffmann, p.113). The satanic father and the benevolent father are two faces of the same figure, which, in Nathanael's mad mind, finally become indistinguishable.

The good fathers of *Frankenstein* are venerated patriarchs, the principle figures in domestic groups. It is his refusal to be a father to the Monster, that is Frankenstein's undoing. The religious connections to the Father–God are ubiquitously present in the novel through the references to Milton's *Paradise Lost*. The Monster tries to situate himself not only in relation to his Maker but also in his role as the good son or the bad son. 'I am thy creature; I ought to be thy Adam, but I am rather the fallen angel, whom thou drivest from joy for no misdeed' (Shelley, p.100). The making of the Monster by artificial rather than natural sexual means leads Frankenstein to cause the murder of the woman he supposedly loves. The detail I want to emphasise here, however, is the fact that in both *The Sandman* and in *Frankenstein* the beloved woman is a sister figure. Elizabeth and Clara are both insinuated into their lovers' families as a result of their fathers' (and mothers') deaths. Clara and Lothar are 'the children of a distant relative' (Hoffmann, p.99) who enter Nathanael's family after the deaths of his father and their own. Clara and Nathanael grew up together. Elizabeth, an orphaned aristocrat, is actually given to Frankenstein by his mother 'as a present' during the father's absence. She is the love child given by the mother to the son. And this is recognized in the text where she is described, several times, just so that we acknowledge the implicit presence of an incest-taboo, as 'my more than sister' (Shelley, pp.35, 36). Spalanzani chooses Nathanael as a suitor for his daughter–doll, Olimpia. The woman is provided by the father figure. She is the sexual gift, offered to the male protagonist by the family or their substitutes. The object of desire is part of a complex sexual exchange, which takes place within the family.

The equivalent figure to the Monster in Shelley's *Frankenstein* is the doll, Olimpia. The Monster is eloquent, articulate, rational, well read and considerably more humane than his maker. Moreover, the Monster has many virtues, which are associated with the feminine in Shelley's ideological structure: domesticity, rationality, the desire for a family; but he is created male. Olimpia, on the other hand, possesses that combination of feminine characteristics, beauty and idiocy, that mark her out as a tool created by the patriarchy. She is the perfect, blank body, brainless, eyeless, lifeless, the pastiche feminine that is bound up with male narcissism. Nathanael falls in love with a projection of his own desires, just as Spalanzani knew he would. Nathanael is in the grip of his own narcissistic egotism, as was Frankenstein when he created the Monster. The Monster, however, turned out to be an independent individual, thinking and judging for himself. Olimpia's discourse reflects Nathanael's own vacuous nonsense. And Hoffmann says so. 'She utters few words, certainly; but these few words are true hieroglyphs, disclosing an inner world filled with love and lofty awareness of the spiritual life led in contemplation of the Everlasting Beyond' (Hoffmann, pp.111–12). Here Hoffmann is jeering at one of his own tropes, the Muse who is a living symbol, a cryptic sign that represents all that is eternal, endless and sublime. In Olimpia's case she is the Muse who is the female mirror of the male ego, reflecting men at twice their natural size. All she ever says is 'Oh! Oh! Oh!' But that is enough for Nathanael, who declares 'only in Olimpia's love do I recognize myself' (ibid.).

The Monster, as I have emphasized, is male, and, except in the cinematic afterlives of the text, Frankenstein is unable to make a female monster. He begins to do so in response to the Monster's just request for a mate, but rips his handiwork to bits. Significantly, he does so at the moment when he reflects that they may breed and fill the world with baby monsters.

The Monster's enraged threat is a direct response to Frankenstein's betrayal of his own sexual hopes and is also sexually explicit: '*I will be with you on your wedding night.*' (Shelley, p.168). And it is here that the symbolic structure of *Frankenstein* is at its most suggestive. This phrase '*I will be with you on your wedding night*' is repeated again and again. And as the moment when Frankenstein and his bride should retire to bed approaches, Frankenstein becomes more and more agitated, terrified and deranged.

> I had been calm during the day; but so soon as night obscured the shapes of objects, a thousand fears arose in my mind. I was anxious and watchful, while my right hand grasped a pistol which was hidden in my bosom. (Shelley, p.194)

What agitates a man whose wedding night is the stuff of nightmare and who paces the passages of the house, terrified? As he insists, 'this night, and all will be safe; but this night is dreadful, very dreadful' (Shelley, ibid.). On the night of the making of the Monster, Frankenstein had dreamed of embracing his 'more than sister' and then realizing that he held the corpse of his dead mother in his arms. This is a classic oedipal dream. It is the fear of a woman's sex, not fear of the Monster, that has taken possession of Victor Frankenstein. As soon as his wife is dead his desire is released: 'I rushed towards her and embraced her with ardour' (Shelley, p.196). The woman in his arms, whether he is dreaming or waking, is always a dead woman. In Frankenstein's unconscious mind he has already destroyed all the women he loves. The Monster is the physical extension of his unconscious will. Women and their sexual capacity to reproduce are, and always have been, monstrous. They must be murdered, terminated.

Shelley's women are all noble victims of men and the monsters they either are, or have made in their own image. This is disturbing and depressing to read. Hoffmann's critique of constructed femininity is more radical. The doll is never alive. It is a cyborg, a created thing, a man's version of a woman. Hoffmann distinguishes between Olimpia and Clara, but Nathanael is finally unable to do so. When he sees her through the father's eyes, that is Coppola/Coppelius's spyglass, she becomes a 'wooden dolly', to be hurled into the abyss. The father is the real perpetrator of destruction. He kills at one remove. Nathanael is merely the tool, the physical extension of his unconscious will. He becomes an automaton in the father's hands. Nathanael's apparent return to precarious sanity is a return to adolescence. 'He was lying in bed in his room in his father's house' (Hoffmann, p.116). Note that Hoffmann insists that it is still the father's house although the father is long dead. Here Nathanael believes that he is secure. But, as Hoffmann, Shelley and Freud have argued in very different ways, we are not secure in the father's house. We are not secure in the father's love. The father's eyes turn women's bodies into corpses or into wooden dolls.

Clara is the woman who survives. We are told that she has 'a very acute, discriminating mind' (Hoffmann, p.99), and that her critique of Nathanael is to be trusted. She has the narrator's confidence and by extension that of the reader. She writes like a psychoanalyst. In her letter to Nathanael she warns of that 'dark power' which leads us astray and, intriguingly, takes 'the same form as we do' (Hoffmann, p.95). We make our own *doppelgänger*, it is a 'phantom of our own self' (ibid.). The father's double, Coppelius, is the 'dark power' who mirrors the father and holds him in thrall. The eerie presence of the double becomes, as Freud points out, 'the uncanny harbinger of death' (Freud, vol. 14, p.357).

Ridley Scott's *Blade Runner* (1982) is one of the twentieth-century afterlives of both *Frankenstein* and *The Sandman*. This film uses all the main themes from both texts. The setting is futuristic, the monsters are perfect cyborgs returning in search of their makers. It is now impossible to tell a man from a monster. 'More human than human' is the slogan of the Tyro Corporation, which makes the cyborgs. Significantly, there are no human women in the film. They are all replicants, living physical creatures, which are not born, but made. One of their makers recognizes the replicants, because they are flawless: 'You're so different, you're so perfect.'[3] The male cyborgs are all perfect killing machines, bent on acquiring longer lives and, if not, then on revenge. The females come in two versions, the updated model, which is loving and self-sacrificing—and the killer doll. The updated state-of-the-art female cyborg doesn't even know that she is replicant. She has been given that which the film courageously suggests makes us human: memories. Memories are our identity, memories of our childhood, our parents, our first piano lesson, Freudian memories of infancy and adolescence, memories that indicate the process of time and our extended existence within its limited trajectory. This is what makes Shelley's Monster human, his vulnerable narrative of his first memories. This is what lies at the core of Nathanael's identity and destiny, his childhood memory of his eyes, menaced by Coppelius and his father's death.

I happen to disagree with this, the central contention of the film. Memories can be manufactured, inherited, invented, passed on. Memory is notoriously partial and inaccurate. There is such a thing as a false memory, often related to the uncanny waking dream. And, indeed, although this comes as a devastating shock to her, the replicant's memories are not her own.

I was not interested in the replicant with memories for the simple reason that she represents many women's worst fears, a made-to-measure woman, the product of male fantasy, replete with wall-to-wall femininity, sex-bomb figure, intellectual banality above and beyond the call of duty, and no desire to be anywhere except in Harrison Ford's bed. The killer doll on the other hand is what many men fear: the basic pleasure model, which is indistinguishable from the loving version, but which is waiting to kill you. The message of *Blade Runner* is simple: identify the killer doll and kill her first.

In the sequence where Deckard (Harrison Ford) kills Pris she disguises herself as what she is, an artificial being, and in her death throes she pounds the floor like a robot running down. Interestingly, the final shot of her body, terminated or murdered, depending on your sympathies, makes her look like a woman, shot down in cold blood. I can only echo Roy's (Rutger Hauer) point, 'That's not very sporting, to fire on an unarmed opponent.'

All the humans in *Blade Runner*, apart from Harrison Ford, who may or may not be a replicant, but who must have a very clever and demanding film agent, are slobs, freaks, dwarves or bullies. No one could argue that the film promotes humanity. Tyro himself, the head of the replicant Creation Corporation, is a tiny freak in large glasses. He lives at the top of a gigantic tower block, which is as near to heaven as he will ever get. When he is faced with his creation, the beautiful Roy, he says, 'It's not an easy thing to meet your maker.' But the opposite is also true. Especially when the created being arrives unexpectedly, making demands. The scene, which takes place in the maker's bedroom, is reminiscent of the sequence at the beginning of chapter 5 in *Frankenstein*. Tyro refuses to hand over the gift of the gods, long life. And so Roy kisses his father–maker, then symbolically castrates him by putting out his eyes and killing him. The maker, the father, the figure of God become one in all these texts. The creator and his creation are locked together for ever. The son must kill the father, or the father and his agents will seek out and kill the son. But whatever happens to either of them, the doll is always switched off, shot down or ripped to bits. Even in the original narrative of *Oedipus* by Sophocles, Jocasta ends up as the corpse while the blinded king goes on to become a well-known saint and martyr in another play. The woman always dies.

In *The Pleasure of the Text* Roland Barthes casually claims the centrality of oedipal fantasies of paternity in all narratives. 'Death of the Father would deprive literature of many of its pleasures. If there is no longer a Father, why tell stories? Doesn't every narrative lead back to Oedipus?'[4] I am beginning to agree with him. In his interpretation of *The Sandman*, Freud insists on the connection between castration, blinding and the fear of the father: 'For why does Hoffmann bring the anxiety about eyes into such intimate connection with the father's death?' (Freud, vol.14, p.353). The first person who the replicants of *Blade Runner* find and kill is the man who makes their eyes. And the only way that you can recognize a replicant is by watching their pupils as you try to catch them out with trick questions about their families and memories. The truth about their humanity, or lack of it, is revealed by their eyes.

Both *Frankenstein* and *The Sandman* are dissenting texts. They are at odds with contemporary Romantic ideologies of creativity, and while they both embody oedipal fantasies of paternity, they also represent critiques of that fantasy. Most interestingly, both tales articulate radical critiques of the male creator and his relation to the feminine. Ridley Scott's *Blade Runner* takes up all the potentially radical elements in Shelley and Hoffmann, but does not develop them. Instead the film simply regurgitates a very ordinary pornographic and murderous misogyny. Deckard can slaughter women with impunity, because they are not women, they are replicants. Had he bothered to read Simone de Beauvoir or Monique Wittig he would know that we are not born women, we become them. And, as some radical feminists, including myself, have always argued, we are encouraged to spend a lot of time and money getting ourselves up to look like daughter–dolls, or like replicants. This was Hoffmann's point. Nathanael cannot distinguish between a woman and a replicant, even, or rather especially, by staring into her eyes.

The ideological poles of *Frankenstein* and *The Sandman* are exactly the same. On the one hand, domesticity, home, married happiness and the balanced social group, on the other, ambition, isolation, science, the search for knowledge and the inevitable results of that search, madness and perdition. Clara is spared for the fate of 'quiet domestic happiness', that Mary Shelley would recognize as the heavenly reward for which all women yearn. I think it was something Shelley did truly desire. It was not something she herself ever enjoyed until she was a widow. But Hoffmann's ending is quietly ironic. Was this what Clara really wanted? Or is this just the happy ending of popular cliché? Hoffmann leaves the question open. It is easy to overlook his explicit feminist critique, because it is wrapped up in a comical-satirical aside and the uncanny elements of the story are far more compelling. But this passage has remained with me and strikes me more forcibly every time I read it.

> Many esteemed gentlemen were not so easily reassured: the story of the automaton had made a deep impression on their minds, and a detestable distrust of human figures became prevalent. In order to make quite sure that they were not in love with wooden dolls, several lovers demanded that their beloved should fail to keep time in singing and dancing, and that, when being read aloud to, she should sew, knit or play with her pug-dog; above all, the beloved was required not merely to listen, but also from time to time, to speak in a manner that revealed genuine thought and feeling. The bonds between some lovers thus became firmer and pleasanter; others quietly dissolved. (Hoffmann, p.115)

Men, Hoffmann suggests, unless they value and respect women with acute and discriminating minds, who may be their sharpest critics, are just as likely to be satisfied with wooden dolls. I agree with him. What makes us human, I venture to propose, is not what we can remember but the fact that we can both feel and think.

II
SEXUALITY AND CONTEMPORARY WOMEN'S WRITING

5.
REIMAGINING THE FAIRY TALES

ANGELA CARTER'S BLOODY CHAMBERS

> I started to write short pieces when I was living in a room too small to write a novel in. So the size of my room modified what I did inside it and it was the same with the pieces themselves. The limited trajectory of the short narrative concentrates its meaning. Sign and sense can fuse to an extent impossible to achieve among the multiplying ambiguities of an extended narrative.
>
> Afterword to *Fireworks: Nine Profane Pieces* (1974)

The Afterword to *Fireworks* (1974) and the Polemical Preface to *The Sadeian Woman* (1979) are both literary manifestos, maps for the territory and enterprise of Angela Carter's fiction. In the writing she produced at the end of the 1970s, a period during which her oblique arguments with feminist themes is most clearly evident, she wrote a collection of modern fairy tales: *The Bloody Chamber and Other Stories* (1979). These tales have two sources: first, her translations of the fairy tales of Charles Perrault (1977). Perrault's tales consist of ancient wisdom reconfigured as didactic little pieces of enlightened self-interest, the short tale in which sign and sense become utterly fused, with the moral, often a contradictory one, chugging along behind like the guard's van. The second source is to be found in Carter's own writing and that is her critique of sexual mythologies. This investigation spreads across her fiction and non-fiction. In her novel, *The Passion of New Eve* (1977), a fantastic Gothic quest across an America rent apart by the approaching apocalypse, she mounts a voyage into the forbidden places of sexual taboo. The psychology of pornography and the Gothic, submerged in the sexual translations of Eve, are subjected to speculative, non-fictional treatment in *The Sadeian Woman*. And out of this last metamorphosis come the fairy tales of Charles Perrault, rewritten by the woman disguised, self-styled as the moral pornographer, the tales in *The Bloody Chamber*.

We must stand back to applaud her ambition, for the success of her enterprise, reshaping and reimagining the archetypes of imagination, recasting all the bricks of our inner worlds, would require extraordinary resourcefulness. The lure of her chosen form, tales rather than short stories, is easily explicable. For Carter, the strength of the tale lies in the fact that it does not sink into the slough of dailiness, rather, it unfetters the imagination. For the tale interprets rather than presents everyday experience, through 'a system of imagery derived from subterranean areas behind everyday experience, and therefore the tale cannot betray its readers into a false knowledge' (Afterword to *Fireworks*). But here, I believe, she is wrong. The unconscious is not a treasure vault containing visionary revelations. It is rather the cesspool of our fears and desires, filled with the common patterns that are also projections of the ways in which we have been taught to perceive the world.[1] And the deep structure of those patterns will reflect the political, social and psychological realities within which we exist as best we can. The unconscious mirrors these changing realities. And so the fairy tales, forming part of the received collective wisdom of the past, which, as Carter rightly perceives, reflect the myths of sexuality under patriarchy, have been and still are used as the text books through which those lessons are learned. Thus the tale, especially the fairy tale, is the vessel of false knowledge or, to put it more bluntly, interested propaganda.

Andrea Dworkin, in *Woman Hating* (1974), discusses the process by which women are taught fear as a function of their femininity—through the fairy tales.

> The lessons are simple, and we learn them well.
> Men and women are different, absolute opposites.
> The heroic prince can never be confused with Cinderella, or Snow-white, or Sleeping Beauty. She could never do what he does, at all, let alone better... Where he is erect, she is supine. Where he is awake, she is asleep. Where he is active, she is passive. Where she is erect, or awake, or active, she is evil and must be destroyed.[2]

The fairy tales, with all the unfettered cruelty that is permissible in fantasy, spell out the punishment for rebellion or dissent. Here is Dworkin again.

> There are two definitions of woman. There is the good woman. She is a victim. There is the bad woman. She must be destroyed. The good woman must be possessed. The bad woman must be killed, or punished. Both must be nullified.[3]

Her analysis is perfectly correct. So far as she goes. She sees the fairy tales as parables handed out to children as working tools, ways of dealing with the world, the way to knuckle down into uncongenial shapes, rather than as weapons of understanding and change. The fairy tales are about power, and about the struggle for the possession of women, by fair or by magical means. And even the fairy (more properly folk) tale itself, as the narrative art of the people, communally owned, has been appropriated by the ruling class at a specific point in history, transformed, sanitised and rewritten. For the fairy tales became children's literature at a particular moment in the history of their transmission. Originally, they were nothing of the kind.[4]

The German term *Märchen*, fairy tale, comes from the Old High German word, *mâri* (or Gothic *mêrs*, Middle High German, *Mâre*), which means news or gossip. The term Volksmärchen, or folk tale, acknowledged the people, das Volk, as its rightful owners. The English term fairy tale comes from the French 'contes de fées', most probably derived from the Countess d'Aulnoy's collection *Contes de Fées* (1698), translated into English in the following year as *Tales of the Fairys*. The term fairy tale is now used to describe both the orally transmitted folk tales and the literary productions of bourgeois and aristocratic writers in the late seventeenth and eighteenth century. The important distinction between these two forms in which the tales appear lies smothered under the blanket term, fairy tale. It is the result of a process, that occurred gradually in Europe, coinciding with the invention of childhood and the rise of the bourgeoisie. The classical notion of *paideia*, education, and of childhood as a time of preparation and initiation into the adult world was not generally held during the Middle Ages.

Our world is obsessed by the physical, moral and sexual problems of childhood. This preoccupation was unknown to
medieval civilisation, because there was no problem for the
Middle Ages: as soon as he had been weaned, or soon after,
the child became the natural companion of the adult.[5]

But during the Renaissance there was a new emphasis on education for the middle and upper classes. The reinforcement of
patriarchy under Protestantism endorsed a more rigid hierarchy
within the family and the state. Eventually the fairy tales became
part of that order and were absorbed into the structure of educational propaganda for children. Thus, a radical current in popular
culture was appropriated and contained. But it is of course
extremely difficult to gauge the intention behind these aristocratic
borrowings from popular culture. Peter Burke poses the questions:
'When Perrault draws on French folklore for his contes, what is he
doing? Equating the common people with children? Striking a blow
for the moderns in their battle with the ancients?'[6] The implication
here is that whatever Perrault is doing, his intentions are anything
but innocent.

In Germany there is a significant distinction between the
Volksmärchen, the traditional tales of the people, and the
Künstmärchen, a specifically literary form that was of crucial importance to the German Romantic Movement.[7] The Romantiker
grasped the revolutionary potential of the folk tale; they wrote
their own. And in the work of Novalis, Brentano, Eichendorff,
Chamisso and particularly Hoffman, the Märchen becomes a
critique of bourgeois society and the vehicle for philosophical and
aesthetic theories.[8] But alongside this radical reclaiming of a current
in German literature went the larger process through which the tales,
trapped in the anthologies by literary archaeologists such as the
Brothers Grimm, were captured for consumption by an educated
audience and finally relegated to the nursery.[9] The original folk tales
were a collective enterprise, produced by both audience and narrator, which articulated the aspirations of the people and their fight
against social injustice. The world of these tales reflects the solid
walls of feudalism: it is ruled by kings and queens, bound by fixed
class hierarchies, filled with peasants, soldiers, dragons and magic.

It is a predominantly rural order; there are no signs of industrialisation. The trades are traditional: weavers, millers, shepherds, peasants, merchants. And the tales stress inequalities, extremes, excess, in superlative terms.[10] The kings are always the wealthiest and most powerful in the world, the poor shepherds and peasants the most helpless, destitute and underprivileged mass nature ever suffered to survive upon the earth. Yet fairyland is also an unstable world in which appearance crumbles before magic; Cinderella becomes a princess. The miller's youngest son becomes the Marquis of Carabas, the frog becomes a prince. Fairy tales deal in transformations that subvert the apparently unalterable social realities. Magic translates, fragments, inverts. The lower classes are upwardly mobile, official morality is calmly set aside, cunning and deception pay off, as it does for Puss-in-Boots, his master, and for the common soldier, who deceives the twelve dancing princesses.

But although the fairy tales show a fantastic inverted world where every pretty chambermaid can aspire to be queen, the hierarchies themselves remain resolutely intact. The King (the Father) will always hold absolute rule over his subjects. Translation into another state is always a process of forgetting. The wicked kings may be deposed. But the memory of the peasant/swineherd/shepherd's previous existence never influences his rule once he becomes the New King. Except that he will govern wisely and well in order to forestall another fairy-tale revolution.

Charles Perrault and the Countess d'Aulnoy, both writing in the last years of the seventeenth century transcribed the tales from a living oral tradition. As did the Brothers Grimm, who rewrote and reshaped the Rhineland tales in their collection for a supposedly more sophisticated audience. But the tales, coming out of history, continued to mirror the times that produced them. There is nothing particularly remarkable about stepmothers in a period when lives were short, childbirth often fatal and a surviving husband would probably marry again; nor, in a medieval community, is there anything extraordinary about wells as the centre of village life, or marriage at puberty. But the fairy tales became, inexorably, the property of childhood. And now, whether they are read or told, they have become narratives passed on from adults to children. The teller traditionally bears the face of age. They are the parables of

wisdom and experience addressed to the apprehension of innocence, in which the pleasure of fiction is carefully fenced off and
contained within the ritual parentheses, 'Once upon a time' and
'They lived happily ever after'. These are the limits of fantasy, and
the fairy tale is necessarily fantastic, a world of extremes, excess,
an inversion of dailiness. But the tales continue to expose the raw
nerves of real conflicts between classes, families, men and women,
mothers and daughters, fathers and sons. The transition from
adolescence through puberty to adulthood is brutally taught through
the tales in which inequalities are painted unambiguously in the
characters of excess. The sexual symbolism of the fairy tales may
now appear to us to be ludicrous, transparent, but to the child
their meanings remain mysterious. Carter's rewriting of the tales
for adults is an exercise in making the mystery sexually explicit.

Apart from 'The Erl-King', which she presumably adapts from
Goethe's ballad, Carter chooses a sequence of classic tales, most of
which are to be found in Perrault. She gives centre stage to the story
of Bluebeard and his wives in 'The Bloody Chamber'. There are two
versions of 'Beauty and the Beast' in 'The Courtship of Mr Lyon'
and 'The Tiger's Bride'. An operatic Puss-in-Boots deliberately
suggests the Baroque ornamentation of Rossini's music. 'The Snow
Child' capitalizes on the mysterious absent father in Snow White
and the motif of necrophiliac desire, which is there in the source.
Sleeping Beauty is a Gothic vampire in 'The Lady of the House of
Love'. There are two versions of Red Riding Hood, and a tale that
combines motifs from several versions of the woman and the wolf
stories: 'Wolf-Alice'. The animal aspects of human sexuality are her
particular concern; thus the wolf and the lion roam through the tales
seeking whom they may erotically devour. Carter's style is genuinely
original. Her deliberate, ornate overwriting is the most startling
departure from the simplicity of form and directness of expression,
characteristic of Perrault's narratives, which are as stark and uncompromising as ballads. Perrault's morals may be knowingly smug:
his narratives are not.

Carter's tales are rewritten as elaborate pieces of pure Gothic,
in the manner of Poe. 'Character and events are exaggerated beyond
reality, to become symbols, ideas, passions. Its [the Gothic tradition of Poe] style will tend to be ornate, unnatural...Its only humour

is black humour' (Afterword to *Fireworks*). But the infernal trap inherent in the fairy tale, which fits the form to its purpose, to be the carrier of ideology, proves too complex and pervasive to avoid. Carter is rewriting the tales within the straitjacket of their original structures. The characters she re-creates must, to some extent, continue to exist as abstractions. Identity is defined by role, so that shifting the perspective from the impersonal voice of an anonymous third person narrator to the inner confessional narrative, as she does in several of the tales, merely explains, amplifies and reproduces rather than alters the original, deeply sexist psychology of the erotic. Here is an example of how this happens. The disarming of aggressive male sexuality by the virtuous bride is at the root of 'The Frog Prince' and 'Beauty and the Beast'. Beauty and virtue translate into power over men's desires. 'Red Riding Hood', on the other hand, is a warning to little girls not to talk to strange wolves in forests. Note that in the original tale the Wolf's behaviour is neither questioned nor challenged. The Wolf consumes little girls because it is his nature so to do. Carter transposes the moral from 'Beauty and the Beast' and 'The Frog Prince' into the erotic confrontation and reversal at the end of 'The Company of Wolves', her version of Red Riding Hood. The encounter of the Wolf and the Woman becomes a meeting of mutual sexual aggression and the cliché of the Wolf as rapist is endorsed. Carter celebrates female heterosexual erotic ingenuity in a backhanded way. Red Riding Hood sees that rape is inevitable, so she decides to strip off, lie back and enjoy it. 'The Wolf is carnivore incarnate' (*Bloody Chamber*, p.116). She wants it really. They all do. That is the message spelt out.

'The Tiger's Bride' presents a variation on the original bargain in Perrault's tale, where the heroine is sold to the highest bidder in the marriage pact. But Carter's bride, like her Red Riding Hood, also strips off all artifice, which are the civilized lies inherent in borrowed garments, the veils of female hypocritical modesty. She reveals herself to the Beast as she really is, the mirror image of his feline predatory sexuality. Authorial comments surrounding this encounter is contradictory. On the one hand Beauty's body is 'the cold white meat of contract' (*Bloody Chamber*, p.66) but, on the other, 'I, white, shaking, raw, approaching him as if offering, in myself, the key to a peaceable kingdom in which his appetite need

not be my extinction' (*Bloody Chamber*, p.67). I would suggest
that all we are watching, beautifully packaged and unveiled is the
ritual disrobing of the willing victim of pornography. Carter's tales
are, supposedly, celebrations of female erotic desire. But male
sexuality has too long, too tenaciously been linked with power and
possession, the capture, breaking and ownership of women. The
explicitly erotic currents in her tales mirror these realities.
Pornography, that is, the representation of overtly sexual material with the intention to arouse prurient, vicarious desire, uses the
language of male sexuality.[11] Even the women's equivalent of soft
porn, romance novels, bodice-rippers, and fantasy romances, all
conform to recognizably male patterns of domination, submission
and possession. The women's fantasy variant is of course the
submission of the male, or his disarming, by her beauty and her
power. The Beast is rendered gentle and tender. But he is only
desirable if he remains the beast beneath the skin. Carter envisages women's sexuality simply as a strategic response to male
arousal. She has no conception of women's sexuality as
autonomous desire. Heterosexual feminists have not yet invented
a satisfactory alternative, anti-sexist language of the erotic. Indeed,
without some drastic change in the social order, I am not sure
how this could be done.

One of the most deft and disturbing pieces in *The Bloody
Chamber and Other Stories* is Carter's version of Snow White:
'The Snow Child'. Here she exposes the oedipal conflict between
Mother and Daughter, a central theme in all the fairy tales. The
snow maiden is the father's child, 'the child of his desire' (*Bloody
Chamber*, p.92) who threatens to usurp the Mother's place. With
one small touch Carter reveals the Mother as a sister to Sade's
Juliette, the sexual terrorist, with a motif taken from the literature
of pornography, 'she wore high, black shining boots with scarlet
heels and spurs' (*Bloody Chamber*, p.91). If the Mother ever fails
the child in the fairy tales that child's life is always in jeopardy. In
Carter's version the Mother offers up the child, as her sexuality blos-
soms in the rose, to the Father's lust. And it is the Father's desire
that destroys her. Interestingly, he only fucks the daughter when she
is dead. Not even Snow White can be accused of leading the men
on. But it can still be said of her and her counterpart, Sleeping

Beauty, that they want it really they both do, for they are awoken from sleep and death by men's kisses. Carter removes the supposedly comforting denouement to the original tale in which the mother is destroyed and the child successfully navigates the dangerous transition into marriage and sexual maturity. But she doesn't question the ideology implicit in this story, that the Mother and Daughter will, of necessity, become rivals for the Father's love and be cheerfully prepared to countenance one another's destruction.

The division between Mother and Daughter, and between Sisters, is one of the cornerstones of patriarchy. The fact that so many of the tales endorse these old enmities is both sinister and predictable. Cinderella, Snow White, Beauty and the Beast all argue the case for women beware women. The logic of the fairy tales continues in the structures of our literature. *King Lear* is cast in the fairy-tale mould of the old father dividing his kingdom among the three daughters. The two older daughters, the Ugly Sisters, are destructive and predatory, only the youngest daughter, carefully constructed out of masculine desire as the Snow Child had been, remains loyal to the father. Carter rings the sexual changes cheerfully enough, and they are entertaining to read. Red Riding Hood sleeps between the paws of the Wolf, the Grandmother actually is the Wolf, Beauty becomes the Beast. But Carter still leaves the central taboos unspoken. She could never imagine Cinderella in bed with the Fairy Godmother.

Carter's peculiar fascination with de Sade simmers at the root of what is both disturbing, reactionary and unoriginal in her work. She knows that 'the tale has relations with the subliterary forms of pornography, ballad and dream' (*Fireworks*, p.122). This is why the tales are both fascinating and dangerous material for women writers. In *The Sadeian Woman* Carter suggests that the Devil is best slain with his own weapons and argues the case for the moral pornographer, who is, curiously, given that she is clearly thinking of herself, envisaged as male.

> The moral pornographer would be an artist who uses pornographic material as part of the acceptance of the logic of a world of absolute sexual licence for all the genders, and projects a model of the way such a world might work. A

moral pornographer might use pornography as a critique of current relations between the sexes. His business would be the total demystification of the flesh and the subsequent revelation, through the infinite modulations of the sexual act, of the real relations between man and his kind. Such a pornographer would not be the enemy of women, perhaps because he might begin to penetrate to the heart of the contempt for women that distorts our culture even as he entered the realms of true obscenity as he describes it.[12]

This is, I would suggest, utter nonsense. Pornography, indeed, the representation of all sexual relations between men and women, will necessarily 'render explicit the nature of social relations in the society in which they take place'.[13] That is why most bourgeois fiction concentrates upon the choices surrounding courtship and marriage, for it is there that the values and realities upon which a society is based will be most sharply revealed. All we need to do is read the bourgeois marriage novels. We don't need to dig out the pornography.

But Carter's claims for the possibilities of the moral pornographer are very far-fetched. What does pornography reveal? The realities of power perhaps, will be revealed by the pornographic text, but not the imagined experience of desire. Pornography, heightened, stylised, remote, mirrors precisely these socially constructed realities, the realities of male desire, expressed through aggression and force; the reality of women's masochistic and submissive complicity with that desire. Where then shall imagined desire, the expression of feminist eroticism, be found, apprehended, expressed? Andrea Dworkin argues that this can only emerge when the divisions of sexual polarity are destroyed, when male and female sexual identities are reborn.

We will have to abandon phallic worth and female masochism altogether as normative, sanctioned identities, as modes of erotic behaviour, as basic indicators of 'male' and 'female'.

As we are destroying the structure of culture, we will have to build a new culture, nonhierarchical, nonsexist, noncoercive, nonexploitative—in other words, a culture which is not based on dominance and submission in any way.

And as we are destroying the phallic identities of men and
the masochistic identities of women, we will have to create,
out of our own ashes, new erotic identities.[14]

This passage, taken from her essay 'The Politics of Fear and
Courage', is Utopian, but very much to the point in that the fairy
tales are used to teach precisely these things: phallic worth, female
masochism, fear and courage. The fairy tales are bridges across the
straits of adolescence into adulthood. The child becomes a man or
a woman; the rite of passage is always conceived as heterosexual
marriage and sexual maturity, but within the architecture of the fairy
tale this will have a different meaning for a boy or a girl.

Tom Thumb and Puss-in-Boots are fairy tales addressed to boys.
They transmit the classical oedipal message of puberty. The Father
or the Ogre must be slain by the adolescent who then possesses his
inheritance, the ogre's castle and the captive princess. The Father
is never killed by name in the fairy tales, but his threatening, confin-
ing destructiveness is emphasized in the Father figures. He is masked
by the usual superlatives, that is he is more powerful, dangerous,
vicious than any other Ogre/Father in the fairy tale world, but with
courage, ingenuity and strength he may be overcome. So the tales
send the boys out into the world to seek their fortunes, create their
wealth, possess their women. The boys must be taught courage. The
girls must be taught fear.

For girls the critical metamorphosis is sexual: menstruation,
puberty, marriage. For Sleeping Beauty the symbolic curse that
comes upon her is puberty, that first shedding of blood, the curse
that can only be redeemed by marriage, which is her rightful place.
Sleeping Beauty is the first of the tales in Perrault's collection
Histoires ou contes du temps passé (1697). Perrault tells the tale
up to the 'happy ending' of the Prince's kiss, which redeems the
time and awakens the Princess from her long stupor of adolescence.
All the women have to do is wait. She must not seek out sexual
experience, a potential she now possesses, for that is fraught with
danger. She must wait and sleep out the years until she is claimed
and possessed. Perrault, with all the unctuousness of a civil servant,
adds the moral: 'The tale of Sleeping Beauty shows how long
engagements make for happy marriages, but young girls these days

so want so much to be married I do not have the heart to press the moral.'[15]

But Perrault only tells us a version of an older Neapolitan story to be found in Basile's *Pentamerone* (1636). In that version a king is out hunting, he passes the locked and deserted castle, his falcon flies in through the open window, he follows the bird and comes upon the sleeping princess. He is unable to rouse her or to control himself, rapes her, leaves and forgets her. The result of this little exploit is twins, Sun and Moon, who awaken their mother. The king eventually returns, but he is, unfortunately, already married to an ogress, a sister of Medea, who tries to organize a meal in which his two children are served up in a pie. The Sleeping Beauty is to be burnt. The link here between Sleeping Beauty and Snow White is clear. In both cases she is the oedipal child of the Father, who arouses his desire and therefore the hatred of the Mother. Perrault's method of curtailing the narrative before it became too unpleasant need not be attributed to prudery. His stories were addressed to the Court, where it was scarcely tactful to speak of cannibal queens and rapist kings, especially if they were sitting in front of him.

Carter's Gothic version of Sleeping Beauty enacts the peculiar nemesis of radical feminism. Killing women has been largely the prerogative of men. 'The Lady of the House of Love' is both the Sleeping Beauty and the Vampire Queen, the voracious witch of Hansel and Gretel. The reader expects a revenge tale, a reversal of Bluebeard, in which the siren vampire, an aristocratic countess, lures handsome princes to an appalling blood-soaked, but erotic finale. 'Everything about this beautiful and ghastly lady is as it should be, queen of night, queen of terror—except her horrible reluctance for the role' (*Bloody Chamber*, p.95).

In fact what the Lady of the House of Love longs for is the alternative Grande Finale, the conclusion of all snuff movies in which the woman is sexually used and ritually killed, the oldest cliché of them all, sex and death. Then she can abandon her predatory sexuality, which is an unnatural force, as her own blood flows. She wants the symbolic breaking of the virgin hymen, the initiation into sexual maturity and then the escape into death. She wants it really. They all do.

In death, she looked far older, less beautiful and so, for the first time fully human.

I will vanish in the morning light; I was only an invention of darkness.

And I leave you as a souvenir the dark, fanged rose I plucked from between my thighs, like a flower laid on a grave. On a grave. (*Bloody Chamber*, p.107)

Only in death does she pass into womanhood, and the handsome British cyclist who does the deed departs the innocent security of fairy tale into the terror of history and the trenches of the First World War. They were both doomed.

The most successful narrative in Carter's collection is the most elaborate and expansive, the modern version of Bluebeard, 'The Bloody Chamber'. This is the finest tale in the collection. It is a *tour de force*. The confessional voice of the tale is that of experience, the woman recalling her initiation as a young girl into the adult world. Carter's story, and indeed all the earlier versions, are about women's masochistic complicity in male sexual aggression—and about husbands. Perrault was in no doubt about this either. He draws the moral from the story; an admonition to nosy women who seek to know the truth about the men they marry: 'Curiosity is the most fleeting of pleasures; the moment it is satisfied, it ceases to exist and it always proves very, very expensive. It is easy to see that the events described in this story took place many years ago.' He than adds, embarrassed, 'no modem husband would dare to be half so terrible'.[16] Carter's Bluebeard is simply a husband; he is given no other name.

There may well have been an historical Bluebeard. One possibility is Gilles de Rais (1404–40), a Breton aristocrat who fought alongside Joan of Arc at Orleans. But this seems unlikely, for although he was hanged in 1440 for multiple murder—his victims were numbered at 140—he only had one wife, and she survived him. Apparently his beard was red and not blue, and his victims were usually little boys, whom he liked to fondle as they died. The other candidate for the role of Bluebeard is Comorre the Cursed, another native of Brittany, who lived in AD500. He was given to murdering his wives as soon as they were pregnant and supposedly decapitated the last one, Tryphine. She was restored to life by St Gildas, a local abbot, eventually founded a convent and was, in the fullness of time, canonized by the Church.[17]

Carter's *Bloody Chamber* uses all the iconography of the Gothic: the remote castle, the virgin at the mercy of the tormented hero–villain, the enclosed spaces, hidden atrocities, women voraciously, masochistically eager for the corruption of sexuality. All the pervading themes of pornography are there too: domination, control, humiliation, mutilation, sexual possession through murder. All perpetrated on willing, eager victims. The marriage bargain as licensed prostitution is made explicit. The bride is the bought woman, acting out the 'ritual from the brothel' (*Bloody Chamber*, p.15). Carter's tale carefully creates the classical pornographic model of women's sexuality, the child bride responsive to her husband's desire, ready to be 'impaled' among the lilies of death, the face with its 'promise of debauchery' and a rare talent for corruption. Here is the sexual model that endorses the 'normal and natural sadism of the male, happily complemented by the normal and natural masochism of the female'.[18] But this story is the closest Carter ever comes to demonstrating the possibilities of her role as the 'moral pornographer'. And 'The Bloody Chamber' is one of the least erotically violent and explicit tales in the sequence. True, the husband of 'The Bloody Chamber' is a connoisseur and a collector of pornography. When the child bride peers at the titles in his bookcase she finds the texts for the knowledge she eventually reads in the blood of her sisters, Bluebeard's former wives. Her husband's books are a guide to her fate—*The Initiation, The Key to Mysteries, The Secret of Pandora's Box*—imaged in the Sultan's murdered wives. But there are two other figures that Carter has created in her rewriting of the tale, whose actions and presence alter the terms of the unequal conflict between husband and wife.

In Perrault's original version the bride's sister Anne, about whom we are told nothing but her name, looks out from her tower as Bluebeard sharpens his cutlass in the courtyard, to proclaim the galloping arrival of the bride's two brothers. In Carter's version this figure becomes the blinded piano tuner, Jean-Yves, who loves the child bride not for her ambiguous beauty, the veil across her corruption, but for her single gift of music. Only with the blinded boy who humbly serves her music can Carter envisage a marriage of equality for Bluebeard's bride. Men as invalids are constant figures in women's fiction,[19] most remarkably in the writing of Charlotte Brontë. Her heroes suffer on the point of her pen, she blinds them, maims them, drowns them. This element in women's fantasies is easy to understand: if a man is damaged and hurt a woman is released from the habitual sexual constraint. She can take action, initiate contact, speak out. If the man is flat out in bed and dependent upon her the situation becomes even simpler. The power imbalance, inherent in all heterosexual relationships, is neatly levelled off.

This attempt to break down the traditional erotic identities is also implied by the pervasive transvestism in Brontë's novels.[20] Rochester dresses up as a gypsy woman, de Hamal as a nun. Shirley, the wealthy landowner, brazen behind the ambiguous sexuality of her name, talks, acts, commands, woos, swaggers like a man. Ginevra Fanshawe is seduced by Lucy Snowe, in front of everyone, when Lucy takes the part of a man in the school play. The man whose eyes are extinguished can no longer evaluate, dominate, control. He is reduced to dependence. Only when Rochester is blinded can Jane Eyre return. Blindness is the curse of Oedipus, a symbolic reckoning. But the blinded man has a further significance. This figure suggests that although men observe women constantly they do not see us; they do not perceive who we really are, we remain invisible. But while blindness, as symbolic castration, may signal the end of male sexual aggression, it is also mutilation. As such it cannot be offered as the answer, the new male erotic identity.

In the case of Bluebeard's bride it is as well that her lover cannot see her, for she carries the mark of her complicity and corruption for ever. This is the complicity of women who have been made in man's image, who have desired to be possessed, who walk after the diva of Isolde, the model of Montmartre, the Romanian Countess, into the arms of the Marquis and who meet the reward of that complicity in the bloody chamber.

It is not the brothers who arrive armed with muskets and rapiers to save Bluebeard's bride, but a figure that never appears in the fairy tales, the mother as saviour and as travelling heroine.

My eagle-featured, indomitable mother; what other student
at the Conservatoire could boast that her mother had outfaced
a junkful of Chinese pirates, nursed a village through a visi-
tation of the plague, shot a man-eating tiger with her own hand
and all before she was as old as I? (*Bloody Chamber*, p.7)

This is the mother who invests in her daughter's career rather than
her price on the marriage market; it is the mother's spirit, the
courage incidentally of the Gothic heroines who pass unraped,
unharmed down into the dungeons of the castle, that accompanies
her daughter to learn the truth of the bloody chamber. 'My mother's
spirit drove me on, into that dreadful place, in a cold ecstasy to
know the very worst' (*Bloody Chamber*, p.28). The hand of
vengeance against Bluebeard is the woman's hand, the mother's
hand bearing the father's weapon. Only the women have suffered,
only the women can be avenged: 'without a moment's hesitation,
she raised my father's gun and put a single, irreproachable bullet
through my husband's head' (*Bloody Chamber*, p.40).

Here Carter is transforming the sexual politics of the fairy tales
in significant ways. The mother of Bluebeard's bride never deserts
her child. She has the wisdom to give her child the freedom
demanded by sexual maturity, the freedom denied to Sleeping
Beauty by her royal parents when they seek to protect her from the
fairy's curse—that her hand shall be pierced by a spindle—and
from sexual maturity. Carter's mother arrives with melodramatic
timeliness. She is not her daughter's rival, but her guardian, giving
the lie to Papa Freud's oedipal realities. The child felt that she had
indeed lost her mother: 'I felt a pang of loss as if, when he put the
gold band on my finger, I had, in some way, ceased to be her child
in becoming his wife' (*Bloody Chamber*, p.7). But, in fact, the bond
between Mother and Daughter is never broken. Carter's tale,
perhaps unwittingly, carries an uncompromisingly feminist message.
If women, especially mothers and daughters, were to protect and
defend one another against men, we would seal up the door of the
bloody chamber for ever.

All Carter's books to date are either short novels or tales, fantastic narratives. The short narrative is her forte. Her style is innovative,
daring; as lavish and ornate as the detail on the architecture Puss-

in-Boots finds so easy to climb. Her texture is complex, but it looks effortless. 'Nothing to it once you know how, rococo's no problem' (*Bloody Chamber*, p.69). This is her great strength. Her reimagining of the fairy tales, had she studied the ambivalent sexual language that is there in the originals, could have been far more telling and suggestive. Take Perrault's 'Le petit Chaperon rouge'. What is the significance of her red hood? At the moment when the ritual words are uttered—'draw the bolt and the latch will open'— she is the one who enters. She is an agent. She chooses to enter. We have a transvestite wolf, that likes wearing old ladies' clothes. In later versions the woodcutter finds Red Riding Hood and the grandmother safe in the womb of the wolf. The male gives birth to the female. Or was the wolf really a woman after all? These ambiguities are acknowledged in 'The Company of Wolves', but there is much more sexual fun to be had. Follow the sexual symbolism of Cinderella thrusting her foot into the envoy's slipper. Cinderella or the Prince? Which one of them is the foot fetishist? Could the cat in Puss-in-Boots be gay? See Bluebeard's wife penetrating the secret menstrual space of the bloody chamber. She is seeking out the other women. Whatever happened to Snow White's dwarves? This is a woman who sleeps with seven men. These undercurrents are there in Carter's tales. She cannot avoid them. But she could go much further than she does.

Carter chooses to occupy a tiny room of her own in the house of fiction. For women, that space has always been paralysingly, cripplingly small. I think we need 'the multiplying ambiguities of an extended narrative' to imagine every aspect of ourselves, the entire Dark Continent of women's lives. We cannot fit neatly into patterns or models, as Cinderellas, ugly sisters, wicked stepmothers, fairy Godmothers, and still acknowledge our divers existences, experienced or imagined. We need the space to carve out our own erotic identities. And then to rewrite the fairy tales,[21] but with a bolder hand.

6.

QUEER GOTHIC

ANGELA CARTER AND THE LOST
NARRATIVES OF SEXUAL SUBVERSION

Women writers have always dominated the Gothic. It is a form within which the female sign, woman as heroine, shapes the terms of the narrative. A long line of intrepid travellers, witches and ghouls, ghosts, vampires and madwomen have peopled their pages, from Ann Radcliffe in the 1790s, the 'mighty mistress of Udolpho', down to the mighty mistress of post-modern Gothic herself, Angela Carter. Carter was not a naturalistic writer. She used the Gothic and Horror modes of writing in much the same way that the original 1790s writers had done: to make the familiar strange within her narratives and to approach difficult material without the strait-jacket of contemporary political and sexual censorship.

Gothic is a romance form. The narratives are always journeys, tales of flight and pursuit, stories of escape. The iconography of the Gothic is built up out of moss-covered fortifications, which are always symbols of oppression: the locked house, the moated grange, the castle, the convent, the prison. It is easy to see why Carter was interested in the Gothic, and in romance rather than realism. Gothic deals in psychic narratives, the logic of dreams acted out. Within Gothic the writer can take risks with her material because the form itself articulates transgressions and taboos, our primal fears about the violence that is endemic within the family. The Gothic gives incestuous desire a local habitation and a name. The Gothic liber-ates vicarious desire; we become voyeurs, witnesses of the forbidden spectacle. Even unspeakable queer passion appears in the coded discourses of disguise.

For contemporary queer communities written histories, especially fictional histories, are crucial. All too often I am told that to describe any aspect of eighteenth-century writing as 'queer' is both anachronistic wish-fulfilment and ahistorical self-indulgence. Queer is here and now, not then. Yet queer lives, even here and now, are often lived within codes and disguises, masquerades, as well as closets. We are not always out, let alone 'in your face'. We are to be found within gossip, tall stories, freak shows, allegations, cabinets of curiosities, hints, gaps, innuendoes. And in the Gothic we were there. Sometimes overt, named, as in de Sade's fantastic sexual narratives, sometimes hidden in women's romantic or sentimental friendships or cross-dressed as novices in monasteries. When we were hidden in history we were often visible in fiction, coded, but present. I am rather in favour of innuendo for the simple reason that without knowing that they were doing so a heterosexual audience read over the shoulders of the dykes, deviants and drama queens.

As a fictional mode the Gothic also lends itself to tacky melodrama; impossible events and sentiments that are overwritten and overblown were extremely popular on the Romantic stage.[1] The theatrical, indeed melodramatic element in Gothic is crucial to the form. The narratives are linear; each confrontation, discovery or event is exaggerated and overplayed for its own sake, for the immediate thrill, and not for its significance in a tightly shaped and constructed plot. The form is episodic, building up to local climaxes, rather than a final catastrophe involving all the dramatis personae. Even within the prose narratives the important unit of meaning is *the scene*.

The narratives of late eighteenth- and early nineteenth-century Gothic fiction and melodrama often hinge upon transvestism, seeming, and disguise. Transformations are in themselves revelations. Who you are depends upon the role you are playing at the time. Identity becomes a stage property; it is changeable, fluid and unstable. The male characters in Gothic are either guilty of deliberately 'seeming' to be other than they are, faking it behind an elaborate facade. Or they are men on the run, bristling with guilty secrets. M. G. Lewis' Ambrosio (*The Monk*, 1796) pretends to be a pious abbot, but is eventually revealed, even to himself, to be corrupt, lecherous, cynical and murderous. Ann Radcliffe's Schedoni is no priest, but a guilt-ridden aristocrat with a lurid past. Frankenstein looks like a bourgeois intellectual, engaged in gentlemanly, scientific pursuits, but proves to be a secret maker of monsters. The good women of sensibility on the other hand are presented as touchstones of integrity. These are the travelling heroines, adventurers, with interchangeable names—Adeline, Emily, Ellena, Ellinor, Matilda. Intriguingly, although they are always being locked up in cells, attics, castles or dungeons, they cannot be contained. They break out.

The heroines of sensibility are supposedly pure, innocent, helpless and sexually naïve, but the possibility that they might be otherwise is not excluded from Radcliffe's romances. Emily of *The Mysteries of Udolpho* falls into the villain's hands because her aunt has married him. And it is not only the aunt who falls for Montoni: 'He was called handsome; and it was, perhaps, the spirit and vigour of his soul, sparkling through his features, that triumphed for him. Emily felt admiration' (*Udolpho*, i, p.125). She must have given some indication of her admiration, because one of the other brigands accuses her of being in love with Montoni. Not surprising, for she insists on her right to his protection even when his intention to rob her of her estates has been made clear. She never allows him to forget her. She continually seeks him out and reminds him that she is there. The sexual attraction that she feels for Montoni and his men becomes explicit when she is watching them mounting their horses from a casement window. Emily reflects that

> As he...[Cavigni—notice that it is a different man every time] managed his horse with dexterity, his graceful and commanding figure...had never appeared to more advantage...As she was hoping, she scarcely knew why, that Montoni would accompany the party, he appeared at the hall door. (*Udolpho*, i, p.307)

The motif of the voyeur, the hidden spectator, whose secret gaze appraises the sexual scene, is very fashionable in the art of the period, especially the work of Fuseli. Emily is far from passive or quietly submissive. Despite her terror and excitement at the prospect of being raped by one or more of Montoni's band, she goes looking for trouble. Radcliffe presents Emily as fearless and desiring. Was the writer aware of the implications of her own narratives? Certainly, she makes no bones about the sexual politics that rule the book: 'understand the danger of offending a man who has an unlimited power over you' (Udolpho, i, p.310).

Notoriously, the absent figure in Gothic is the mother. This is a fiction of oedipal fathers, adoring daughters and the immoderate passions unleashed between them. Here is the father: 'he caught Emily to his bosom, their tears flowed together; but they were not tears of sorrow'(Udolpho, i, p.61). And here is the daughter: "His voice faltered, while Emily, still weeping, pressed his hand close to her heart, which swelled with a convulsive sigh; but she could not look up' (Udolpho, i, p.77). When he dies she mourns not a parent, but a lover. 'She continued to gaze wildly; took up the cold hand; spoke; still gazed; and then burst into a transport of grief. La Voisin, hearing her sobs, came into the room to lead her away, but she heard nothing' (Udolpho, i, p.85). Of course, Radcliffe exploits the discourse of sensibility to the full. But it allows her to enter that Gothic sexual twilight zone where it is impossible to chart the moment at which cruelty becomes sadism, admiration becomes desire or when an excessively emotional filial attachment becomes an incestuous passion.

Even in The Italian (1797) Radcliffe writes scenes that have a resonance and potency as intriguingly shocking as any produced by M. G. Lewis, whose novel, The Monk (1796), caused such a scandal in the mid 1790s. The scene in The Italian that captured the imagination and applause of the critics and reviewers was the moment when Schedoni was about to murder Ellena: 'the horrible sublimity which characterises the discovery made by the former that Ellena was his daughter, at the instant in which he was about to stab her, is perhaps unparalleled'.[2]

Nathan Drake characterises this instance with the emotions usually associated with the catharsis of tragedy, pity and terror: 'Every nerve vibrates with pity and terror, especially at the moment when, about to plunge a dagger into her bosom, he discovers her to be his daughter'.[3] Again, the emphasis is upon the dramatic potential of the individual scene. And this scene is certainly very suggestive. Schedoni's preparation to stab the sleeping woman is described as an act of ritual violation. He draws aside her garments to reveal her flesh, finds he cannot do it, thinks of the man she loves, then works himself into a fury of jealousy and resentment: 'vengeance nerved his arm, and drawing aside the lawn from her bosom, he once more raised it to strike" (*The Italian*, p.234). The suggestion of rape and incest is there in Radcliffe's fiction. In M. G. Lewis' *The Monk*, the events actually occur. Ambrosio rapes then murders his sister in the charnel vaults of the convent of St Clare.

In his essay *Idée sur les Romans* (1800) the Marquis de Sade speaks of 'the strange flights of Mrs Radcliffe's brilliant imagination'.[4] The only writer he admired more in the Gothic genre was M. G. Lewis. *The Monk* was translated into French within a year of its original publication. In Britain the book caused a sensation. Lewis was threatened with prosecution for blasphemy. The novel, in expurgated versions, rapidly went through four editions and cheap pirate chapbooks abounded. In his review of the romance Coleridge denounced the Gothic in general and Lewis in particular:

> Tales of enchantment and witchcraft can never be useful: our author has contrived to make them pernicious, by blending, with an irreverent negligence all that is most awfully true in religion, with all that is most ridiculously absurd in superstition.[5]

The fact that Lewis, then only nineteen, had the nerve to sign himself 'M.P.' only added fuel to the scandal. Here is Coleridge again: 'Nor must it be forgotten that the author is a man of rank and fortune—Yes! the author of the Monk signs himself a LEGISLATOR!—We stare and tremble".[6] The sequence in *The Monk*, that was most admired by its original audience was the seduction of the supposedly pious abbot, a gripping and lengthy business that takes up all of chapter 2. In this episode, Matilda, a young aristocrat, who has fallen in love with the abbot, dresses up as a boy, insinuates herself into the convent and, armed with equal measures of lust and self-delusion, sets out to seduce him. This narrative became the basis of the cheaper nineteenth century re-prints which carried many sexy illustrations; see, for example, *Rosario, or The Female Monk* (1 vol., 1865).

Most seduction narratives are stories of hubris and nemesis. In this case the abbot Ambrosio is asking for it. Supposedly, he can withstand anything, but in fact he is already sexually bewitched by a portrait of the Madonna, which, unknown to him, and at this stage to the reader, is of Matilda.

> Oh! if such a Creature existed, and existed but for me! Were I permitted to twine round my fingers those golden ringlets, and press with my lips the treasures of that snowy bosom! Gracious God, should I then resist the temptation? (*The Monk*, p.41)

Temptation, in the form of the beautiful youth Rosario, then walks through the door. Rosario is the feminine boy, who arrives in the abbot's cell, intent on a little flower arranging. Ambrosio, naturally enough, is falling for the boy while insisting on the paternal nature of his tenderness.

> Rosario, I lay aside the Monk and bid you consider me as no other than your Friend...From the moment in which I first beheld you, I perceived sensations in my bosom, till then unknown to me; I found a delight in your society which no one's else could afford. (*The Monk*, pp.57–8)

Queer passion is often articulated within the shifting code of disguise, or of masquerade. Gender cross-dressing gave Lewis the freedom to explore desire between men while giving him the anatomical escape clause. The body beneath the habit is female. But the destabilisation of the *relation* between sex and gender, the element of performance described by Judith Butler in *Gender Trouble: Feminism and the Subversion of Identity* has already been achieved. Rosario/ Matilda is performing a part. He is in drag. Transvestism cuts gender off from its origins in biological differ-ence and turns it into performance.[7] In her essay, 'Gender as Performance: Shakespearean Ambiguity and the Lesbian Reader', Paula Bennett argues that 'when a man plays a woman or a woman a man, the apparently natural and prediscursive links between sex and gender are disrupted, bringing into question, not only the roles we play, but the desires we feel'.[8] This disruption is the basis of M. G. Lewis' eroticism. In this particular tale of seduction Ambrosio and Rosario are plunged into all the titillating ambiguity of queer desire. And no amount of biological revelations about sex can dissolve this infinite ambiguity.

How can the erotic scenario be resolved? One possibility for Rosario/Matilda is the continuation of her/his role as the desirable boy. Ambrosio speculates, 'Will it not be easy for me to forget her sex, and still consider her as my Friend and my disciple?' (*The Monk*, p.66). Lewis continually returns to this; the setting aside of sexual difference. His seduction narrative is resolved in very suggestive terms. Ambrosio is bitten by a heavily symbolic serpent while plucking an equally melodramatic rose for Rosario/Matilda. He is about to perish from the poisons when he is miraculously cured. But how? Rosario/ Matilda is mysteriously cheerful.

> 'You are in spirits, Matilda.'
> 'Well may I be so: I have just received a pleasure unexampled through my whole life.'
> 'What was that pleasure?'
> 'What I must conceal from all, but most from you.' (*The Monk* p.74)

The expensive spirit in this waste of sexual shame is of course the sucking out of Ambrosio's poisons while he was asleep, sucking spirit is the 'pleasure unexampled'. His spirit has entered Rosario/Matilda and is working his/her downfall. Even the moment of Ambrosio's capitulation is closer to queer passion than conventional heterosexual declarations of passion. Ambrosio proposes something very original: 'Let us forget the distinctions of sex, despise the world's prejudices and only consider each other as Brother and Friend' (*The Monk*, p.89). Rosario /Matilda takes the sexual lead, using the language of male demand. 'I prize you no more for the virtues of your soul; I lust for the enjoyment of your person...I feel with every heart-throb that I must enjoy you, or die' (*The Monk*, p.89). It is usually the man who longs to 'enjoy' the woman. Lewis's cross-dressed seduction masks one erotic transgression by ferociously insisting upon another. Ambrosio is supposedly celibate. Any kind of sexual fall, be it heterosexual or homosexual, accomplishes his religious defeat and the abandonment of his monastic vows. Rosario/Matilda enables Lewis to breach the sexual taboos on representing queer desire without appearing to do so. The seduction sequence is a series of suggestive erotic tableaux, like a game of charades. There was so much else in *The Monk* to inspire outrage, fury and disgust that Queer Gothic was not among the accusations. No one appears to have suspected anything. But Lewis's narrative is suggestive and charged. For all his hesitations and his ultimate withdrawal into a conservative and conventional resolution Lewis' seduction sequence remains peculiar and explosive. Lewis knew that he was thinking queer. He knew it was dangerous, and, for him, it mattered.

The Marquis de Sade, already imprisoned for sex crimes when he wrote his vast tracts of Queer Gothic, was genuinely gripped by the possibilities of lesbianism and sodomy. He was far too courageous, evil and mad to care about the danger. However, he published his manuscripts anonymously, for his version of queer Gothic was not only violent, uncompromising and explicit but also replete with republican philosophy. De Sade admired Monk Lewis. Carter admired De Sade. This is the literary lineage of Queer Gothic.

Ambrosio's transgressive passion, Emily's daring, the persecuting oedipal fathers and openly incestuous desires, all found within the Gothic, are part of a pattern; the psychic narratives of romance, what Michelle Massé calls the 'Ur-plot' of Gothic. This involves 'separation from the known, exposure to horror, alliance of horror and romance plot, and often conservative resolution—…(as) examples of the involuntary repetition Freud associates with the uncanny.'[9]

The repetitiousness and irresponsibility of dream allows us to entertain forbidden guests. The Gothic, even the Gothic of sensibility, is therefore a romance form that allows us to take vicarious pleasure in unspeakable things: the prospect of gang rape, willing or resisting victims and the psychology thereof, incestuous passions, persecution and insanity, ritual sadistic murder, sexual transformations, forbidden desires. This is Angela Carter's literary territory.

And this is her radical feminist inheritance: the unbreakable link between women's economic oppression and our sexual disadvantage. In Ann Radcliffe's *The Mysteries of Udolpho* the evil Montoni tries to bully and intimidate Emily into signing away her estates. She refuses. With extraordinary courage and using all the rhetoric of the 1790s Jacobin radical discourse, she insists on her rights.

> 'You may find, perhaps, signor,' said Emily with mild dignity, 'that the strength of my mind is equal to the justice of my cause; and that I can endure with fortitude when it is in the resistance of oppression.' (*Udolpho*, ii, p.51)

Emily knows that holding on to her inheritance is her only chance of survival, of controlling Montoni and escaping his grasp. Her economic liberty guarantees all her other freedoms. Surprisingly, the circulation of money and estates in Radcliffe's romances is as carefully charted as the ghosts. Radcliffe knows that the basis of women's oppression is economic and that financial security represents liberty. She says so.

Carter says so too. The critical relationship between women and men in Carter's fictions, whether the women be wives or whores, is always economic: the heterosexual cash nexus, where cocks and cunts carry price tags. The act of sex is always a question of performance. Most women are able to perform award-winning orgasms to order, faking it so successfully that the limits of authenticity are placed in doubt. Most men neither know nor care whether they are getting a command performance or the real thing. Prostitutes often run their sessions as an endless repetition of performances with careful attention to detail. And, more often than not, Carter's women expect to be paid for their performances. Here is Jeanne Duval, Carter's Black Venus, dealing with her Daddy:

> 'Jeanne, get it up for me.'
> Nothing is simple for this fellow! He makes a performance worthy of the Comédie Française out of a fuck, bringing him off is a five-act drama with farcical interludes and other passages that make you cry and, afterwards, cry he does, he is ashamed, he talks about his mother. (Carter, *Black Venus*, p.21)

But no one performs to an empty house, or to an empty bed. And where there is a performance there must always be a public. For the show to go on the punters must be there, demanding their money's worth. Each act must be perfected as spectacle. The climaxes are a sequence of endless repetitions. The central unit of meaning in the sexual performance is *the scene*.

Carter is particularly sharp on the economics of sex, the exact cost of the performance. Coolly unsentimental, she knows, and says, that men like sex and women like money. Consider Fevvers from *Nights at the Circus* (1984): '"A pretty face is one thing, our Liz," opined Fevvers, trying on the bracelet at once, "but diamonds is another. 'ere's a punter good for a touch." Her pupils narrowed down to the shape of £ signs.'[10]

Jeanne Duval, the Black Venus, survives Baudelaire surprisingly well by selling off the poet's trivia and manuscripts. She liquefies her literary assets with admirable insouciance. The culture that valued his writing never valued her, nor imagined her realities. And Carter herself, occupying the ambiguous position as both writer and woman, endorses what she does. The respectable old age of Jeanne Duval is pure performance; that of the successful prostitute, semi-retired, with that pre-requisite of freedom, hard cash, amassing in the bank. Jeanne Duval was the mistress–muse of a famous writer, and it is in that role, that her performance has been valued. Carter asks us to admire the remote indifference of the whore, the woman without ethics or desire, who patches herself up, buys new hair, fresh teeth, carries on, survives.

In her two tales, 'Black Venus' and 'The Fall River Axe Murders,' which frame the collection *Black Venus* (1985), Carter takes two historical women, Jeanne Duval and Lizzie Borden. We know very little about these women in history. They are both mysterious, exceptional. They are remembered in writing, through Baudelaire's sonnets and the children's rhyme of Lizzie Borden with her axe. Carter transforms these women into heroines by giving back to them a psychic drama, an inner narrative of necessity and pain. Interestingly, like the heroines of sensibility, they are locked up, confined within the house, the attic apartment. They are both killers. Jeanne Duval, disseminating syphilis, is finally, casually revenged upon 'the most privileged of the colonial administration'

(Carter, *Black Venus*, p.23). She has a charming house, a vine-covered veranda, an obsequious gardener. She is the whore who makes good. She wins.

Lizzie Borden's revenge upon her Daddy is less subtle, but more thorough. She hacks him to death with an axe. Her motives remain mysterious. Carter speculates on the inevitable question, 'why-did-she-do-it?', with ingenuity and verve, tossing off every kind of reason from heat to hormones. Was she unhinged? Was her endless virginity oppressive? Was her corset too tight? Did the house smell foul? Was she simply avenging her slaughtered pigeons? Most of us, I suspect, at some time or another, have needed very little reason to slaughter our parents. These are the first people who own us, rule us, thwart us. Lizzie Borden hacked them to pieces. She meant to do it.

Every woman writer creates a woman who meant to do it. Remember George Eliot's Laure, the French actress, tucked away in one tiny episode in *Middlemarch*,[11] the subject of what John Blackwood, Eliot's publisher, described as Lydgate's 'tremendous French adventure'. Laure is a performer. Her part requires her to stab her husband on stage, before the paying public. The actor really is her husband. She stabs him to the heart, then terrifies both Lydgate and all her readers since, with the admission, thrillingly printed in italics, that '*she meant to do it*'. We are the punters, getting our money's worth. Lizzie Borden meant to do it. She is akin to Bertha Rochester. She is not the travelling heroine of the Gothic, Jane Eyre on her quest for a home. Lizzie is trapped, back in Massachusetts, her adventure, her tour of Europe is over. Frustration and imprisonment in the Gothic lead inevitably to action and escape.

> It is in vain to say that human beings ought to be satisfied with tranquillity: they must have action; and they will make it if they cannot find it...Millions are condemned to a stiller doom than mine, and millions are in silent revolt against their lot.[12]

Like Bertha Rochester, Lizzie Borden is confined to a 'stiller doom' than that of Jane Eyre. She cannot have action, and she makes it as she cannot find it. Even as Jane Eyre broods on women's rebellion she hears Bertha's mad laugh. Bertha spends the entire novel trying to bump off Mr Rochester. Bertha and Lizzie neither explain nor justify themselves. They act.

Carter's ironic, self-conscious method continually calls attention to the theatricality of her prose, the fabrication of her scenarios. Carter's writing is deliberately episodic, her great moments march past as a sequence of set pieces. She insists on the primacy of the scene. Sometimes her cast of characters are professional performers as in *Nights at the Circus* (1984) or *Wise Children* (1992). Sometimes they are accidentally caught up in the action of the play, as is the Herm in her "Overture and Incidental Music to Shakespeare's *Midsummer Night's Dream*'. Carter's voice is that of the director, insisting on the presence of characters, staging, props, script. The characteristic narrative mode of the Gothic is confessional first-person narrative. The events of Mary Shelley's *Frankenstein* are poured out in emotional floods: from Walton to his sister in intimate, private letters, from Victor Frankenstein to Walton as a warning, an appeal, from the Monster to Frankenstein. Each narrative is a demand for sympathy, understanding, justice. Passion, desire, remorse, ambition, murderousness, all the emotions of excess, are painted large. This confessional mode is entirely unironic. But Carter is never unselfconscious. She manipulates her readers with calculated, knowing charm. We, her public, stand on her stage sets, looking about. She tells us what she is doing and where to look; she explains her methods, her intentions. When she is removing an historical character she tells us why: 'Write him out of the script. Even though his presence in the doomed house is historically unimpeachable, the colouring of this domestic apocalypse must be crude and the design profoundly simplified for the maximum emblematic effect' (Carter, *Black Venus*, p.105). Carter's insistence on the scene, the set piece, the confrontation, persists in her fiction, even when the big scene is sometimes forever deferred, as is Lizzie Borden's deed or Shakespeare's play, *A Midsummer Night's Dream*. She insists on the primacy of the voice—her own, that of the storyteller and that of her star performers—telling tales.

Carter's Gothic presents identity in flux. The instability of metamorphosis is always possible, always present. There are no boundaries between the animal and the human; there is a slippery continuum. Carter often civilises the beasts, but makes monsters out of men. She does not need the feminised monster of Frankenstein, for her version of femininity is in itself capable of becoming monstrous. Lizzie Borden is the oedipal Gothic daughter. She gives her Daddy a ring, which he always wears, for the love of his daughter. She is the miser's Achilles' heel, the monstrous flaw into which he pours his money, for 'no extravagance is too excessive for the miser's younger daughter' (Carter, *Black Venus*, p.118). It is always the favourite child who is monstrous. Mary Shelley's tale dealt with monsters, loose within the bourgeois family. Lizzie Borden is still on the loose.

But what of queer desire? Queer Gothic? What of the seductive confusion into which Monk Lewis plunged his abbot? This was not Carter's territory. She uses the themes, the iconography, the methods of Gothic, she gives us the marvellous, the monstrous and the nakedly (hetero)sexual, tough, mercenary women and Oedipal passions. But she constructs heterosexuality as the maze, the labyrinth within which we must find answers to the questions: what is a man? what is a woman? what is a bird? what are the shapes of desire? The heterosexual questions, to use Carter's own metaphors, keep us on the tracks in an English wood.

> For example, an English wood, however marvellous, however metamorphic, cannot, by definition, be trackless, although it might well be formidably labyrinthine. Yet there is always a way out of a maze, and even if you cannot find it for a while, you know that it is there. A maze is a construct of the human mind, and not unlike it; lost in the wood, this analogy will always console. But to be lost in the forest is to be lost to *this* world, to be abandoned by the light, to lose yourself utterly with no guarantee you will either find yourself or else be found, to be committed against your will—or, worse, of your own desire—to a perpetual absence from humanity, an existential catastrophe, for the forest is as infinitely boundless as the human heart. (Carter, *Black Venus*, p.68)

The forest becomes the lost queer space, which you can seek out of your own volition or to which you can be committed against your will. If to be human is to be heterosexual, and there is plenty of historical persecution and available legislation that suggests it is not human to be otherwise, then queer is not quite human. Carter has never been an unequivocal advocate of all things human; indeed many of her tales suggest that beauty belongs to the beasts.[13] But even bestiality proves to be heterosexual.[14] Gothic deals in monsters, freaks, the language of excess. So does Carter. But, oddly enough, Carter's frolics in the exotic world of the weird conclude by domesticating, diminishing or even denying the dangers of difference. I have heard her work described as dangerous, subversive, radical, and most fashionably of all, transgressive.[15] Transgression has a religious echo, of blasphemy, of overreaching. A transgressor crosses a forbidden frontier, creates a breach in the boundary. But we have to be in agreement as to what that boundary actually is in order to admire the radical transgression. We also have to be convinced that some new and extraordinary step has been taken in order to be impressed or, better still, shocked. Elizabeth Wilson points out that there is a

> more general weakness and a political inadequacy in the way in which 'transgression' has operated or may operate, or rather can't operate: it can't deal with the systematic or structural nature of oppressive institutions. On the contrary, it reaffirms or may even reinforce them.[16]

Carter's writing is transgressive within her own terms, and she does indeed question the political meanings of the very modes within which she writes. Lorna Sage is absolutely right when she says, 'The world of outsiders is not, for her either, so securely marginal, or so confined as that. Her writing, in short, unravels the romance of exclusion.'[17] But the consequence of this it to re-establish the traditional hegemonies. Carter and her advocates may say that she boldly goes where no woman writer has gone before, but the frontiers she transgresses are, for some of her readers and many other woman writers, not even on the map. They have been traversed and left behind. Some of us abandoned the English wood for the pleasures of the forest years ago.

At first glance there is enough cross-dressing, transvestism, spanking sessions, and general physical freakishness in Carter's fiction to keep the most demanding of perverts happy. But Carter usually resolves her transvestite mysteries in conventional ways, as Monk Lewis had to do. In 'The Merchant of Shadows', *American Ghosts and Old World Wonders* (1993), she presents a sequel to Tristessa, the screen icon in *The Passion of New Eve* (1977). These cross-dressed men impersonate women, with grace and ease, because womanliness is in itself a masquerade. And only men can imagine and create the women they desire.

> *That* was why he had been the perfect man's woman! He had made himself the shrine of his own desires, had made of himself the only woman he could have loved! If a woman is indeed beautiful only in so far as she incarnates most completely the secret aspirations of man, no wonder Tristessa had been able to become the most beautiful woman in the world, an unbegotten woman who made no concessions to humanity. Tristessa, the sensuous fabrication of the mythology of the flea -pits. How could a real woman ever have been so much a woman as you?[18]

Tristessa is therefore both man and woman. Only more so. This is convincing and suggestive. Femininity is performance. Women are men's creations. But it's been said before. Many times.[19] Disguise is therefore not a subversive means to achieve that obscure object of queer desire as it is in Monk Lewis's novel, but a method of pandering to egotistic narcissism.

It is a moot point what sex hermaphrodites actually are if they are literally, physically, both man and woman. In the eighteenth century the term 'female hermaphrodite' was a euphemism for Lesbian.

> It is certain, that in some Women, especially those who are very salacious, the *Clitoris* is so vastly extended, that by hanging out of the Passage, it is mistaken for a Penis, such have been called *Fricatrices*: By *Caelius Aurelianus*, *Tribades*: By *Plautus*, *Subigatrices*, and accounted Hermophrodites (*sic*), because, as said before, they have been able to perform the Actions of Men with other Women.[20]

There is an intriguing sexual history here, and I would have thought a good deal of sexual fun to be had with the myth of the giant clitoris. But Carter's Herm in 'Overture and Incidental Music to Shakespeare's *Midsummer Night's Dream*', despite his double genitals, is male, the golden Indian boy, as he was in Shakespeare's play, inspiring lust in either sex, wherever he goes. Shakespeare is, arguably, a lot kinkier than Carter, in that Titania falls for an ass, a beast with a thrillingly long penis. At least everyone else in Carter's clever, strange tale is generically a fairy.

Carter never attempts to imagine queer subjectivity, although male subjectivity presents no problems. She was not interested in doing so. Fair enough. Why should she be interested? But if your subject is sex and sexuality in all its forms, and if you are anxious to present your writing as subversive, transgressive, radical, and if the literary lineage of Queer Gothic is one of your sources, then that silence begins to speak.

Carter's women don't get a good deal out of heterosexuality, but they fight back with energy, verve and imagination. However, Carter carefully constructs her English maze so that, as Mrs Thatcher once argued, there is no alternative. But there is. Queer gives us another alternative territory from which to investigate that fallacious conjunction of the heterosexual and the human, to think of other, and different ways to be human and to explore the weird. The questions: what is lesbian? what is queer? who is homosexual? take us off the map of the woodland maze and plunge us into the forest. Here it is not difference, but sameness that is dangerous. But thinking queer, thinking in terms of same-sex desire also means thinking radical difference. Homosexuality has its own scripts, its own traditional performances; but because queer affirms, celebrates, rejoices in the freak outside nature, the script can be perpetually rewritten, the performance re-rehearsed, the act reimagined. The scene is fluid. The parts can be swapped around. You can even get to play both parts in the same scene.

Carter's refusal to make the leap into the forest of Queer Gothic was a lost opportunity, for there were the lost narratives of subversion.

Carter's women still have their heads full of men. Even if the men are only there to be fleeced and butchered, they are still the punters, demanding their money's worth, the public who have paid to see the show. But Carter's saving grace is to be found in her heroines. These are the women who stay wild: Jeanne Duval and Lizzie Borden, the kept whore and the pampered daughter, whose hearts never belonged to their respective Daddies; the Wolfwoman who unknowingly chooses savagery, wildness, freedom; the cook whose soufflé—at last, second time around counts—for more than the ducal desires. I murmur just as he does, *Quelle femme!* Women's work, on our feet, on our backs, is warmly valued and precisely priced. Lizzie Borden got away with it. So did Jeanne Duval. There she is, in Carter's elegant final sentence, dressed in respectable black, on her way to the bank.

7

HETEROSEXUALITY: FICTIONAL AGENDAS

MARGARET ATWOOD *THE EDIBLE WOMAN*
AND *LIFE BEFORE MAN*, AND JENNY DISKI
NOTHING NATURAL

NOW AND THEN

Yes, yes, of course there's a story behind this. Why am I talking about Margaret Atwood and Jenny Diski? Why these particular writers and why these particular fictions? What about Atwood's more recent novels? That one that carried off the Booker Prize? Are Atwood and Diski supposed to be quintessentially heterosexual? Of course you want to know. So I'll tell you the story. Ten years ago I got a new job. It was then a relatively decent new job in a University Department of English. My most immediate senior colleague suggested that I might feel moved to talk about Margaret Atwood's fiction on the first-year lecture course as she was tired of doing so. I was anxious to please. I agreed at once.

Every university has a heterosexual agenda. And no one is lesbian unless she says she is. But every woman is who even mentions the word. Lesbian is no longer a word that cannot be spoken. But it still cannot be spoken with impunity. Or without consequences. Unfortunately, there is always someone out there, at least one of them, maybe more, who already hates you, simply on account of who you are. Or who wants to go to bed with you just to see what it's like. You have to find out who he, or alas, she, is.

And so there I stood, ten years go, ready to deliver my inaugural lecture to a mass of expectant first years, all of whom I was to assume were heterosexual. My unspoken institutional agenda was to suggest to them that if they weren't they ought to be and to tell them what to expect of relationships between women and men by talking about fictional representations of heterosexuality. If you don't mention the alternative, there isn't one. In fact, on our first-year course in the early 1990s we did mention the gay alternative. We taught William Golding's *Rites of Passage* (1980), a Booker Prize winning book by a Nobel Prize winning author. The homosexual man represented in that fiction is made drunk, sucks off a handsome sailor whom he's had his eye on and subsequently dies of shame. So much for the gay alternative. Ten years ago the lesbian alternative, as a subject for a lecture, was quite unthinkable.

Gender and all its attendant power structures are one of the main concerns of the literature that we teach. Male homosexuality rises up from time to time from the canon of English Literature and is either given a fair hearing or passed over in respectful silence. Shakespeare helps. But inevitably the Sonnets were used to prove that gay desire is ultimately no different from heterosexual desire. The torments of lust, anguish and jealousy are pretty much the same. And, so the more liberal version of the argument used to go, as we're all in some way bisexual, insisting on homosexual difference is to make a loud noise about nothing.

But here I really do think that there has been a sea change. The Sonnets are now about being queer. One of my (straight) colleagues speculates boldly about Tennyson and Hallam. The Fin de Siècle has become very queer indeed. Oscar Wilde is on the new Genre course. We teach him twice oe'er. Once as a 1890s writer and again as our queer forefather. Our new first-year course on Contemporary Writing, which was designed by my gay colleague and myself, contains an equal number of male and female writers. We teach Black writing in an overwhelmingly white department, which, to me, presents a multitude of contradictions. We have no Black lecturers and very few Black students. We now have one out lesbian lecturer and one out gay one. If there are any others lurking in the photocopy room then they certainly haven't declared themselves. We now teach Jeanette Winterson's *The Passion* and Jonathan Harvey's *Beautiful Thing*. The students enjoy reading and discussing the texts. They were all hooked on the Manchester TV soap *Queer as Folk*. No one has complained. Flicking through the courses in most university departments could become a pleasant exercise in self-congratulation.

But the structures of heterosexuality are still there, and if they are neither analysed nor questioned then all the queer alternatives remain just a colourful forum for the politically correct, an interesting sexual experiment, something you might like to try at the weekend.

To declare yourself a feminist in the academic literary world is now to be part of the Jurassic past. We have all moved on. Queer studies are not confined to Sussex University and America. Ten years ago I was the third woman to be appointed in my Department. Now there are ten of us. We are not all feminists. Some of us don't even see the point of studying women's writing. I find it hard to view this as radical progress. But ten years ago when we used to teach Margaret Atwood I was asked to do the lectures because Atwood was seen to be in some sense irreducibly feminist: a woman writer who talks about women and heterosexual sex from the woman's point of view. Better give her to one of the women.

'Margaret Atwood,' I began ponderously, 'is a writer who has always been intriguingly ahead of her times.' And what now follows is the lecture that I did not give.

THE LECTURE I DID NOT GIVE

By an accident of literary history Margaret Atwood's first and fourth novels were published together in Britain during 1979–1980. *The Edible Woman*, written and set in the mid-sixties, when the women's liberation movement was no more than a tingle of desire, was first published in Canada in 1969. *Life Before Man* (*sic*), set in the years 1976–1978, was first published in 1979. Both books are urban Canadian novels, set in Toronto. They have the same theme; they are novels of sexual manners, which offer an analysis of the heterosexual contract. This is white, middle-class fiction, which sometimes resembles Leni Riefenstahl's Nazi propaganda films. No one is Black, disabled or homosexual. No one is ugly or old. They aren't unemployed either, but that reflects the economies in the West before the 1980s. In *The Edible Woman*, the cast are all in their early twenties. The young men are busy making it. They are either lawyers and soap men on the verge of being successful or they are intriguing, alienated sensibilities writing their graduate theses in English studies. The women, so far as the action is concerned, sit on the rim of the book. They are either wives, or women waiting to be made wives, or underpaid, undervalued employees. The novel centres on women's perceptions and experiences, but makes it clear that we cannot significantly influence the conditions within which we live our lives. We will never get to be the boss. By the time we get to *Life Before Man*, the lawyer has given up his job and taken to making home crafts in the basement. The women have apparently progressed, been to university, attended the obligatory off-stage women's group, stopped going to it and got decent jobs. It is ten years on. They are all thirtysomething or pushing forty.

In *The Edible Woman* the decision is still up for grabs. Should our appallingly normal heroine (Maid) Marian opt for marriage to the lawyer and a life of dull, predictable respectability? Or not? What else is there? By *Life Before Man*, we are caught: we have been married ten years, have two kids and are contemplating divorce. In *The Edible Woman* the heterosexual contract could still be negotiated, repudiated or recast in another form—but in *Life Before Man* marriage is a set of bars in and around which the cast has to negotiate their various lovers and mistresses. In *The Edible Woman* the women still fight back indignantly. And in doing so it was clear that they had the writer's whole-hearted support. In *Life Before Man*, Atwood's narrator takes up an ironic distance from the characters, male and female alike. The women are now either blood-curdling ballbreakers, who have certainly lost the narrator's approval, or vaguely suicidal, or both. The sparky rebelliousness of *The Edible Woman* has gone. Cynicism and despair are now the name of the game.

Margaret Atwood writes a form of late twentieth-century Jane Austen: neat, smug prose, sex and marriage, class and manners. Except of course the dramatis personae writhe around in beds rather than simmer with repressed sex in drawing rooms. And, as in Jane Austen, atrocities never happen on the doorstep, but offstage. In *Life Before Man*, the ex-lawyer, Nate, has a mother with a social conscience. She pins up the off-stage nightmares on a map of world horrors. The closest manifestation of social protest is a petition against the Mounties, who have overstepped the mark in Québec. Nate's gloomy assessment of the public's attitude is probably accurate.

> He knows that most people will allow six million Québeckers, Pakistanis, union leaders and transvestites to have their finger-nails pulled out rather than admit that the paint is chipped on the bright red musical Mountie of their dreams. (Atwood, 1982, p.305)

Queers aren't explicitly included in the list, unless we are covered by transvestites, or indeed, the Mountie. Heterosexuals are most people. We are part of the rest.

In Atwood's fictional world people have careers and enough to eat. Marian, our heroine in *The Edible Woman*, does her degree then gets a job in advertising. Now advertising is always about selling you things that you don't need. And often about making the unacceptable desirable. The consumer and the thing consumed must correspond; therefore advertising produces images, images of ourselves and images of the product. Masculinity must be as carefully constructed as femininity if heterosexuality is to work. Take the example of the Moose Beer ad.

> After a preliminary ringing, buzzing and clicking a deep bass voice, accompanied by what sounded like an electric guitar, sang:
> *Moose, Moose,*
> *From the land of pine and spruce,*
> *Tingly, heady, rough-and -ready...*
> Then a speaking voice, almost as deep as the singer's, intoned persuasively to background music,
> *Any real man, on a real man's holiday-hunting, fishing or just plain old-fashioned relaxing-needs a beer with a healthy, hearty tasty, a deep-down manly flavour. The first long cool swallow will tell you that Moose Beer is what you've always wanted for true beer enjoyment. Put the tang of the wilderness in YOUR life today with a big satisfying glass of sturdy Moose Beer.*
> *The singer resumed:*

Tingly, heady,
Rough-and-ready,
Moose, Moose, Moose, Moose, BEER!!!
and after a climax of sound the record clicked off. It was in
satisfactory working order. (Atwood, 1980, p.26)

Here we have heterosexual Canadian man, the huntin', shootin',
fishin' type who has mastered the wilderness. The Moose Beer
advertisement demonstrates the social construction of this particular version of masculinity. Hunting, drinking and consuming
nature are the signs of sexually successful masculinity. The deep-
down manly flavour is associated with casual killing.

Advertising constructs women too: as heterosexual, available to
men, docile or wild according to male preference, both desirable
and domesticated. Marian's story, like many early feminist texts,
is about the experience of being socially constructed as a heterosexual woman. This is a universal experience. All women are
brainwashed from infancy to be heterosexual. Those of us who
refuse to perform as required slide into the category labelled deviant.
The interesting thing about being socially constructed as a heterosexual woman is that it is not just something other people do to
you. You do it to yourself. For social expectations operate both
within and without.

Marian spends a whole chapter brain-washing herself. The result
is that she can no longer manage to tell the story. The narrative
ceases to operate in the first-person-singular confessional mode, the
usual voice in which feminist escape stories are narrated, and lapses
into the third person, the impersonal voice. Thus, the narrative
moves from within to without—from I to she. Until we reach the
end of the book and our heroine shakes herself free from the odious
lawyer.

Life Before Man takes the three points of the conventional heterosexual triangle to tell the awful tale: wife, husband, other woman.
Atwood uses first-person narrative very rarely and sparingly because
this would crack the ironic surface that holds her characters at a
distance. In fact the material is too dangerously violent to risk
narrating instantaneous feeling. Some of the violence happens
offstage: Elizabeth (the wife)'s lover Chris blows his brains out, the

event that unleashes the novel. He reappears in flashback, a hairy Canadian Heathcliff, all penis and menace. In her heterosexual loneliness after his suicide, Elizabeth, who is given to slumming it sexually, tries a one-night stand with a naughty-knickers salesman. This is a disaster. Elizabeth is a monster, a vampire, a bitch: she is what happens to women who go for respectability at all costs, but she is still vulnerable to casual sexual assault.

> 'Hey, don't you want your turn?' the man says. His hand scampers like a spider up her thigh. 'I'm good,' he says. 'Take a break and enjoy yourself.' His left hand holds the microphone, as if he's expecting her to sing.
> 'Get your hand off my crotch,' Elizabeth says. She feels as if she's opened a serious-looking package and a wind-up snake has jumped out. She's never appreciated practical jokes. (Atwood, 1980, p. 229)

The encounter is presented as funny. And we all laugh. But the undertow in the incident is nasty. She is alone with a man at night in his car. She wants to get out and walk home. She can't. Elizabeth is portrayed as a loathsome woman. Most of her readers, many of them women, have been set up to think that she's asked for it— and that she deserves all she gets.

Both *The Edible Woman* and *Life Before Man* are written within that extraordinary, peculiar moment of sexual history when contraceptives were fairly easily accessible for women and before the advent of AIDS. Both Ainsley, our heroine's best friend and confidante in *The Edible Woman*—no, not her lover, that's unthinkable—and Lesje, the other woman in *Life Before Man*, decide to get pregnant of their own volition and in their own time. Anisley actually picks, stalks and gets her man. Both women control their own reproductive force. This is (hetero)sex before AIDS in the style approved by heterosexual feminists. We can all entertain and act upon our desires, fairly fearless of the consequences. But in *Life Before Man* the sinister aspect of the heterosexual pact, and an aspect of male sexuality, that was completely absent in *The Edible Woman*, is male violence. When Lesje's live-in lover William understands that Lesje is having an affair with Nate, his immediate response is to rape her.

'William, that hurts,' she says; then, 'William, cut it *out*!'
He's got her jeans worked halfway down her thighs before it
occurs to her that William is trying to rape her.

She's always thought of rape as something the Russians
did to the Ukrainians, something the Germans did, more
furtively, to the Jews; something blacks did in Detroit, in dark
alleys. But not something William Wasp, from a good family
in London, Ontario, would ever do to her. (Atwood, 1982,
pp.185–6)

Here, respectability cracks. The veneer of civilised, sexual manoeu-
vring breaks down to reveal the ugliness of sexual force beneath.
Atwood is telling the truth, most of us are raped by men we know
well. And when it comes to heterosexual sex women aren't ultimately in an equal negotiating position. It's not that easy to have
sex with men on our terms—which is Atwood's point.

Behind every woman stands another woman, and behind every
man stands his mother. This is Atwood's form of literary psychoanalysis, which has intriguing implications. In *Life Before Man* she
elaborates her three points of consciousness, moving back into
their childhoods and memories. Behind Elizabeth is Auntie Muriel,
the evil stepmother, the witch she has to slaughter, the monster she
is in the process of becoming. Behind Nate's awful, concerned
understanding is his mother with her selflessness and noble causes:
Save the Korean Poet. Behind Lesje are her passionate grandmothers
and her divided identity: Latvian/Ukrainian, Gentile/Jew. It is their
voices, that come back to her in her rage:

'She was too angry. If she tried to say anything at all, it would
come out in the form of her grandmother's curses: *Jesus asshole
poop! I hope your bum falls off! I hope you die!*' (Atwood,
1982, p.292)

In fact, this naked fury that erupts from time to time is the only
thing that makes Atwood's analysis of the heterosexual contract feel
clean. Her writing is a study in muted tones, fiction in ironic grey.
The texture of her prose is dispassionate, unloving, cynical. What
matters? What are the values being asserted? What is being argued

for in this long grey stream of heterosexual misery? Should fiction argue for values? What indeed is the point of it all?

Adultery becomes a civilised arrangement if we can all sit on our feelings effectively. Religion becomes Auntie Muriel's torrent of hypocrisy, culminating in her black comic funeral. Sex is always disappointing. After ten years of making heterosexual love the earth has ceased to move. It all culminates in Lesje's theoretical reflection that,

> Man (*sic*) is a danger to the universe, a mischievous ape, spiteful, destructive, malevolent. But only theoretical. Really she believed that if people could see how they were acting they would act some other way. Now she knows this isn't true. (Atwood, 1982, p.293)

Atwood uses a capital for Man. It's generic. The gloom, which has been deepening throughout the novel, is now complete.

So what *did* happen to feminism by 1978? Where have they gone, the women who caught the thinking disease? The women who said that post-feminism meant that you could wear your bra and burn your brains. Well, they have walk-on parts in Lesje's head.

> Lesje is doing something seedy…Or even tacky. Very tacky, to be having an affair with a married man, a married man with two children. Married men with children are proverbially tacky, with their sad stories, their furtive lusts and petty evasions. Tackier still to be doing it in a hotel, of necessity a comparatively tacky hotel, since Nate is, as he says, a little broke. Lesje hasn't offered to pay the hotel bill herself. Once, long ago, her women's group might have sneered at this reluctance, but there is a limit. (Atwood, 1982, p.124)

Feminism belongs to 'once and long ago'. Whatever may have happened to the women's group, she certainly doesn't frequent it any more. She opts for the clichés instead. And the sadness of this book is in the irony of lines being spoken, situations acted out, which are all pre-determined elsewhere. The script is already written; feelings are waiting to be felt, reproaches waiting to be

venomously delivered. And that's the subject of *Life Before Man*—
Atwood is examining the way in which heterosexuality doesn't
evolve, doesn't change, doesn't develop. The way in which women
and men, in the hopeless attempt to love one another, slink help-
lessly, miserably, into ruts.

What saves 320 pages of cynical, grey, ironic fiction from being
a torrent of sexual discouragement? Two things: naked rage and
the wilderness. And this is a pattern in Atwood's fiction. Remember
the abysmal Moose Beer advert in *The Edible Woman?* Well, there
the wilderness was made safe for men who drink the right beer. It's
a billboard wilderness with no blood or fear. At the climax of *The
Edible Woman* our heroine and the awful lawyer give a party, the
first and last they ever give together. By this time our heroine can
no longer eat. Her mind has been brainwashed beautifully, but her
body rebels. Refusing or being unable to eat is always a form of
self-punishment, but it is also a bid for control. Marian is in a situation where she can no longer control what is happening to her.
Her identity is about to be swallowed up in marriage, her body
consumed. She does the sensible thing. She runs.

It is a good sign in Atwood's fiction when anyone does a bolt.
It is always a bid for freedom. Marian runs to the moody, loony
English thesis-writing graduate, who is another parasite, but at
least an interesting one. And he opens the door into the wilderness.
He takes her across snow-covered Toronto to one of the ravines.
This is a startling scene. It is as if the urban text opens up, the city
cracks to reveal the wilderness beneath. The moment of danger is
also the moment of liberation.

> Marian gasped and took an involuntary step back: they were
> standing on the very edge of a cliff. The ground ended abruptly
> beyond their feet. Below them was a huge roughly circular pit,
> with a spiral path or roadway cut round and around the side,
> leading to the level snow-covered space at the bottom....It
> seemed wrong to have this cavity in the city...It made her
> suspect the white-pit bottom also; it didn't look solid, it looked
> possibly hollow, dangerous, a thin layer of ice, as though if
> you walked on it you might fall through. (Atwood, 1980,
> p.262)

The city breaks open and so does the sexual system between women and men. The alternatives exist in the cracks. The alternatives are unknown, unsafe: 'you might fall through'. But there is no question of marrying the lawyer once she has seen the ravines.[1]

The same wilderness metaphor of ancient time exists in *Life Before Man*. Underneath urban Canadian civilisation lurk the dinosaurs, who exist as bones in the museum and as living beings in Lesje's imagination. Their presence suggests that there is a propositional element in human being. We have not always existed. In the chain of evolving life we are insignificant, a tiny recent addition, and we may not always continue to exist. The heterosexual contract between women and men has become alarmingly tenuous, brutal and uncaring. Stripped of its property arrangements and economic rationale the western ideology of heterosexual love begins to look preposterous, negligible, bizarre. We may as well head for the wilderness.

During the 1970s there were women who decided to be lesbians, seeing the commitment to other women as the way out of the impasse of heterosexual feminism. Some of them never went back on this decision. Some of them did well out of the bargain. But not everyone survives this wilderness. Some found that they had chosen to live in a particularly gruesome horror comic. Some became professional lesbians, and even give lectures and sermons about being lesbians. As the economic climate of the 1980s darkened and they too became thirtysomething, like Atwood's characters many decided to go back to the lives that they had left. They chose heterosexuality. Others chose to have children. At the beginning of the 1980s there was a veritable lesbian baby boom. I now teach some of those children who had two mothers. My point is that the wilderness is an unstable, illusory place. We still have to bring it into being.

Should we care about the continuing—appalling—state of relations between women and men? Should we be bothered with heterosexuality? Well, yes, I think we should. We have to be concerned, for the following reasons. That most men prefer men seems to me to be an observable fact. Men prefer to work with men, to socialise with men, compete with men, write for men, read men. Sadly, it is also true that most women prefer men, even when they are not forced economically to do so, nor obviously brainwashed beyond repair. They work for them, wait upon them, take care of them, sleep with them, puff up their egos and bear their children. No one can deny that it is largely in our economic interests to do so. Heterosexuality is both a social and a sexual institution. We all live within it, in varying degrees, whether we want to or not. If you don't live with a man you will usually work for one or with one. You are probably related to one that you love.

At the moment there is no world elsewhere.

Back in the 1970s feminists took upon themselves the terrifying task of changing the institution of heterosexuality from within. That project was the basis of the seven original demands of the women's liberation movement. We demanded equal pay with men, equality of opportunity, state-funded childcare facilities, control over our reproductive capacity, security from men's violence, the right to determine our own sexuality, rather than being forced to be heterosexual in forms decided upon by our so-called masters, and an end to discrimination against lesbians. None of this was ever achieved. What we all failed to realise in the early 1970s was that these conditions of women's existence were the actual bricks of the heterosexual institution, the prison itself. They therefore cannot be changed. We can negotiate better conditions: no more slopping out, more frequent parole reviews, educational opportunities for long-term insiders, and we have done that for some. But the women's prison will always be there without a more radical rearrangement of all our lives.

I believe that ignoring the heterosexual world, however much we may loathe its customs, is madness. Section 28 must have proved that even to the most sanguine and apolitical among the queer community. The wilderness women, the women who refused to conform, have gained the few rights that we have by insisting that we too are human and have the right to exist. We do not exist in large numbers in many countries. We have only to be placed in another category to lose the right to live; we will, at best, be forced back into economic dependence with our children on the ends of the umbilical cord and violence as the threat if we put our noses outside the door.

Margaret Atwood, always ahead of her times, has already said this too. In 1985 she published her eerie dystopia, *The Handmaid's*

Tale. In the Republic of Gilead, religion rules. Identity becomes role; the women are wives, aunts, marthas, handmaids. Heterosexuality is enforced. Women with viable ovaries become walking wombs. In a scenario resembling de Sade's fantasies, but without his sense of humour, the handmaid lies between the wife's legs, to be ritually fucked in the desperate attempt to breed. The only lesbian character in the novel fails to escape and is confined to a brothel, 'Butch paradise' as she ironically describes it, where the women can amuse themselves when the men have been sufficiently serviced. Lesbians are idealistic failures, with sentimental dreams of liberty. But Atwood is not going to abandon her heterosexual reader. In true Lawrentian style the chauffeur Nick turns up trumps. Freerange het sex is still interesting and erotic; we are led to believe that he helps our pretty heroine escape.

Women and men, in an egalitarian society, would resemble each other. We would look alike, talk alike and move about in similar ways, dress in much the same clothes and earn the same pay. In Atwood's dystopia women and men are sharply differentiated. They are not the same species. And it is this division, this brutal polarisation, which is at the crux of the argument in another significantly successful heterosexual text. In the same year, 1986, that Margaret Atwood's terrifying vision of a theocracy, *The Handmaid's Tale*, was published in Britain, Jenny Diski published a well-turned piece of realist fiction, which was marketed as adult reading: an incisive analysis of a sado-masochistic heterosexual relationship. It was suggestively, indeed brilliantly, entitled *Nothing Natural*. It had wonderful reviews: hard sex, well written. The reviewers gloated. It is still in print, still selling well; there is a new paperback edition.

Nothing Natural is about being imprisoned in institutions and feeling well-off and secure inside them. Diski's novel takes up the same arguments about sexual difference and the ways in which it is oppressive to women that Atwood discusses in *The Handmaid's Tale*, but this time heterosexuality is discussed as a private sexual contract rather than as a state institution. But the idea that heterosexuality is an institution manipulated by the state is not absent from the text. The novel does a tour of various institutions: a home for abandoned, disturbed young people—in the sub-plot, our heroine befriends an alienated boy who shits himself—prison, the mental ward of a hospital and a heterosexual relationship that is based on ritual patterns of violence, dominance and submission. The man gives orders, the woman bends over. Diski is absolutely explicit about what he does to her; spanking: 'Christ,' she thought, 'this is new. What is this?' (Diski, 1990, p.21); buggery over the kitchen table: She felt everything: violated, released, hugely and darkly excited' (Diski, 1990, p.30); and, eventually, a rape scenario, her idea, in which she is tied up, beaten and then sodomised.

Nothing Natural is also about being programmed to respond in certain ways, playing along up to a point, then refusing to play the game any more. At the beginning of their relationship, Rachel, our heroine, feels that Joshua, her night visitor, not only has absolute control over what happens between them but that 'He had directed the evening as if he had had a script in his hand' (Diski, 1990, p.33). At the end of the novel when she suspects that Joshua is being hunted for rape she sets him up by informing the police and writes the script for the rape scenario herself. The script is a web of pornographic clichés, and Joshua falls for them. The most astonishing thing about pornography is its repetitiveness: all the great classics, including de Sade, Bataille et al. propose the same scenarios.

Diski also suggests in the true Sadeian manner that the woman is really the mirror image of the man, with the same desires. It is essential that she should be like him, hard, cold, remote, for there is no pleasure in persecuting an entirely unwilling victim; to explain this she gives them both brutal, unloving childhoods. Again and again Diski insists that 'it was precisely what Joshua revelled in that she wanted too' (Diski, 1990, p.84). They both know the script. 'They were acting out a pantomime and they both knew it, although it wasn't to be said. As a pair of sophisticated post-Freudians they were giving each other therapy' (Diski, 1990, pp.85–6). What remained implicit in *Life Before Man* now becomes explicit: the fact of the heterosexual script.

Unfortunately the post-Freudian S&M therapy results in Rachel's severe and desperate suicidal depression. And just in case we were telling ourselves that mutual, loving, equal heterosexual sex was the answer, our heroine's confidante, Becky, discovers that her husband, who has lost interest in her, is having an affair. Round she comes for comfort and here we have the Lesbian Sex Scene.

Pornography often presents lesbian sex as apéritif, the intriguing appetiser before the heterosexual main course. In most pornographic representations lesbianism is portrayed as the fun-and-games end of heterosexuality. Male homosexuality, apart from its representation in the work of de Sade, who was genuinely gripped by the possibilities of buggery, is treated with caution in heterosexual pornography, because it involves penetration, the 'real thing', and therefore introduces an unstable element into the drama of power and persecution.

This time, for her lesbian lovemaking, Diski uses the metaphor of the mirror and of Alice entering the Looking-Glass world.

> And as she stroked and touched and felt her own body being caressed, she became enchanted by the confusion. She was Alice at the moment when the looking glass dissolved, kneeling on the mantelpiece, pressing her palms against the glass and feeling the reflection of her own flesh, touching another, touching herself, familiar but quite different, creating a third neither one nor the other, making love in a glass that became a liquid refracting pool, not you, not me, strange and strangely known. (Diski, 1990, p.152)

This is as finely written a passage as anything in the book, but what interested me was the fact that, apart from a little nipple-sucking, Diski became uncharacteristically vague about describing what it is that the two women actually *do*. She is utterly explicit about the heterosex, but when she describes the lesbian act the lovers are 'shockingly naked, shockingly women together, female form wrapped around itself' (Diski, 1990, p.153), as if her lovers were a sculpture. They are not two women, but one flesh.

Heterosexuality, in this text at any rate, violently differentiates male from female, even while Diski insists that Rachel and Joshua are critically alike. Their natures are supposedly the same, but what they do to each other is different. So are their roles in the script: he commands, she obeys. I thought about this for a long time, because something critical about the construction of heterosexuality had emerged from the text of *Nothing Natural*. Let me explain.

One of the great nineteenth-century operas of heterosexual love is Wagner's *Tristan and Isolde*. I love it. So do many queers who are in the habit of going to the opera. Why? At first glance it is not promising territory. I am not at all keen on the idea that the only way in which illicit passion can be consummated is in death, whether that passion is homosexual or heterosexual. So far as women, are concerned, our history is packed with far too many tales of noble self-sacrificing lesbians who either achieve greatness and respectability by dying off, or demonstrate that justice can and should be done by getting killed off. What is particularly extraordinary about *Tristan and Isolde* is the suggestion that what prevents their passion is the fact of sexual difference. And it is his idea, not hers. He demands to be '*Nicht mehr Tristan, sondern Isolde*' ('No longer Tristan, but Isolde'). Homosexuals admire *Tristan and Isolde* because the opera argues that *difference* is unworkable, impossible, insoluble, to be resolved only in death. The lovers exchange names and identities. Passion is about being the other person. Not being different, but being the same. No longer locked inside the ego or the self, but transformed into the other person. Here, as far as I am concerned, is the answer.

The usual accusation levelled at homosexuality is that it is narcissism. I don't quite understand this objection, as, if it is a question of mutual passion, some one else is always involved. It is not narcissism to love the other who resembles you. To love the other as yourself, is to love yourself. The other has the same needs, the same desires, the same passion, and, were sexual difference dissolved, whether the other is man or woman would not matter. You are the other person. Sexual difference has ceased to exist.[2] The other is yourself.

But of course, in Jenny Diski's text, which conforms to the heterosexual fictional agenda, Rachel gives Becky the push. She turns chilly and cold. Becky is the loving other who must be shaken off: '"Rachel, what is it?" Becky insisted. I want you away, out of here, she thought; I want you to stop being so fucking pathetic, so fucking warm, so loving' (Diski, 1990, p.155).

When required to explain, Rachel argues that they are both 'hooked on men' (Diski, 1990, p. 157), as if heterosexuality were an unfortunate drug habit. As indeed, as far as the sado-masochistic relationship with Joshua is concerned, it is. Sameness cannot be perceived as erotically gratifying. Or as a long-term proposition. If it were, Diski would have to rethink heterosexual sex and the plot of the book.

'Nothing's a natural thing to do,' snaps Diski's heroine. I think that's absolutely true, which is why any sexual act is as much about politics as it is about feelings. The urge to perform one particular sexual act rather than another doesn't rise up mysteriously from the gulf of our inward natures. There's a script. There is *always* a script. This is why we have to be precise about what it is that we do with one another, in novels, in bed and elsewhere, and even be prepared to argue it out.

There is no easy way of disentangling heterosexuality as sexual practice from the rest of the institution. But how could heterosexual sex be transformed so that it did not turn women into willing victims and men into monsters? Unlike a substantial proportion of the human population, queer and straight, I don't think that pleasure and pain are inseparable. I believe that gentleness is preferable to violence in all sexual circumstances, and that because sexual fantasies are dangerously linked to actual sexual acts, we must even be prepared to interrogate our fantasies.

There is nothing intrinsically horrible about fellatio or anal penetration, indeed, even vaginal penetration, if those practices have no political meanings, which are oppressive, humiliating and destructive in the society at large. At the moment they do have such meanings. Should we then be prepared to obliterate heterosexuality as an institution? Well, this means getting rid of sexual difference. It also means abolishing most of the legal system, marriage, the family, most cultural and national traditions, the Christian Church, in all its forms, all sects, and most aspects of all other religions too, for our political systems reflect and follow our religious structures of thought, as the night the day, the tax system, work patterns, child-care arrangements, the distribution of wealth. It means rethinking the language, rebuilding our houses, remaking most of the sculptures, repainting the pictures and rewriting the books. We should have to argue for a radical restructuring of society. It could be done. And I for one will be glad to see it all go. I have been arguing that we should change it all for the last thirty years.

Can we imagine a world without sexual difference? A world in which gender was abolished? A world in which it had ceased to matter if your lover was a man or a woman? A world in which you might not even know? A world in which the polarization of hetero-sexuality in our dress codes, incomes and sexual practices were simply irrelevant? We would have to rethink the erotic. And that too would be no bad thing. This wonderful plan for complete demolition and rebuilding came from the extraordinarily simple insight that the private, sexual space between two human beings is not free from external, public, political meanings, or to put it more succinctly: 'The personal is the political.' These two cartographers of heterosexuality's fictional agendas, Margaret Atwood and Jenny Diski, suggest that the sexual space is the political space. I agree.

8.
'THE LONG LINE OF BLOOD/ AND FAMILY TIES'
GRACE NICHOLS AND THE LONG-MEMORIED WOMEN

Let me begin with a recipe: saltfish and ackee, the national dish of Jamaica. My mother knew how to cook this, but she never did any cooking at home. In the Jamaican household where I was brought up the cooks with authority were Miss Vi, Dolly Brown, Lur and, when she wasn't in a mood, sulking or complaining, Virginia. This is what you need.

> 2 dozen ackees in pods
> I half lb (250g) salt cod
> 2 tablespoons (1oz/ 25g) butter
> I qtr cup (2fl oz/ 50ml) oil
> 2 onions, sliced
> 1 sprig thyme
> 3–4 slices hot pepper
> I small tomato, chopped (optional)
> black pepper

And this is something that you must be careful to do:

> Choose ackees that are completely open, with the black seed and yellow fruit clearly visible in the scarlet pod. This is important, as unripe ackees contain a highly toxic substance. Remove the ackees from the pods. Discard the seeds and the pink membrane found in the cleft of each fruit. Wash them and put them to boil in a large pot of water with the salt fish. (Benghiat, 1985, p.77)

Now reflect upon a sexist Jamaican riddle: *'Me fadre send me to pick out a wife, tell me to tek only those that smile, fe those that do not smile wi kill me.'* What is he talking about? The answer of course is ackees, the national fruit of Jamaica. And ackees are like women or, more specifically, wives. Delicious when ripe, vulnerable, split open, showing their pink membranes, but when they are closed, locked, unripe, they are highly toxic and dangerous. It is wise to throw away the water in which ripe ackees have been boiled. When a wife decides to murder her husband she will often try poison and will usually do it in the kitchen. Women's cooking can make for dangerous eating. A wise man would beware even of the smiling ackee.

When I was a child, breadfruit, plantain, yams, cassava, guava, pawpaw, saltfish and ackee were all daily foods. There was nothing exotic, 'Other' or different about them. We had pineapples out the back, coconuts and avocados on the estate, a banana above the gully behind the bathroom. But in the High School where I began my education in the 1960s we never read any Caribbean literature. We studied *Julius Caesar* and Wordsworth, thus giving me very strange ideas about England, the so-called mother country, the motherland. England was the other country, the Mother Country, a nation of heroes where everyone was rich.

It is dangerous to construct Caribbean literature as exotic, different, 'Other'. Who is the 'Other' against whom we measure our difference? By what right do we designate the 'Other' as different? Who are 'we', anyway? When I was a child, Patwah, Creole or nation language—and they all have political implications, whichever term we choose—was the language spoken by the people, many of whom were Black women, who had authority over me. Nation language was the language in which I first learnt the meanings of permission and denial; the language in which I first grasped the implications of the word no. Writing by Caribbean women that seems exotic and extraordinary to a white, western middle-class audience may, to Caribbean readers, simply be the articulation of dailiness, daily words, daily foods. Or it may be just as strange as Shakespeare's *Julius Caesar*. The question of audience is crucial.

For whom do Caribbean writers working in Britain actually write? The audience for their work may not be the people addressed by that work. And although the sensation of performing like a freak in a circus may be confined to an older generation of writers I find it hard to believe that it has entirely disappeared. James Berry, who came to Britain in the 1950s, writes: 'The audience I crave/ compels exhibits' (Berry, 1979, p.20). In her most recent book of poetry, *Sunris* (1996), Grace Nichols is forced to add a four-page Glossary explaining who all the gods she invokes actually are. A Caribbean audience would have heard of 'Papa Bois' and would know what 'Mas' meant. I find it sad that neither she nor her publishers are even able to assume that we have all heard of Cortez and Montezuma. Tales of liberation struggles begin to lose their significance if the historical memory of colonial atrocity has also vanished.

The writing of women, whether they be ripe, open ackees, or the closed-up, toxic, dangerous variety, may well be revelatory, embarrassing, threatening to men, black, white, or any other race and colour. But to women this writing may have another meaning, a shared meaning. It is often this secret, shared knowledge, which Byron called the freemasonry of our sex, that is written large on the wall. So who is the 'Other' against whom you measure your difference? Well, that depends on where you are standing. The 'Other' is not easy to define nor easy to consume. And not every ripe smiling ackee is safe to eat. You can make no assumptions.

What is the Caribbean? Clearly more than the necklace of islands and coastal states encircling the gulf. There is no single Caribbean nation language, no single national culture, identity, landscape. The islands were exploited and possessed by Spanish, French, English colonists, leaving a legacy of difference. Many of the black people now living there, who are the descendants of the slaves, trace their ancestry, music and languages back to Africa. But not all the islands are black nations dominated by Afro-Caribbeans. Trinidad is more or less divided between people of African and Indian descent. The latter were imported from Asia as indentured labour after the end of slavery. There are also substantial minorities of Lebanese and Portuguese origin. Tobago on the other hand, a part of the independent nation of Trinidad and Tobago, is 90 per cent black. The national slogan of Jamaica desperately demands one nation, while recognizing endless diversity: 'Out of many, one people.'

The Caribbean is also a presence, a psychic space within the prescribed boundaries of the ex-imperial nations. Thus the

Caribbean is also present in many cities and districts throughout Britain: Brixton, Birmingham, Bristol, Liverpool and gloriously, completely, once a year, in all of Notting Hill. And the scale beats Jamaica Masquerade. James Berry (1979, p.59) takes it upon himself to explain 'Mas' to his white audience.

> Mi dear, yesterday I did go Carnival
> or Mas, as the Trinnies call it.
> Mas comes from Masquerade, you know.
> But Jamaica Masquerade is pickney
> party, compared to royalty occasion.
> Mi dear, this elaborates big big.
>
> A whole London district
> in street jumpup, in costumes,
> in ordinary clothes, even barefoot.
> A dozen costume ban's, floats galore
> like stars. Should see kaftans an' gowns.

Here, James Berry recreates a voice, a woman's voice, speaking in her own nation language. The poem is a letter, but the woman writes as she speaks.

Caribbean writing is rooted in oral cultures, oral traditions and in music. The most crucial black medium for self-expression and protest has, of course, been music; from the slave songs through to the union of rhythm and voice, which is the basis of rap. Most black Caribbean artists in Britain unite music and poetry: Linton Kwesi Johnson, the late Michael Smith, Jean Binta Breeze, Merle Collins and Marsha Prescod are all performance poets. The foundation of their work is the voice. Prescod comments,

> Writing about writing seems a bit artificial. Being asked how I see myself as a writer, and why I write, seems like being asked how I see myself as a talker and how I talk. Writing for me is like talking first to myself, then to other people. (Ngcobo, 1987, p.106)

Prescod began writing in the context of the Black Writers workshop in Brixton. She also worked with the Brent Black Music Workshop. Grace Nichols works with Calypso rhythms and the steel-band beat: 'I myself have grown up with the words and tunes and rhythms of calypso constantly in my head—sweet calypso with its wit, wordplay, bravado and gusto. It is the music of my childhood' (1996, p.3). Nichols thus not only writes in the way that she speaks and thinks but as she dances and sings.

What are the implications of producing serious writing within languages that are outside the dialects and hierarchies of standard English? The representation of Creole or nation-language as a literary language remains a crucial issue for Caribbean writers working in Britain. Language for post-colonial writers will always be an area of political struggle. Marlene Nourbese Philip comes from Tobago. She became a lawyer and worked in Canada. Her work addresses the problem of linguistic inheritance and how we read. Overleaf is an extract from her 'Discourse on the Logic of Language' (1993, pp.30–3).

This poem is about the complexity and significance of the mother-tongue. The central text is flanked by two other framing discourses: the slave edicts forbidding the African blacks to speak in their own languages and the mythic, ancestral mothertongue, the long-memoried language passed on from mother to daughter, the secret women's language of the long-memoried women. This is the language beyond the control of The Fathers, the masters. Nourbese Philip finds a solution to the political tensions within her language by dramatizing the conflicting discourses. She places the mythic language of the mother on the left. This language is animal, instinctive, magical. It is also matrilineal. On the right is the fathertongue, the language of punishment and interdiction. This is the white man's language, the White Father's tongue. The language of the mother is the language of love, motherlove, the secret women's inheritance, which is unambiguous, physical, empowering. Tongue here has a double meaning: it is both the language and the organ of speech. English is the double-tongued language. It is both the 'foreign anguish' and the mothertongue, the alien, compromised, hybrid inheritance. Caught between the two, the speaker struggles against silence, stuttering, desperate to find the words, to refuse the paralysis of dumbness, to give tongue.

Discourse on the Logic of Language

WHEN IT WAS BORN, THE MOTHER HELD HER NEWBORN CHILD CLOSE: SHE BEGAN THEN TO LICK IT ALL OVER. THE CHILD WHIMPERED A LITTLE, BUT AS THE MOTHER'S TONGUE MOVED FASTER AND STRONGER OVER ITS BODY, IT GREW SILENT—THE MOTHER TURNING IT THIS WAY AND THAT UNDER HER TONGUE UNTIL SHE HAD TONGUED IT CLEAN OF THE CREAMY WHITE SUBSTANCE COVERING ITS BODY.

English
is my mother tongue.
A mother tongue is not
not a foreign lan lan lang
language
l/anguish
 anguish
—a foreign anguish.

English is
my father tongue.
A father tongue is
a foreign language,
therefore English is
a foreign language
not a mother tongue.

What is my mother
tongue
my mammy tongue
my mummy tongue
my momsy tongue
my modder tongue
my ma tongue?

I have no mother
tongue
no mother to tongue
no tongue to mother
to mother
tongue
me

I must therefore be tongue
dumb
dumb-tongued
dub-tongued
damn dumb
tongue

EDICT 1

*Every owner of slaves
shall, wherever possible,
ensure that his slaves
belong to as many ethno-
linguistic groups as
possible. If they can-
not speak to each other,
they cannot then foment
rebellion and revolution.*

In an essay on her work and the problems she confronts Nourbese Philip argues (1993, p.84) for the same solution Grace Nichols offers in her writing. She says,

> The excitement for me as a writer comes in the confrontation between the formal and the demotic in the text itself...It is *in the continuum of expression* from standard to Caribbean English that the veracity of the experience lies. (author's italics)

Both writers tackle the language issue head-on, either by separating out the different discourses or by forcing a shot-gun marriage between the two. Nichols uses the same combative terms as Nourbese Philip: battle, confrontation. Here is Nichols.

> It's the battle with language that I love. When it comes to writing poetry it is the challenge of trying to create or chisel out a new language that I like. I like working in both standard English and Creole. I tend to want to fuse the two tongues, because I come from a background where the two worlds, creole and standard English, were constantly interacting though Creole was regarded, obviously as the inferior by the colonial powers when I was growing up. (Ngcobo, 1987, p.97)

Creole or nation-language is both class marked and race marked. Standard English and Creole are in conflict. But Nichols makes the subversive move of undermining the power one language has over another in her poem sequence *i is a long-memoried woman* (1983). She gives both languages back to her mythic figure, the slavewoman who is the voice in her narrative of memory. Thus, the slavewoman knows the master's language; she has the mastery of his tongue and her own.

The voice introduces herself in Creole (Nichols, 1983, p.4):

> From dih pout
> of mih mouth
> from dih

> treacherous
> calm of mih
> smile
> you can tell
> **i is a long-memoried woman**

Sinister, menacing, the voice remembers cruelty, injustice, monstrousness. The entire sequence is written in the woman's double tongue. A woman's calm is treacherous. Here is the closed and open ackee, the one passing for the other, the smiling woman who is also a killer. Ancestral memory contains both horror and joy. Memory is a dangerous thing.

Some of the poems are incantations, spells, ritual exorcisms. Any gesture of passivity or submission should be read as a threat. 'I COMING BACK' is directly addressed to 'Massa'—ferociously ironised in inverted commas—and the text holds out the promise 'I coming back', which is also a threat. The woman's power is metamorphic; she can become anything she desires. She is a shape-shifter. She is a 'dog howling outside/yuh window', a 'ball-a-fire' a 'skinless higue' (Nichols, 1983, p.43),

> hiss in yuh ear
> and prick in yuh skin...
> bone in yuh throat
> and laugh in yuh skull

Notice that she is inside his skin, his skull; she is a form of possession. The poem SKIN-TEETH is written in standard English. Here the woman presents herself as the smiling, open ackee. But the smile is a snarl: *i is a long-memoried woman* deals with abjection, suffering and revolt. Nichols uses the same psychic narrative technique that Toni Morrison develops in *Beloved* (1987). She gives the power, awareness and solidarity of contemporary Black consciousness back to the slaves, so that memory spans history, moving forwards and backwards in time. Nichols' prologue describes the passage from one continent to another, from Africa to the Americas, as a birth. It is not a defeat, but a 'Black beginning' (1983, p.6).

> Child of the middle passage womb
> push

In the Epilogue she describes a resurrection into language. The slavewoman's tongue is torn out, but a new one grows from its root. She possesses a new language, a new tongue. (1983, p.80)

> I have crossed an ocean
> I have lost my tongue
> from the root of the old one
> a new one has sprung

A people who have been severed from their language have been severed from their myths. There may be no choice but to create new ones. Nichols' long-memoried woman sets out to create these new myths. She is 'mistress of the underworld' (1983, p.43) priestess, sorceress, 'woman-keeper / of dreams' (1983, p.65). Crucially, the slavewoman / memorywoman is the woman who forges connections with other women. Nichols comments on her deliberate transformation of the slavewoman into memorywoman and the strategy of giving supernatural powers to the apparently powerless (Ngcobo, 1987, p.102):

> The woman is something of a mythic figure. She breaks the slave stereotype of the dumb victim of circumstance. She is a woman of complex moods who articulates her situation with vision. Her spirit goes off wandering meeting women from other cultures. She's a priestess figure and employs sorcery when necessary.

The trajectory of Nichols' long-memoried woman is from slavery to freedom. But throughout her history the woman has been no man's possession. She has never been fully conquered, never been completely colonized. Memory is the enabling power, that guarantees the possibility of vengeance. Her consciousness now moves across historical time. She wins.

Nichols' second volume of verse, *The Fat Black Woman's Poems* (1984), employs a feminist strategy of moving the figure on the margins into the centre. To be both fat and black in white, racist Britain is to be vast, monolithic and yet quite invisible. The fat, black woman occupies the intersections not only of race and gender but also of body politics. Fat is hated and feared in western culture. If women are enormously fat they are regarded as both disgusting and stupid, and certainly not sexy. Obesity is akin to obscenity. Nichols transforms the conventional racist, sexist meanings of fat and black—that is, ugly, insignificant, grotesque—into beauty, power, autonomy, control. She does not use her fat, black speaker's voice as the only perceiving consciousness. She sees the fat, black woman from the outside and the inside. The fat, black woman is both the perceiver and the perceived. Thus, she is both an actor within as well as an observer of white western culture and her Caribbean motherland. She is the standard, the measure, the size to beat. Nichols and her fat, black woman redefine what beauty is: all the earth adores the fat, black woman. The sun lights her path (1984, p.7),

> while the sea turns back
> to hug her shape

Fat and black become the adjectives, that both define and judge the world. The fat, black woman has the voice of authority. In 'The Assertion' she is claiming her place not in the teeth of the exclusion and resentment of thin people or white racists, but the white-robed chiefs of her own tribe. She has chosen the golden stool, the position of power and authority. She refuses to move. She is 'heavy as a whale', and all her weight is behind her refusal (Nichols, 1984, p.8).

> *This is my birthright*
> says the fat black woman
> giving a fat black chuckle
> showing her fat black toes

Fat and black are thus being given new meanings. They are potent signs, of power, pleasure, freedom.

Nichols takes on the stereotype, so beloved by Hollywood, of the fat, black mammy, dedicated to her white masters—the jovial jemima—the fat, black woman of white, racist memory. She is held up, remembered and mocked in American double negatives: 'but this fat black woman ain't no jemima' (Nichols, 1984, p.9). And here again (ibid.) is the sinister edge that was there in the long-memoried woman, the echo in the fat, black woman's

> happy hearty
> murderous blue laughter

This fat, black woman is a traveller, a voyager. She is both the closed and open ackee. She is also fearless.

Nichols places her mythic fat, black woman in ordinary scenarios. In 'The Fat Black Woman goes Shopping' the poetry moves in and out of Creole syntax, indicating the inner voice of the fat, black woman, and a framing narrative. The oppositions set up by the poem are frozen, cold, thin, against fat, black, breezy sunlight, bright, billowing. Here black and fat signify freedom, warmth, the erotic.

The fat, black woman is universal, multilingual. She speaks Yoruba, Swahili, nationlanguage. There is a pernicious prejudice, widely held in the white west, that you can only have good sex if you're thin. But the fat, black woman's come-on in 'Invitation' demonstrates a powerful, autonomous sexuality. She celebrates and enjoys her own body (Nichols, 1984, p.13).

> My breasts are huge exciting
> amnions of watermelon
> > your hands can't cup
> my thighs are twin seals
> > fat slick pups

Her heterosexual desire is neither suppliant nor submissive. She is a challenge, difficult to grasp. She overflows. In 'The Fat Black Woman's Instructions to a Suitor' she sets the tests like a fairy-tale princess. Her men have to undergo a dance competition, to perform for her. There's no shortage of suitors. But she does the choosing, taking over Mae West's immortal line, 'Come up and see me sometime'.

All the discourses of patriarchy that have defined woman and black as other, suspect, second class, are transformed and dominated by the fat, black woman. In 'Thoughts drifting through the fat black woman's head while having a full bubble bath' the fat, black woman playfully fantasizes about taking over the opposition. The fat, black body, her back, feet, breasts push aside anthropology, history and the capitalist slimming industry. Notice that it is the power of her physical presence rather than argument that displaces the discourses that deny her, her enormous buttocks massively present in the surrounding natural world (Nichols, 1984, p.13):

> Steatopygous sky
> Steatopygous sea
> Steatopygous waves
> Steatopygous me

I had to look up 'steatopygous' when I first read this poem and roared with laughter on discovering that it meant 'fat buttocked'. For the first time in my life I felt ruefully thin. I wanted to be 'steatopygous'. Obscurity becomes insolence. The joke was on me.

The fat, black woman confronts the white west with Caribbean values, colours, perspectives. Hers is an oppositional discourse. Her standards are dominant, and the west stands judged. There is no doubt, neither in her mind, nor in that of her readers, which land is the motherland, the land of her roots, origins, identity, her nation (Nichols, 1984, p.19):

> T'he fat black woman want
> a brilliant tropical death
> not a cold sojourn
> in some North Europe far/ forlorn...
>
> In the heart
> of her mother's sweetbreast
> In the shade
> of the sun leaf's cool bless
> In the bloom
> of her people's bloodrest

The motherland is the tropics, the landscape of breezy sunlight and hibiscus. Many Caribbean texts, published in Britain, address precisely this tension between two worlds. But many of them do not resolve the dilemma of belonging with such certainty as the fat, black woman. Many Caribbean texts are fictions of displacement and alienation, which describe the knowledge of exile, the realization that there is no nation, no motherland, to which the traveller entirely belongs. And to this condition of 'unbelonging' there are different solutions.[1]

Nichols' first piece of adult fiction, *Whole of a Morning Sky* (1986), is set in the early 1960s and deals with the fate of the Walcott family amid the political unrest and race riots at the time of independence. She portrays the Guyanese people struggling to create a national identity out of a disparate population whose political schisms were carefully orchestrated by the British. The Walcotts live in the same Georgetown yard as a wealthy Asian family and a poorer hoard of Blacks. Nichols uses the yard as a metaphor, a microcosm of the state. Despite her sceptical reading of the liberation struggle—nobody's politics are ever disinterested, and Nichols says so—this portrait of a community is optimistic and there is a revealing comic sequence describing the flowering of the city after the looting and the riots (Nichols, 1986, pp.114–15):

> All around Georgetown at this time, there's a rustling among the poorer segments of the population, a burgeoning of new clothes, new shoes, new dresses, new shirts and trousers, nighties and hats: a resurrection of the smaller items looted in the recent fires. People who had been nowhere near the scene of the looting came into little bonanzas through friends of friends, relatives of relatives, and other far-reaching connections...the smaller items begin to circulate generously, unexpected gifts coming to even those who had condemned the looting.
>
> On Easter Sunday morning blind Mrs Costello, leaning on Mr Costello's arm, stepped out in a pair of bright blue leather wedge-heels which fitted her like a soft glove...On bended knee she prayed generously, praying not only for her devoted Mr Costello...but praying also for the contentious neighbours in the yard, praying for the country ('Lord, stop the strife and

troubles and guide us through to peace and harmony')...

The children were all unbelievably proud of these clothes, even Dinah, old as she was. Lying around in her red-flowered housecoat, she felt as though she was wearing a piece of her country.

Here, it is the circulating pleasure of stolen goods that makes the nation. Burglary and looting become a method of redistributing the wealth of the country; they create a community of good will. The connections between the disparate populations, even if they remain 'far-reaching' and 'unexpected', are celebrated and cemented in a 'burgeoning of new clothes', a flowering of national identity. Theft brings reconciliation. Mrs Costello prays both for her yard and her country. Everybody suddenly belongs in the magical rebirth, the generous resurrection of the nation. Dinah feels as if she is 'wearing a piece of her country'. The sharing of their inheritance unites the community. Out of many garments, one nation.

It is difficult to separate the idea of the nation from the hope of belonging. The political term nation now generally refers to the modem nation state. The Latin root is *nasci, natus*, the verb 'to be born'. And the original meaning is 'a body of people born of the same stock'. The second meaning is 'the people inhabiting the same country, or under the same government'. The problem here is that these two meanings are directly in conflict. Let me explain.

I was born in Jamaica of mixed English/West Indian parents. I have lived more than half my life in other countries. I look and sound English, which is a convenient and privileged white mask to wear. But I have no emotional investment whatsoever in 'Englishness'. When I was a child I used to believe that England was my motherland and that English was my mothertongue. I now think otherwise. I have lived for many years in France. I speak French. In France my 'Otherness' is perceived as 'Englishness'. To be 'English' in France, especially if you speak fluent French and live at ease within French culture, is a convenient comfortable, privileged 'Otherness' to occupy. To be Arab in France, of Moroccan, Algerian, Tunisian origin, even if you were born in France, raised there, educated within the French educational system and speak no language other than French, is to remain a stranger, an outsider and to suffer the sharp end of French racism.

French becomes the 'foreign anguish'. And often, for the children of second-generation immigrants living within French culture, there is nowhere else to go. So there are different degrees of otherness and exile, and different knowledges of what it is to be alien.

National character, a national essence, or even a national literature cannot exist as pure, fixed absolutes except within the racist imaginations of the politically self-interested. Race, languages, traditions, even landscapes, are living things. They are too diverse and shifting to constitute a stable, identifiable community. Yet people, especially men, die for their nations, fight wars on behalf of an idea, kill and abuse other people in the name of their nation, and write poetry and fiction justifying their invented homeland. Nation must be defined against that which is 'not nation', the 'other', the alien. Sometimes there are nations within nations. And to sign up for one is to declare yourself an alienated exile from another. Lesbian nation is an Utopian ideal, the invisible international sexuality/ nationality, with its own codes, languages, music, customs, literatures, rituals. Queer nation is a more diffuse version of sexual dissidents. One of Antonia White's characters (1978, p.122) has this to say concerning Catholicism: 'I'd never advise anyone to become a Catholic...if you're one, you've got to be one. But you can't change people. Catholicism isn't a religion, it's a nationality.' And the same might be said of Judaism. There are Jews who repudiate the state of Israel, but who will still affirm the idea of the 'Jewish nation', a nation that exists across races, languages and international frontiers.

Benedict Anderson points out that the attachment to this imagined entity[2] is always expressed in terms of kinship, family, parentage, home. We speak of motherland, fatherland, Heimat, patria. But your family is the one group you don't choose, can't change and for which, thank God, you cannot be held responsible. But isn't this the point? Ties that are not chosen cannot be said to be self-interested. Self-sacrifice for your nation is noble, heroic, sweet, glorious. Theoretically, you can choose your nation. You can become 'naturalised', sign up for national belonging, learn nation language. But this never works. Not entirely. I can apply for French citizenship, speak impeccable French, settle down somewhere in France. But I will never become French. In a country that is intensely aware of itself as a nation, whose public national ideology is exclusive, rigid, racist, intolerant, I will remain foreign, alien, other. But in my case conveniently accepted as 'English'.

Grace Nichols (1984, p.30) addresses this phenomenon of 'unbelonging', being the foreigner, the alien, the other, in 'We New World Blacks'.

> The timbre
> in our voice
> betrays us
> however far
> we've been
>
> whatever tongue
> we speak
> the old ghost
> asserts itself
> in dusky echoes

But she goes on to locate herself and the community of exiles in their motherland, the tropics. And she does this by referring to the old proverb we had in the Jamaican household into which I was born. We said that you would never leave the place where you had buried your navel string. For this was both the place where you had given birth and the place that had given birth to you. You will always find your way back. You will be called back (Nichols, ibid.):

> we know the way
> back to
>
> the river stone
>
> the little decayed
> spirit
> of the navel string
> hiding in our back garden

I love this poem, even though I know that, for myself and for many like me, black and white, women and men, this is just sentimental wish-fulfillment. There is no 'way back'. And for us this is especially poignant because the navel string is the mother's cord, the link not only with the nation but also with the mother and the mother's garden.[3] We have no motherland, no mothertongue. The separation from the mother is final, irreparable, complete.

For Nichols, the dilemma of identity and nation is resolved by this link with the mother's body, which in turn becomes the motherland. Thus, the return is not only to a nation but a return home. In 'Praise Song for My Mother' (Nichols, 1984, p.44) she praises the mother in terms of landscape, food, the sea, the earth.

> You were water to me
> deep and bold and fathoming...
> You were
> sunrise to me
> rise and warm and streaming
>
> You were
> the fishes red gill to me
> the flame tree's spread to me
> the crab's leg / the fried plantain smell
> > replenishing replenishing
> Go to your wide futures, you said

Nichols is using present participles as adjectives. Thus the mother is not only a noun but also a verb, a process of mothering, nurturing, just as 'mother' is both person and action. To mother is the task of a lifetime, a lifetime of making and replenishing. Significantly, this is the mother who lets go, sends forth her daughter:

> Go to your wide futures, you said

It is the daughter who has the future tense. She is commanded to set out on her voyages of conquest and adventure. She is given the boy's role of the fairy-tale prince.

Alongside these love poems to the mother is a love poem to her daughter, 'Hey There Now' and there the daughter occupies the present continuous tense. 'My young stream / headlong/ rushing' (Nichols, 1984, p.45). She too is part of the natural world: 'my brownwater flower', 'my sunchild'. Nichols celebrates the classic triangle of grandmother, mother, daughter, typical in black women's writing and from which the male is absent, invisible, largely irrelevant. The most erotic relationship described in her poems is with the landscape, and this landscape is always firmly associated with the body of the mother, the daughter, the woman.

Out of her poems Nichols constructs a sequence of intersections, a structure of passion and possession, a continuum between the people and the Caribbean landscape, with its continuities and illusions. Thus there is a bond between the exile in Europe and the navel string buried in the mother's garden, between her mother's breasts and the 'sleeping volcanoes', her father's tears and the 'hurricanes', her grandmother's voice and the 'sifting sand / water mirroring palm' (Nichols, 1984, p.42). This is a primal world of sea, earth, sky and 'strange recurring mysteries' (ibid., p.40) in which nothing is fixed. This is a world of transformations, passings. Watch something that appears firm, and it becomes fluid, shifting, different. (ibid., p.41)

> The heavens are blue
> but the sun is murderous
> the sea is calm
> but the waves reap havoc.

The earth, however, also gives itself up to the inhabitants, as the fish do to the fisherwomen in 'Those Women', because they inhabit the same element (ibid., p.39).

> standing waist deep
> in the brown voluptuous
> water of their own element

The landscape structures the identity not only of the family but also of the nation. This is an identity rooted in a physical geography of continuity and consent. It is an identity that is lived and remembered, rather than chosen.

Nichols defines the nation as ancestral memory and as blood ties,

even across the tapestry of mixed races. In 'Tapestry', her conclud-
ing poem to her third collection, *Lazy Thoughts of a Lazy Woman
and other Poems* (1989), she creates for herself the black identity
and the black nation to which she can lay legitimate claim. This is
the tapestry created in history (1989, p.57):

> The long line of blood
> and family ties
>
> An African countenance here
> A European countenance there...
>
> The tapestry is mine
> All the bloodstained prints
> The scatterlinks
> The grafting strand of crinkled hair
> The black persistent blooming.

But this is, ultimately, a conservative position in which race still
means blood, even mixed race and mixed blood. Nichols opts for
the first meaning of nation—the body of people born of the same
stock, however various. She is arguing for the tribe, for blood ties,
family ties. We can see the 'bloodstained prints' in the face, the
cheek, the eye, 'the grafting strand of crinkled hair'. Nation is
rooted in the body and the blood. Your nation is your birthright,
your inheritance. Nation cannot be chosen.

Nichols and I part company here, in radical and disturbing ways.
I do not see this as a liberating assertion of identity, but as a political
trap with appalling implications. Any writing that does not transform
the conventional meanings of mother, motherland, mothertongue into
a critical discourse that is problematic, disruptive, divisive and frightening will finally endorse a conservative sequence of meanings. Nichols
meanings offer the body as the basis of knowledge, memory and identity. Thus, the good mother, her mother, becomes the nurturing earth
goddess. Did the mother have any desires beyond home and family?
Had she acted upon them she would have become the uncooperative
bad mother, the castrating, neglectful witch of fairy tale. Nichols
nation is a particular patch of mother earth, to which only family

members can belong. It is the motherland in which asylum seekers are unwelcome, and in order to keep the family exclusive we often cover the earth with other people's blood.

We all have a dream of belonging, a fear of unbelonging. Hence the improbable and unreasonable demands we often make of our mothers and of our children. Ironically, this is also true of our dreams of the nation. The 'long line of blood / and family ties' (Nichols, 1989, p.57) is undeniable, irrational, full of mysterious obligations and emotional attachments. It is hard to imagine systems of both kinship and nation that could be based on rational decisions, intellectual convictions and political choice. But that is my revolutionary desire, rooted in a radical dream. I dream of a political nation in which race, blood and family ties are irrelevant; a nation in which there is no element of unbelonging dependent upon the religions we espouse, our sexual desires or on the colour of our skins; a nation to which we can choose to belong.

Nichols does not simply offer a naïve vision of the nation as blood kin and family. The poems contradict their own ideologies. Her Black women characters negotiate the intersections of nation, identity, body politics and (hetero)sex from a position of strength. There are no victims here; no banal, smiling ackees. Beverley claims her right to be one of the black British (Nichols, 1989, p.35).

> Me good friend Beverley
> Come to England. She was three.
> She born in Jamaica, but seh,
> Dis ya she country,
> She ancestor blood help fe build it,
> Dat is history.

Beverley's ancestors spilt their blood for the Empire. She claims kin through sacrifice. It seems, therefore, that the blood claim still has to be made to validate the demand to belong.

'Configurations', however, draws together the politics of heterosexual sex and imperialism in a poem that is comic, erotic and sharp. The metaphor of sexual and colonial penetration, exploitation and possession has been so overused in writing by men—Joseph Conrad, E. M. Forster, Seamus Heaney—that it leaves me irritated, spitting and bored. There is usually a lot of irrelevant heat generated around the issue of rape and the tragedy of a women's body/the body of a nation lying wasted, exploited, discarded and abused. This reinforces the victim status of women in sexual and political discourse. The colonized nation is feminized, then cast in the role of helpless victim. Nichols (1989, p.31) rewrites the encounter between the Caribbean and Europe, the white man and the black woman, along the lines of the 'Song of Songs', which is a celebration of mutual passion.

> He gives her all the configurations
> of Europe.
>
> She gives him a cloud burst of parrots.
>
> He gives her straight blond hairs
> and a white frenzy.
>
> She gives him black wool. The darkness
> of her twin fruits.

This sexual exchange is mutual, reciprocal, a sharing of gifts. It is also very funny. Consenting sex, heterosexual or otherwise, is often comic. When we make love we are at our most vulnerable and least dignified. Nichols (ibid.) knows this and says so.

> He gives her uranium, platinum, aluminium
> and concorde.
> She gives him her 'Bantu buttocks'.

The joke is that the encounter does not end in phallic penetration with all its equivocal overtones of colonization and dominance, but in oral sex, with the man going down on the woman.[4] And as she opens her legs, like the fat black woman taking possession of her 'golden stool', she surrenders the Caribbean, but takes over the Empire (ibid.).

> She delivers up the whole Indies again
> But this time her wide legs close in

> slowly
> Making a golden stool of the empire
> of his head.

Notice that her legs close in like scissors. This is the woman who is the open ackee, but who loses none of her power by revealing her soft, pink membranes. She gives, she takes, she wins.

Nichols' version of black female sexuality is of fullness, generosity, power. The black woman's body, her bleeding, her fat folds, her moles, arse, hair are her own possessions. If she chooses to give her body to a man she gives out of her overflowing wealth, not out of poverty or lack. 'My Black Triangle' is not only a celebration of woman's sexual power, firmly and unashamedly celebrating her wet cunt, it is a gift to the dry, senseless world (Nichols, 1989, p.25):

> My black triangle
> is so rich
> that it flows over
> on to the dry crotch
> of the world

This is typical of Nichols, her playfulness, cheekiness, optimism, generosity, as well as her raunchy sexiness; here she offers the black loving and giving that both possesses and engulfs the world.

III
MAKING WRITING

9.
POST GENDER

JURASSIC FEMINISM MEETS QUEER POLITICS

I was brought up on slogans: slogans shouted in the streets, recreated on badges, painted on walls, political slogans of the radical left and feminist slogans. These varied from the obvious 1960s vintage versions: BLACK IS BEAUTIFUL, SOCIALISM OR DEATH and END THE VIETNAM WAR to the slogans of our sexual revolution: ANY WOMAN CAN BE A LESBIAN and I'M GAY, KISS ME GIRLS. The value of slogans is not obvious, but I want to defend their potency and their function within our historical memory. They are condensed, 'in your face' statements. They are uncompromising, unnuanced, bald, provocative, aggressive. For us they were often political affirmations not only of identity but also of evil intentions. Above all, they represented certainties, the certainties of what I now think of as Jurassic Feminism. We know what we want, and we want it now. Certainty is an aspect of political Utopianism.

Well, now we live in a time without certainties. A time when all identities and subjectivities are suspect, unstable. It is no longer clear what a lesbian is, let alone who is one. And the category woman has long since been dissolved into a splintered mass of possibilities: '*One is not born, but becomes a woman.*' Adding a gloss to de Beauvoir's famous statement I would say that all women are not born straight, but have the experience of being socially constructed as heterosexual. Femininity is socially constructed to mean heterosexual femininity. And the possibility inherent in de Beauvoir's comment is that if we are not born women, but become women, then, either by hazard or by choice, we could become something else. Something other than, better than, different from woman, the subject sex, the second sex. We could become monsters, aliens, freaks, perverts, dykes. If we define ourselves in any sense as feminists then we are in opposition to what the word *woman* has always been held to mean. Post-feminism may not be here yet, but in order to be a feminist in the first place you certainly had to be post-woman.

Monique Wittig represents a current of French feminist thought that has effectively been erased in the Anglo-American concentration on the work of the Holy Trinity: Kristeva, Irigaray and Cixous.[1] It is no coincidence that the high theory produced by this triad can easily be assimilated into a post-modern politics of fragmented subjectivities, in which all political categories, such as woman, lesbian, Black, are suspect, self-indulgent, essentialist. Wittig is a materialist as well as a radical feminist. For her, women and men are social categories; gender difference is a sex-class difference. If we regard gender divisions as a result of social, political and above all economic structures, then the so-called natural differences, upon which the entire institution of heterosexuality is based, collapse. This is Stevi Jackson's point: 'Patriarchal domination is not based upon pre-existing sex differences, rather gender exists as a social division because of patriarchal domination'.[2] We should not then be too preoccupied with trying to transform the prison of gender, but with planning an escape. Here is Wittig's suggestion: '*Les lesbiennes ne sont pas les femmes*'.[3] In German this reads as 'Lesben sind nicht Frauen'. Interestingly, although the ambiguity of this translates into German, it does not translate into English. 'Femme' in French means both 'woman' and 'wife', just as it does in German. In English we have two words. Wittig's pun calls attention to the overlap in the straight mind between woman and heterosexual woman. Lesbian is the emergency exit from the category woman. But Wittig's position, seductive as it is, is a betrayal of that old radical slogan: ANY WOMAN CAN BE A LESBIAN, with its suggestion of ability, power and of becoming: ANY WOMAN CAN. Lesbian represents the decision to cease being a woman altogether, rather than becoming post-woman, and the definition of lesbian, which evolved within lesbian feminism, actually excluded many women who had always thought they were lesbians and who had loved other women all their lives.

We all used to believe, in those days of radical, transforming certainties, that the decision to become something else was boiling in every woman. Radicalesbians' 1970 manifesto produced a compelling definition of lesbian: *What is a lesbian? A lesbian is the rage of all women condensed to the point of explosion.*[4] Setting off that explosion was the name of the game. I wrote the slogan LESBIANS IGNITE over numerous lavatory walls. But this is a version of lesbianism that belongs to a unique moment in women's revolutionary history. Lesbianism is celebrated as far more than an expression of sexuality, more than a way of life. Here it is the revolutionary impulse to liberty, to freedom, a sexual politics that is engaged, committed, dangerous. This is in fact very close to Wittig's position. But it has ceased to be the escape route open to any woman. Lesbian is the chess move out of and away from the rest of the pack. Lesbian is the sexual passport into the vanguard, leaving the category woman to be occupied by fembots, victims, collaborators, wives, mothers, heterosexuals. The refusal to be a woman involves stepping across 'the deadly space between' the normal and the deviant, out of the cage and into freedom.

What does it mean to be a woman? The clichés are clear. Within heteropatriarchal discourse a woman is a wife and mother, submissive, conformist, familial, heterosexual. This is not how being a woman is always experienced, but this is what woman means within that discourse. These are men's myths. Women's lives seem to be made up of men's myths. There are other categories intersecting that discourse: slut, slag, dominatrix, whore, bitch, dyke. And what does lesbian mean within that discourse? Well, it means two things. Firstly, abnormal, deviant, bent, queer. But it also means sexy, titillating, asking-for-it. I worked on a small-scale study[5] of inexpensive non-violent pornography in France and found that lesbian sex was the most commonly represented sexual fantasy in a wide range of magazines. The scenarios, visual and verbal, were largely domestic, familial and everyday: the sexual scene was located at work, shopping, outside the school gates, on holiday, in lifts, at home. The message was always the same. Women like doing it with each other, and men like to watch. Any woman can be a lesbian, and most women are. This was lesbianism as home entertainment. It is simply not true to suggest that male rule is threatened by lesbian sexual desire.

Wittig puts her finger on something important, however, when she argues that lesbians are not women. What makes a lesbian life radically different from a woman's life is that she plays a less significant role in the service industry. Women's lives are spent in service and servitude, learning to be superserviceable, being at the service of others, being serviced. We are a service industry, serving husbands, lovers, bosses, children, aged parents, families, colleagues. Few of us ever escape this entirely. Even if you love women, live with women, spend all your affective life with women you will probably end up working for and with men. And that means working in the heterosexual-ego service industry.

Outside the heterosexual category of woman lies one of the gender myths occupied by radical lesbians, that of the warrior woman. She is the Amazon, the queen, the woman with one breast, the woman who rules, fights, kills. She exists in male myth too, but she is not always under male control. The male myths reproduce the woman tamed, captured, married. Thus Hippolyta is married off to Theseus in Shakespeare's sex-war comedy *A Midsummer Night's Dream*.[6]

The gender system is the political system within which we are all born, within which we all live—whether we call ourselves women, wives, mothers, feminists, straights, queers, dykes. But it is a political system, or, as Adrienne Rich argues, a compulsory political institution, which affects us all differently.[7] Some of us are privileged within it, financially protected by the heteropatriarchal state, if we play our cards right and as long as our luck holds. We are never secure. Some of us are caged, controlled, destroyed. Some of us are marginal to the structures of the institution. It does none of us any good. Of course, there is a difference between heterosexuality as an institution and as lived experience. The two cannot be seen as identical. But neither can they be severed. Heterosexuality is not the only element in the gender system, but it is one of the key elements.

The initial animus of the 1960s feminist critique was directed against three things: men, femininity and heterosexuality, both as a sequence of sexual acts and as a gender system. Men were then perceived to be our masters, our owners and, often, in no uncertain terms, the enemy. Even homosexual men benefited from belonging to the sex class of men. And they often bought into the gendered constructions of femininity. Femininity merely amounted to men's constructions of women. The heterosexual gender system—with all its manifold ramifications of marriage, motherhood, the family, unequal pay, violence against women—was the political regime within which women were kept down. Heterosexuality was endorsed by patriarchal religions, all patriarchal religions. Heterosexuality promoted Noah's Ark, a great sea of happy couples.

We cannot escape these patterns. Many homosexual couples—lesbian, gay and transgendered—reproduce similar heterosexual structures in their relationships and in their lives. But similar is not the same. The hetero-structures reproduced will never be identical to those of the 'real' heterosexuals, whose divisions and power hierarchies are based on sexual difference within the gender system. Some homosexuals, especially men, are busy trying to eradicate that critical difference. Why can't we have the right to marriage, service in the armed forces, respectability in church and at work? These are the arguments of the assimilationists, such as Andrew Sullivan,[8] for whom homosexuals are 'virtually', but not quite 'normal'. Love is love, he says, whomever you happen to love. Love is the same. And no one should be persecuted for loving someone else. This is a very attractive argument. But it is a counsel of defeat and capitulation to the gender system. There is nothing normal about heterosexuality and the gender system. It works to the advantage of a single gendered class. It cannot be in the interests of any sexual dissident, no matter how mild their dissent, to demand inclusion in a gender system that is constructed precisely in order to make their lives wretched and untenable.

The social construction of love is, I believe, one of the key elements of oppression in the gender system. For most of us, our first overwhelming experience of love is for our parents. Our love may not be returned. We may in fact have a harrowing experience of rejection and frustration in our first love. But our love for our parent, or parents, whatever their sex, or indeed their sexual orientation, is also a relationship of dependency and possession. They own us. We have no rights, no redress. Even if we have the good fortune to be loved in return, our first experience of overpowering love is of powerlessness, desire and demand. The love of a child for a parent is a profoundly unequal love. We are helpless in our desires. Hence the aggression that characterises the expression of most children's love for their parents. We are socialized into our heterosexual gender roles in infancy; and this process of socialization will vary enormously from culture to culture, but this nexus of passion, anger and powerlessness seems to be universal—and dangerous.

Women are infantilised within heterosexuality. We are treated like children, or like creatures of diminished responsibility. Think of the belittling patterns of endearment: baby, child, doll, little one. Whores call their pimps Daddy. Marilyn Monroe declared that her heart belonged to Daddy. Even the coded structures of male homosexual love contain ritualized inequality. Greek love was that of the older man for the younger boy. Marguerite Yourcenar and Mary Renault, both life-long lesbians, wrote historical novels of classical antiquity, that celebrated difference and inequality in same-sex relationships between men. It has always been unusual to insist on equality, or on sameness, even in homosexual love.

The traditions of courtly love (*amour courtois*), which apparently involved giving women power, also involved putting us on pedestals and fixing us firmly into men's myths. Even the religious expression of love for God means that men fake the feminine role within the heterosexual structure. God is their (masculine) master. They wait, as women are supposed to do, to be ravished, consumed, possessed. Men's fantasies of God are often homoerotic, even of penetration and rape, but the male poet takes the woman's place. The feminine role is associated with vulnerability, submission, lavish clinging desire. It is the woman's role within heterosexual gender ideology.

This obsession with difference, 'otherness', and inequality in our sexual desires is rooted in childhood, parenting and in our first family relationships. Our primary learning of love is from our parents, or the people who parent us. The first body we love is usually a woman's body. The first passion we have is for another woman. In a lesbian relationship the mother–daughter bond is echoed rather than repeated. It is largely from our mothers that we learn how to be women. And for most of us this is also the first experience of lies and betrayal. For it is the mother who teaches us how to be feminine, second-class, second-rate. And even when she affirms us as agents, as empowered beings who can choose our own lives, it is rare that she will tell us the truth about heterosexuality, about patriarchy, about men. It is rarer still that she will tell us how not to be women, how to get out. The primary relationship between women within patriarchy is ambiguous: an ugly mesh of betrayal, truth and lies. Very often we cannot afford to tell each other the truth. Sometimes we don't dare.[9] No one reared within the gender system will be exempt from this particular sexual pattern, this ubiquitous eroticising of inequality and difference in sexual structures, this pattern of power within desire.

One is not born a Lesbian, one becomes one. I would like to query the existence of the lesbian, and indeed the heterosexual gene. However attractive it might be to imagine that we were 'born that way' and however fiercely some of us might feel this to be the case, I think it is a biological dead end. Heterosexuality is no more natural than lesbianism or any other kind of sexuality. Sexuality is fluid. Sexual identities are radically unstable. And I for one am glad that they are. BIOLOGY IS NOT DESTINY was one of my favourite slogans. I want to go on saying, ANY WOMAN CAN.

It was for only a brief time, ten years perhaps, from the mid-1970s to the mid-1980s, or even barely ten years, that the two political gender categories, *lesbian* and *woman*, came into a radical conjunction within a public and political discourse. *Lesbian* and *woman* were united within feminism as theory and as praxis. To decide to be lesbian was to attempt a different way of thinking, behaving and being. It was in fact an attempt to create another gender that women could choose to inhabit. To decide to be lesbian was to choose women, not as we were, or as we are, but as we could become. Lesbian/woman was something other than woman, to be a lesbian/woman was to be an active creator of revolutionary change, a subversive, a rebel, a saboteur. FEMINISM IS THE THEORY, LESBIANISM IS THE PRACTICE, so the old slogan says. In that particular historical moment the women's movement in Britain was supported by a broad front of left-wing activism,

Greens, trade unionists, environmental campaigners, CND, anar-
chists, Rock Against Racism, Gay Liberation. Socialism was not a
dirty word. Feminists were not the only ones demanding a society
that was freer and more just.

There have always been lesbians, and there have always been
women's communities, but they have not always seen themselves
as part of a revolutionary movement. Lesbians have not always identified with women, nor have they seen themselves as dissidents. To
be different is not necessarily to be in a state of rebellion. In fact,
you may long to mask your difference, be desperate to conform.
Lesbians have, for centuries, existed peacefully within romantic
friendships, bisexual arrangements or closet marriages. Sometimes
we have taken risks, cross-dressed and lived as men.[10] Lesbians have
evolved subtle parodies and masquerades of heterosexual structures in butch–femme lives, and have lived differently, either
flaunting it, or underground.

But the revolutionary moment of feminism, a moment of Utopian
joy and possibility, was unique in asserting that there were no entry
qualifications: that you did not have to cross-dress, be an invert,
be different, cut your hair, be born dyke. '*A lesbian is the rage of
all women condensed to the point of explosion*'. All you had to be
was explosively angry at the way you were treated and the little
that you got. All you had to want was freedom: all you had to love
was women. Whatever that meant to you. And the meaning of
woman was up for grabs. So was the meaning of lesbian. The
prison of gender was apparently breaking down. We were making
our own meanings. All you had to be was a woman in the process
of becoming. 'Woman' was no longer a fixed point of closure, but
a dynamic process. We were women in movement, a movement of
women.

Over the last ten years I have watched the gradual separation of
lesbianism from feminism and, inevitably, lesbian from woman.
Lesbian is now part of a single corporate entity: the new firm,
LESBIAN 'n' GAY, or subsumed into that new product, QUEER.
Lesbians choosing to identify themselves as queers in Britain are,
in the main, young women. They are a post-feminist generation.
And they see feminism as their mother's politics, a politics that
may once have had something going for it, but that is now, like the

somewhat redundant patriarchy—not the monolith it once was—
also outdated and smelling of lies, betrayal, prohibitions and taboos.
Cherry Smyth explains:

> The attraction of queer for some lesbians is flavoured by a
> rebellion against a prescriptive feminism that had led them to
> feel disenfranchised by the lesbian feminist movement...the
> importance of identifying politically as a lesbian had obscured
> lesbianism as a sexual identity.[11]

And sex, indeed SEX, defiant, perverted, flagrant, on your backs,
in your face, is the name of the queer game. Lesbian sex is, in itself
apparently, a subversive, political act. Feminism has atrophied into
boring politically correct rules, mother saying no. Queer dykes are
the new radicals, the new sexual outlaws. Here is Spike Pittsberg
explaining the new frontier. 'We pushed back the borders and talked
about SM, fantasies, taboos, butch/femme, violence in relationships, non-monogamy, penetration, ass-fucking etc.'[12]

Doing anything with anybody in any position might well be fun,
but, despite my generation's experience, as sexual liberationists, I
find it hard to see how sex can be the source of revolutionary change.
It was never the right to screw ourselves senseless in private that was
in question, it was the right to gather socially, organise politically
and dispute the heterosexual hegemony that caused trouble.

But Queer also means 'to fuck with gender', and here I do see
radical possibilities. The binary opposition between masculinity
and femininity is fluid and unstable. It always was. That is why it
is so carefully policed. The pastiche dress codes of queers signal an
engagement with and refusal of heterosexual binary divisions.
Gender is performance. The body becomes ambiguous. Therefore,
power and knowledge cannot be so easily allocated to the masculine in queer discourses. Queer is a gender game. Direct action
rather than lobbying is characteristic of queer politics, just as it was
within the original revolutionary moment of feminism.

Here comes the good news. You do not even have to be born
woman to become lesbian. The intriguing encounter between
Jurassic Feminism and queer politics was dramatized for me, when
I re-read Janice Raymond's *The Transsexual Empire*, first published

in 1979 when lesbian feminists were busy occupying the righteous moral high ground of identity politics, and Kate Bornstein's *Gender Outlaw* (1994), that, as the subtitle points out, is about 'men, women and the rest of us'. Bornstein was a male-to-female transsexual, but is now, as she prefers to describe herself, transgressively transgendered. She is endearingly upfront about her onion of identities.

> I write from the point of view of an S/M transsexual lesbian, ex-cult member, femme top and sometimes bottom shaman. And I wondered why no one was writing my story?... I write from the point of view of a used-to-be politically correct, wanna-be butch, dyke phone sex hostess, smooth talking tele-marketing, love slave, art slut, pagan Tarot reader, maybe soon a grandmother, crystal palming, incense burning, not-man, not always a woman, fast becoming a Marxist.[13]

Well, no one can say that she hasn't tried everything, and I wish her good luck with the Marxism. Bornstein's thesis, that she has evolved from this process of social and sexual transitions, is actually very simple. Gender is a violent political system, that is enforced upon us. Gender has nothing to do with sexual orientation or how we actually experience our identities. There are certainly many more than two genders. But only two genders are privileged: male and female, and they operate throughout the world as an hierarchical and unequal system of power. This is the system, that privileges men over women and turns the rest of us into freaks. Bornstein identifies one of the reasons for the peculiar alliances between right-wing heterosexual gender fundamentalists and radical lesbian separatists. They are gender defenders. The Religious Right are busy upholding heterosexual family values and lesbian separatists often base their identity on the gender of their sexual partners. This means that they need to be absolutely certain that the lines of inclusion and exclusion are firmly drawn: women-born-women-only. Please check your chromosomes. According to Bornstein, the real radicals are the gender transgressors, the frontier freaks who insist on the endlessly fluid articulation of gender. Here, gender is perpetual mutability.

Bornstein herself once believed in gender. She must have done or she wouldn't have bothered with genital surgery and made such a determined effort to cease being a man. She charts her move from gender defending—after all, you have to think that you know what a woman is, if you want to become one—to gender scepticism.

> I'm supposed to be writing about how to be a girl. And I sure don't know how to be a boy. And after thirty-seven years of trying to be male and over eight years of trying to be female. I've come to the conclusion that neither is worth all the trouble... A lot of people think it is worth the trouble... And hey, I'm not just talking about transsexuals here. I'm talking about men and women, maybe like you.[14]

There are solid financial reasons for wanting to remain a man and if naked power gives you a thrill there are plenty of reasons for wanting to pass as a straight, white male. Many biological 'women' pretend to be Real Women to avoid being killed. But this is playing the gender game as tactical, survival strategy. It doesn't necessarily mean that you believe in it. Bornstein no longer subscribes to the myths of gender. Jurassic feminists never did. BIOLOGY IS NOT DESTINY. And, interestingly, Bornstein recognizes this in the work of Janice Raymond. One of the most telling sentences in *The Transsexual Empire* reads as follows: 'Men, of course, invented the feminine, and in this sense it could be said that all women who conform to this convention are transsexuals, fashioned according to men's image.'[15]

Exactly. I've spent a lot of time performing the transsexual role of feminine woman. There are considerable rewards attached to a good performance. Raymond argues that lesbian feminism recreates the female in opposition to the man-made invention of 'woman'. This is therefore an alternative gender. I agree. It only becomes prescriptive when lesbian feminists proclaim that it is the only authentic option for females on the run from the prison of gender. And how many of us experience gender not as playful performance, a sequence of costumes we can slip on and off, but as a sexual and behavioural code that is imposed and enforced? I don't want to be told anymore what my gender is and how I should therefore conduct my life.

Bornstein had the cash and the medical industry on hand to buy herself another gender. She charts her history from transsexual to transgressively transgendered queer artist as a progressive conversion experience. She is now neither man nor woman. She is a gender performer, a post-feminist figure, a maker of queer theatre, both as live entertainment and life in the raw. She does all this with panache and charm. But I did ponder the significance of the fact that she had no real sense of what male privilege actually was until she lost her prick and balls, the penis and the phallus all in one. She is honest enough to say so. Is that going to be generally true before we can get to a post-gendered world? I wonder. Legitimate protest and rational argument, from Mary Wollstonecraft onwards, appear to have had remarkably few results. Who willingly dismantles their gender privilege?

But what gives me heart is the sense of *déjà vu* I had while reading Bornstein's book. Yes, I have read it all before. Here, queer theory re-presents the central demand of Jurassic Feminism: the destruction of the gender system and the end to male privilege. We can only do that by ending the existence of the categories men/women. The post-gendered world, which has been the subject of so many fictional feminist utopias,[16] would look very different to our world. Maybe Bornstein's dream of a multiplicity of genders, of each one of us giving radically different performances, in any register, whenever we like, could then come true.

Bornstein stresses the risks that the transgressively transgendered take in negotiating the gendered world. She's right. They do. And they are courageous people who decide to breach the limits of gender. But—and this is the one point that makes it utterly clear that a Jurassic Feminist did not write *Gender Outlaw*—if you are born into the gender class of woman you are neither safe nor free, *simply because you are female*. You are not at risk because you are radically questioning the structures of gender, although you may be doing that too, but because your assigned place within those structures is female. And you did not choose your place. It has been imposed upon you by force. Some of us, myself included, would much rather not be 'women'. We have spent our lives trying to change the meaning of 'woman'. And, in some parts of the world, we have had some success.

The break with feminism is complete if, as Stevi Jackson cogently points out

> queer theory ultimately displaces patriarchal gender hierarchy in favour of heterosexuality as the primary regulatory system. It is vitally important for feminism that we see heterosexuality as a gendered hierarchy and not just as a normative construction of cross-sex desire.'[17]

Being queer may well be an alternative to femininity, to being woman within the heterosexual ideology, but we cannot escape the political regime of gender by wishful thinking, or even by wishful theory.[18] Unless we pack our bags and head for the Greenwood, as some women have long since decided to do. Separatism is both an important strategy and a radical solution. But it can't be our only solution. Subversion is the other alternative.

The energy of queer politics is delightful and obvious to everyone. I would rather be surrounded by the slogans that proclaim: SILENCE = DEATH and CHEERS QUEERS, the slogans that taste of opposition and dissent, than retreat into privacy and seclusion as many ex-radicals have done before me. And I am all for putting the sex back into sexual politics and the camp into campaigning. Queer theory has put Lesbian and Gay studies on the academic map, invaded cultural politics, advertising, television, cinema, given homosexuals of both sexes a new visibility. The suggestive queer politics of cross-dressing, theoretical and literal, has liberated queers of every gender and has provoked new debates about essentialism and the gender system, which is all to the good.

But...

And here are my Queer Caveats.

Every revolutionary movement appears to pass through eerily similar phases: the first years of celebration and manifestos when the old order totters, or at least has the grace to appear to do so. Demands are drawn up, and the Golden Age is at hand. Then come the darker times of impatience at the slowness or absence of change, the rigid imposition of what had once been the radical dream, finally the brutal divisions into the pure and the impure with purges to prove the point. Then, if the movement is not defeated altogether there are the years of underground struggle; long, slow years of hard work, disappointment and imperceptible change. And so it has always been with Jurassic Feminism. Political and sexual structures do not, unfortunately, exist only in the mind. And even lies that have been recognized as such take centuries to displace. Change need not be progressive. Women's movements and radical gender challenges have been obliterated, suppressed, vanished —without trace.

Queer is a politics of demand. But all too often that demand ends with the group who makes that demand. Where else can we begin but with our own agendas? I believe, passionately, that the old Jewish saying is right: 'If I am not for myself, who will be for me? And even if I think of myself, what am I? And if not now, when?'[19] No one else will fight for us, unless we fight for ourselves. But I cannot desire my own freedom without desiring the freedom of every 'woman' who is not free. However she defines herself. I want a world in which ANY WOMAN CAN BE A LESBIAN. If we achieve this it will automatically follow that ANYONE CAN BE ANY GENDER. And we are still very far from enjoying a post-liberation honeymoon with the heteropatriarchy. A large purple slogan in my study declares: I'LL BE A POST-FEMINIST IN POST-PATRIARCHY. We're not there yet.

When I first called myself a radical feminist I was—I still am— a privileged, educated, white woman. When we marched, campaigned, argued, took direct action, wrote books, we were not only championing ourselves, although that was our point of departure. Insane as this now sounds, twenty-five years on, we did it in solidarity with all the women of the world. We did it for women who were not like us, women of other races, nations, faiths, women whose difference was often unimaginable, women who would probably not have recognized their commonality with us, women who defined themselves in completely different ways. We could not speak for them, but we were on their side.

JURASSIC FEMINIST: DON'T FORGET US!

10.

ON NARRATIVE STRUCTURES IN CONTEMPORARY FICTION

J. M. COETZEE *DISGRACE* AND PAULINE MELVILLE *THE VENTRILOQUIST'S TALE*

I want to begin with the reader. A piece of writing, whether it be a letter, a work of prose fiction, a song, a ballad, a lyric or an epic poem always constructs an audience, in other words, readers. Some writers like to remind readers of their role as listener or confidante: 'Reader, I married him.' (*Jane Eyre*, 1847). Other writers create a narrator who will explain the narrative pact and do a fair bit of showing off, as does Chico, Pauline Melville's ravishing, vanishing narrator of *The Ventriloquist's Tale* (1997). This is how he begins: 'You can call me Chico. It's my brother's name but so what. Where I come from it's not done to give your real name too easily.' Here the intimacy of the relationship with the reader is paramount. If you want to tell the reader an appalling tale inhabited by monstrous characters, then the closer you are to them the better. Establish an intimate, narrative voice and the reader will trust you, travel with you. It is all a question of confidence. Other writers like to woo, persuade and cajole their reader from a safe distance. Some writers only talk to their readers through a series of masks. Some prefer to remain almost invisible, undercover, hiding behind a carefully established point of view. 'For a man of his age, fifty-two, divorced, he has, to his mind, solved the problem of sex rather well.' This is the first sentence of Coetzee's *Disgrace* (1999), which establishes the narrator's relationship with the central character and the narrator's relationship with the reader. Solved the problem of sex, has he? That's what he thinks. We, the readers, and I the narrator, behind whom the writer hides, know that he hasn't solved the problem of sex at all. And that he's in for trouble.

Here is the simplest possible version of the narrative chain, indicating the uneasy, unstable link between author and reader. Notice that the person who is furthermost from the writer is the reader.

AUTHOR—implied author—narrator/speaker
—characters/ event—implied reader—READER

The implied author, sometimes referred to as the textual author, is a piece of virtual reality constructed in the text. The implied author and, of course, the narrator may have a quite different age, gender and even different attitudes from those of the author outside the text. Think of Chico in Melville's *The Ventriloquist's Tale*. I used an unnamed male student, less than half my age, and certainly a good deal more romantic, as the narrator in my first novel, *Hallucinating Foucault*. The same instability characterizes the implied reader. There may also be a textual reader who is simply a rhetorical strategy and has nothing to do with the implied reader. For example, Walton's sister who is the reader of Walton's letters in Mary Shelley's *Frankenstein* (1818) and the first textual reader of the horror in the tale. Sometimes the narrative chain is a very fluid mass of shifting genders. This is what happens when Marian Evans Lewes, otherwise known as 'George Eliot', takes up the pen.

AUTHOR (Marian Evans)—pseudonymous identity (George Eliot)————narrator (often assumed to be George Eliot, but who operates like a character in the novels)————Implied reader (sometimes a man sometimes a woman often addressed in the plural: the famous 'we' of Eliot's texts)—READER

So the identity of the author may be exceedingly ambiguous. But so is that of the reader. Readers are subtle, difficult people. They have two identities: their living selves, the one that goes shopping, has sex and dies—and their reading selves. Their reading self is the extraordinary, shape-shifting, gender-bending self. The reading self is infinite, multiple and immortal. This is the implied reader. This multiple identity is the one you, as the writer, offer to the reader for her or him to inhabit. Some writers/authors have an ideal reader in mind when they write, some write purely to please themselves.

But for whoever you write, even if it is for yourself, it is for yourself as a reader. You forget your reader at your peril. My first advice to young writers is very simple, very straightforward and absolutely crucial: imagine your reader. Remember where you have positioned your reader in relation to your narrative. Be courteous. Give her a gender, a sex, an identity and something to do. Don't abandon her. Don't forget to address her. Tell her your story.

What is a narrative? The definition that is usually given in narratological theory is 'the representation of a series of events'. But I'd like to look more closely at the classic statement made by Aristotle in the *Poetics*. He's talking about dramatic tragedy, but we can still learn much that is relevant to the construction of prose fiction. He lists the elements of a dramatic piece that are important, things like spectacle and song, but comes back to the narrative, here translated as 'plot', or as he puts it 'the ordered arrangement of the incidents', as being the most crucial element.

> The most important of these is the plot, the ordering of the incidents; for tragedy is a representation, not of men, but of action and life, of happiness and unhappiness—and happiness and unhappiness are bound up with action...Tragedies are not performed, therefore, in order to represent character, although character is involved for the sake of the action. Thus the incidents and the plot are the end aimed at in tragedy, and as always the end is everything... Another point to note is that the two most important means by which tragedy plays on our feelings, that is, 'reversals' and 'recognitions', are both constituents of the plot (mythos)...
>
> The plot, then, is the first essential of tragedy, its life-blood, so to speak, and character takes second place.[1]

As a writer, and indeed as a reader, that is, another creator of meanings, I am very intrigued by this definition of narrative: 'the ordering of the incidents...a representation not of men, but of action and life'—and his insistence on the primacy of plot over character. There are some kinds of narrative, that we are used to reading for the plot, fairy tales for instance, and most children's books. In those texts identity is subordinated to role. Who you are is what you do.

You are either the miller's son, the princess, the ogre or the witch, and you act accordingly.

I think Aristotle is right. The narrative structure of a piece of writing is the spine upon which the entire body of the work depends. It is the central nervous system, nourishing the intelligence of the writing. It upholds the bones of character, the muscles of the descriptive passages, it supports the heart and the circulation of the blood that is the emotion and tension in the text. A narrative must have tension and emotion if it is to survive the test of being read and re-read.

Must we always have a plot? Here is Peter Brooks on plot: 'Plot is the principle of interconnectedness and intention, which we cannot do without in moving through the discrete elements—incidents, episodes, actions—of a narrative...Plot is thus the dynamic shaping force of the narrative discourse.'[2] Peter Brooks appears to believe that plot, is an essential element in prose fiction. But I am working with a slightly tighter definition of plot and I think that we do not always need a plot. No, not always. And how do plots differ from narratives? Plot is causal. It is the rational intelligence ordering the narrative and answering our petulant demands for reasons why. Narrative is the arrangement of the incidents. Plot implies intention and motive. You do not always need a plot. But you must have a narrative. Even the smallest, briefest, most delicate lyric poem has a narrative. The narrative is what happens.

Virginia Woolf famously commented. 'And as usual, I am bored by narrative' (A Writer's Diary, Thursday 28 March 1929). Well, how would you summarise the events of To the Lighthouse? Here is a large family and assorted guests on holiday, supposedly on the Isle of Skye. They decide to go to the lighthouse, but put off the expedition. One of them starts a picture. They eat dinner. Time passes, many die. Those that are left return to the house. They go to the lighthouse. The picture is finished. That's what happens. Apparently very little. So clearly the interest, tension and emotion, even the action of the narrative, lies elsewhere. To the Lighthouse is a narrative driven by desire, but not strictly by a plot. That is part of Woolf's theme. There is no plot. The motiveless malignity, that controls our lives, is terrifyingly random. There is no God, and therefore no plot, and no providence. And in the face of that void we make art.

Plot, and J. M. Coetzee's *Disgrace* has a tightly structured, carefully patterned plot, is a very interestingly charged word in English. To plot is to chart a course, to plan something with intent, to conspire and to be part of a conspiracy. Common to all these meanings is the idea of boundaries, demarcation, the drawing of lines to mark off and order. There is also an interesting whiff of threat. If someone is the victim of a plot, or involved in a plot, they are either done for or intending to do for someone else. There are literal plots in both Melville's and Coetzee's fictions. There are rapes and murders.

If someone is raped or murdered in your tale then your reader will want to know who did it and why. You may have good reasons—and Coetzee does have good reasons—both artistic and political, not to tell your readers what happened or for obfuscating the entire issue. But it would be unwise to forget that your reader will want to know the answers to these questions. You must address her desire, even if you wish to puzzle her. Yet a reader who is baffled and puzzled is not necessarily a reader who is bored. They can be curious and excited. It is not a crime to baffle your reader. But it is a crime to bore her.

An American writer once commented to me: 'There are only two kinds of narrative, either the heroine leaves home, or a stranger comes to town.' I brooded on this distinction and on the master-narratives of our culture and came to the following conclusions.

The paradigmatic narratives that stand at the source of our western traditions of writing are the Bible and the Homeric epics. These are our master-narratives, our master texts. The Bible is the ultimate Book. It contains all things: lyric, epic, myth, history, law, song, war stories, love stories, biography, epigrams, parables, elegies, prophecies, apocalypse. It is a sacred text. And therefore better read than pillaged.[3] Although there has been extensive activity by raiding parties down the centuries. Homer's epic narrative poems are secular texts. *The Iliad* and *The Odyssey* give us the two giant patterns on which to base our own tales: Siege Narratives or Quest Narratives. *The Iliad* is a war story and, quite literally, a siege narrative. The siege of Troy has lasted ten years. Stalemate. Heroic and treacherous deeds form the basis of the narratives. Mortals are at the mercy of the cunning of the Gods. The ruse of the Trojan

Horse leads to the sack of Troy. And the bloodbath leads to other narratives. *The Odyssey* is a quest narrative, which tells of a search for home. Odysseus becomes the wanderer, a voyager searching, moving from land to land. What awaits his return to Ithaca? Both the journey and the arrival matter.

Here are some of the key characteristics of these types two types of narrative. And some of the traps they set for unwary writers.

SIEGE NARRATIVES

This kind of narrative can be thrillingly claustrophobic, and if it is well constructed will give you tension and intensity. Siege narratives in prose fiction work best with a limited cast and not too many sub-plots. Many war stories are siege narratives. All submarine dramas are. Family sagas are nearly always siege narratives. So are love stories, marriage and divorce narratives. Siege narratives can turn into escape narratives. Make sure that the sources of danger, pressure, tension are believable. Even if it is quite fantastic it must be convincing. Life and death matters must be plausible if they are to be harrowing. A siege narrative can intensify your sense of place. Your description or detail can become terrifying, uncanny. Beware of bathos. The most common problem with a siege narrative is that the writing goes flat, the tension goes out of the narrative, and the reader is bored. If you are anxious about losing the tension then put a clock on your narrative.

> Great Siege Narratives
> *High Noon*
> *Twelve Angry Men*
> *Camus' La Peste*
> *Hamlet*

QUEST NARRATIVES

Quest narratives are usually driven by desire. The most powerful of these is the desire to go home. Everyone longs to go home. Very few people have homes to which they can return—your endings can therefore be either joyous or horrific. Quest narratives can be lost and found narratives. You can extend your cast of characters. It is easier to introduce new characters. It is easy to lose them. You need a strong central character to hold the quest or the multiplying narratives together. Your narrative can travel. You can introduce many changes of place, many startling adventures. Coincidences are easier to fabricate. Beware of writing that is rambling or diffuse. The danger is reader confusion. If your quest narrative contains too many characters, too many events you may lose the focus and the tension. Beware of open endings with a quest narrative. Readers who love quests also love closure. Please them.

Great Quest Narratives
Gawain and the Green Knight
A. S. Byatt's *Possession*
Jane Eyre
Star Trek Voyager

But, of course, as a writer you cannot simply choose what kind of narrative you wish to make. The material, the raw matter of your narrative, often dictates its shape. *Disgrace* is a siege narrative. J. M. Coetzee's historical-subject position as a white Afrikaaner in South Africa is that of a man in a classic siege situation. The white Afrikaaners in South Africa have no other country. They are now an African tribe, like any other. Yet they created a siege situation that left them isolated and threatened. They built their walls themselves. Now the walls are down, and Coetzee's *Disgrace* describes his nihilistic vision of the New South Africa, which is about what happens when the enemy is not only within the gates but also owns them, controls them. And not just the gates, but the walls and the land around. White law and white justice no longer have any meaning. The Beast's hour has come round at last. Coetzee's most recent novel clearly relates his moment in history. He chooses a very traditional narrative structure to tell that history. Why? I'll return to that question.

Pauline Melville's first novel, *The Ventriloquist's Tale*, bears the ghost of a quest narrative, but does not fulfil the accepted criteria for a first novel. Let me explain. Publishers want simple explanations of origins. They like to know where a novel comes from.

They like a first novel to be autobiographical, written in first-person narrative, to have a strong link with the author's own background, to contain powerful descriptions of childhood, and to be filled with easily recognizable and universally shared agonies and vicissitudes. Publishers want lots of emotion and a strong sense of place. The key words here are Fresh, Original, Authentic. The book is then God's Gift to the Marketing Department.

The publicity and marketing departments find it easy to sell the book as a convincing representation of the author's experience. Names can be changed to protect the guilty, but, on the whole, the link between representation and reality must appear to be unproblematic. Language should seem to be a transparent material, which renders the author's experience in immediate, fresh and delightful ways. If the material is shocking: starvation perhaps, wife-battery or child abuse, then the marketing key-words are Searing, Outspoken, Courageous. But in either case, selling it to the journalists is plain sailing. The 'Author in the News Features' on the writer's home, family, native landscape, experience of racism, sexuality and drug habit then simply write themselves for the broadsheets. The book sells well, and everyone is delighted.

Publishers do not like first novels to be playful, self-reflexive, parodic or written from a gendered, ethnic or sexual point of view that is absolutely different from that of the author. If you do this you are not writing a first novel. And you are creating problems for yourself. The publishers are not simply ignorant and philistine. A first novel has to establish a name, a name previously unknown to the public. Therefore that name must be given a face and a context, not a mass of confusing, postmodern, disruptive narrative cleverness. My point here is that the market demands something quite specific from a first novel: a particular kind of narrator—usually older and wiser, experience looking back on naïve innocence—and a certain kind of narrative, linear, open-ended; a *Bildungsroman* that is structured like a quest.

The Ventriloquist's Tale does not conform to any of these ideologies. This is what happened when I read the novel for the first time. The book opens with an utterly charming, engaging, provocative narrator, the fascinating Chico. He has a witty, indomitable grandmother. But, having pointed out that what the market wants is realism, he vanishes. I was bitterly disappointed, but read on, convinced that he would return. He cannot, I decided, go to such trouble to beguile and seduce the reader, then abandon us. He must, he will, come back. But in fact he doesn't, except to speak the Epilogue and usher us out of the book. The novel then shifts to Chofy McKinnon and the survival struggle of his people. Chofy sets out on a journey to see his Auntie Wifreda. Ah, here beginneth the quest. Not a bit of it. As soon as we get settled in Georgetown he meets Rosa, the Eng. Lit researcher on the trail of Evelyn Waugh. Shift to Rosa's point of view. Shifting the narrative viewpoint, while not interrupting the tale, thus breaking the illusion of the story, is a very risky business. The reader can become disoriented, confused and alienated. Worst of all she may put the book down. And read something else. You will notice that Coetzee, the old hand at the novel-writing game, never does this. We stick with the same narrative voice, embittered, ironic, detached, and the same narrative point of view, the same trajectory, the limited learning curve of David Lurie. Luckily for me, on my first reading of Melville's novel, it was at this stage that I decided to listen to Arthur Singh, who pointed out: 'You are at the mercy of the random. Don't look for a pattern and don't try to impose one. Wait until something happens and then go with it' (Melville, p.44). Chofy and Rosa have sex in a quite delightful way as if they had been reading Gertrude Stein. I am enjoying an inter-racial love story. Then I am given an essay on structuralist anthropology that 'represents brother-and-sister incest in the form of a copulating sun and moon' (Melville, p.82). Auntie Wifreda begins to remember, and the novel finally gets underway on page 91. We are back in Waronawa with Danny and Beatrice, the incestuous couple of the main narrative, in 1905, all set for tales of the incestuous passion and the mysterious eclipse. But we are nearly *100 pages* into the book. That is a long time to keep a reader waiting for her tale.

The motif of the gendered, incestuous eclipse is not as unfamiliar and exotic as it at first appears. Passion between siblings is a familiar theme in the Great Tradition of English Literature. The two most compelling versions of the myth are Emily Brontë's *Wuthering Heights* (1848) and George Eliot's *The Mill on the Floss* (1859). The siblings always stand for the two severed, lost halves of the

human soul, as a metaphor for our incompleteness and our longing for union, which is often denied by our daylight consciousness.
We are not entirely natural beings. Stories about siblings always side
with the brother-sister passion. This love is often presented as egalitarian, mutual and an irresistible force. It will be associated with
some kind of natural power. Melville uses the eclipse, Brontë uses
the Yorkshire Moors, George Eliot uses the river in flood. But the
lovers never survive. Even when the myths are sympathetic to them,
society is not. The incestuous couple is disruptive, uneasy, frightening.

Melville's novel presents a conflict between two cultures, two religions, two ways of interpreting the world: one that is explained and
endorsed by the natural world around the Wapisiana people, the
other is the alien, imperial religion of Christianity, whose impera-
tives and taboos are hostile to the peoples the Jesuits invade to
convert. The battle is fought out over the bodies of Danny and
Beatrice.

Father Napier as the meddling priest seems to me to be an easy
moral target. Most of Melville's modern readers will be as out of
sympathy with his views as they will be with the global capitalist
ambitions of Hawk Oil, the modern imperial villains. Of more
interest is the way in which Beatrice is constructed not as a victim,
but as an avenger. She doesn't see Danny's new bride as the enemy.
She targets the priest. His poisoning is presented as a form of
natural justice. Koko Lupi hands out the fatal beans (Melville,
p.240):

> They work over a long, long time. I don't like him either. He
> tries to strike the sun out of the sky. Him with his dead god
> on a stick. He thinks he can stand between the sun and moon.
> Give him this and leave the rest to the sun. The sun will finish
> him off.

The patterning of the plot justifies Beatrice and grants her a Phyrric
victory. Her threat against Wifreda comes true. The priest goes
mad. He undoes his own work, horribly, over page after page. The
people turn against him. The moral is clear. Don't meddle with the
sun.

The meanings conveyed by Melville's narrative are essentially conservative. The society of the Amerindians is complete in itself, self-regulating. Outsiders are always intruders, bringing disruption, destruction, certain death. Outsiders can neither understand this society nor live in peaceful harmony with its values. As a narrative *The Ventriloquist's Tale* is rich, exotic, overflowing. The quality of the writing offers many pleasures. But it is an imperfect whole. There is too much jumble, too many minor characters, too many threads. Too much is *named*. This is a fiction filled with things and the names of things. The eco-politics of the narrative, which defend the culture she describes, are remorselessly, unfailingly shaped by post-colonial political correctness, and as such are predictable, simplistic and tiresome. The triumph of the book is Beatrice, a woman who is wronged, but never shamed, a vengeful woman who correctly identifies the main enemy and strikes.

However, for political ambiguity of the most disturbing kind let's turn to J. M. Coetzee's *Disgrace* (1999). This is a short book, just over 200 pages. It could be read in one sitting and that is how I first read it. This book needs to be short, like a parable. Because if it were any longer the silences and absences that haunt the text would begin to scream at the reader, who would, in turn, begin to ask awkward questions. Coetzee's brevity is part of his master-strategy to control his meanings.

The institution of English Literature, which, in Melville's novel, has a walk-on part in Rosa's research on Evelyn Waugh, here becomes central. *Disgrace* begins as a campus novel. All the standard tropes are there. The faded lecher who stars in the novel is disillusioned with his ignorant 'Post-Christian, posthistorical, postliterate' (Coetzee, p.32) students. He takes comfort in Wordsworth and plans an opera on the last days of Byron, another faded lecher whose sexual operations were on a somewhat larger scale. Lurie abuses his position and seduces one of his students, Melanie. The Body. She is dull, mediocre, clearly none too bright, but has a quite wonderful young body. Her body, breasts and buttocks are all that David Lurie really notices. But all through Coetzee's narrative women are only ever noticed as bodies. Lovely young ones like Melanie, or the fat, unattractive, hideous, smelly and disgusting bodies of women who have the misfortune to be over twenty-one.

Here are some examples:

> * Helen, too awful even to enter the text: 'Helen is a large, sad-looking woman with a deep voice and a bad skin, older than Lucy.' (Coetzee, p.60)
> * Lucy herself: 'Ample is a kind word for Lucy. Soon she will be positively heavy, letting herself go' (Coetzee, p.65). Lesbianism is an 'excuse for putting on weight...he does not like to think of his daughter in the throes of passion with another woman, and a plain one at that' (Coetzee, p.86). Presumably it would be more erotic, and pleasant to think about if Helen were better looking.
> * Bev Shaw: 'The veins on her ears are visible as a filigree of red and purple. The veins of her nose too. And then a chin that comes straight out of her chest, like a pouter pigeon's. As an ensemble, remarkably unattractive.' (Coetzee, pp.81–2)
> * Even Petrus' wife gets the lookover: 'She is young-younger than Lucy—pleasant-faced rather than pretty, shy, clearly pregnant.' (Coetzee, p.129)

The studied disgust with which every living thing is described in this fiction leaves the reader with the sensation of having been physically assaulted. Even the animals, that crawl through Bev Shaw's surgery are, by and large, disgusting.

The carefully controlled narrative viewpoint, that of David Lurie, never varies. This perspective is held in an ironic frame, that of the masked narrator. But Lurie's viewpoint is rarely challenged and never displaced. Coetzee's novel is a political parable and susceptible to a Marxist class analysis. Lurie and his daughter represent the bankrupt bourgeoisie, a faded, effete and exhausted class. They stand for the white civilization, that once profited from apartheid and is now overtaken by history. Petrus and his people are the Rising Blacks, the rising class. They are evil, sinister in their rational normality. Petrus, we are led to believe, wants only the land and will use any means to get it. The plot, and here I mean 'the controlled arrangement of the incidents', ensures that we judge Petrus to be the master of the plot. Why was he absent from the farm when the rape and the attack took place? How did the blacks who came know that they would not simply be shot? Why are they all relatives of Petrus?

And here I come to the text's silences. Silence does not necessarily mean absence; silence is not necessarily consent. A text shudders in its silences. These are sometimes the faultlines in the text, the key to its meanings. The text speaks loudest where it says nothing. The most appalling silence is that of Lucy, who considers her rape to be a private matter, a settling of historical scores. But neither David Lurie nor the reader was there. We neither see nor hear from Lucy what happened. This rape, like the incident in the caves in *A Passage to India*, remains unrepresented, silent. But it is not uninterpreted. For Lucy, this is the necessary unravelling of apartheid and of the nation's bloody history. She accepts her fate, which is to live with nothing: 'No cards, no weapons, no property, no rights, no dignity' (Coetzee, p.205). The other silence is that of the blacks. They never explain. They never speak. They act. Petrus admits nothing.

In 1985 I invited one of my friends to the opera. Her name is Wanjiru Ciira. She is a blackwoman journalist from Nairobi. She had never seen an opera. I took her to Mozart's *Die Zauberflöte*. It was an excellent performance. In the interval Wanjiru took me aside and asked, 'Patricia, why is the Black man a rapist?' She had a mocking glint in her eye. It was a rhetorical question. She knew why. I was speechless then. But I'm going to answer her now. Because, Wanjiru, in white racist ideology the black man is always a rapist, voiceless, sinister, one dimensional, grasping, ruthless. He has no complex inner subjectivity. His identity is determined by his role, and his role is that of the rapist. This is how it works in J. M. Coetzee's *Disgrace*. A white man is a seducer, and he is brought to book, disgraced. He pays for his peccadillo. Belittling a white student, seducing her and undermining her confidence is not that important. The punishment is excessive. The university tribunal is a mad forum for the politically correct. But as for the blacks, Lucy's judgement is never challenged: 'I think they are rapists first and foremost. Stealing things is just incidental. A side-line. I think they do rape' (Coetzee, p.158).

Go back to my very first points. Let me begin with the reader. To whom is this novel addressed? Who has Coetzee constructed through the text as his readers? Clearly, his audience in South Africa will read the novel very differently from his audience abroad. But how do we read this novel if we are women? How do we read this novel if we are black? I am quite certain that Coetzee is not address-ing me, as a white woman, or indeed as a woman of any colour. And I would expect that poor blacks, especially illiterate jackal boys, aren't part of his ideal audience either.

And yet, ironically, I think that Coetzee has written a perfect text. Everything is subordinated to the main design. He is describing a society that is breaking down, that is in the last stages before chaos. He predicts a future of waste, loss and death when these people who Petrus describes as 'my family, my people' (Coetzee, p.201) hold sway and eventually inherit the earth. He has written a para-ble that hides behind the authority of realist narrative. Yet if you read carefully and peer into the silences, absences, you will see that it is not a realist text. That is an illusion. The point of view is too partial; there is almost no descriptive writing. The novel is domi-nated by dialogue. It is in fact a novel of debate, where the voices take up positions and argue their case. And here is another absence that haunts the text because the descriptive writing is minimal, the element that is missing from the book: the land. The prize is the farm, the earth of Africa, the land itself. And yet that land is barely present in the text. It is not the looming presence that it is in Olive Shreiner's *The Story of an African Farm* (1883) or Nadine Gordimer's *The Conservationist* (1974). Coetzee's decision to render the land invisible is in keeping with his design. We must not value the prize too highly, as that would unbalance the novel. We would be forced to take sides, to choose between Petrus and Lucy. The land of Africa is emotional territory. Why? Because the ownership and possession of that land and all its wealth is the original point of the imperial enterprise, the scramble for Africa. Love for that land is a dangerous thing. If the reader were to see Lucy and David Lurie as the unambiguous descendants of the white murderers who marched north from the Cape we might think that they deserve everything they get. And more.

And so all the loose ends are tied up. For his conclusion Coetzee uses a classic trope: the return to earlier places. Lurie goes back to find Melanie's family, back to his office at the university, back to the theatre where Melanie is still performing in the appalling trivial play, back to his former house in Cape Town. This too has been attacked and ransacked by 'a raiding party...another incident in the great campaign of redistribution' (Coetzee, p.176). Now Lurie too accepts his fate. His time as the legitimate white master in this world is over.

Let me sum up. These two fictions are post-colonial texts. They are set in dark times, at the end of empires, at the moment where one power cedes to another. In Melville's novel it is the moment when the British have relaxed their grip and the Americans are poised to take over. Pauline Melville has written a brilliant, vivid, broken-backed novel whose narrative uncertainties undermine the strength of her work. Her extraordinary vision of a society in evolution, out of step with their century, but not with themselves, is clouded by the muddle of her fictional structure. Yet rarely have I read a contemporary character with such power and sexual certainty as Beatrice McKinnon. She is not like other textual women. She ends in exile, but she is neither beaten nor defeated.

J. M. Coetzee has written an implacable fable for a doomed society where the new grasping black patriarchs are the most monstrous of all, sinister and intent, defending their mentally deficient jackal boys, inexorably demanding blood for blood.[4] The blacks have no voice. The writer denies them a voice. In the face of Lurie's insults and abuse Petrus remains silent, or simply repeats his demands. Yet these silences are managed, controlled by the author. The structure of this narrative is not neutral in its meanings. The meanings of that black silence are clear: the blacks are fuelled by nothing but a primitive hatred and the longing for revenge. It is a perverse reading, like my own, which sees the patterns in the silences, resents the calculated assault upon her emotions and becomes enraged by the deliberate silencing of two groups that are already denied justice in the world: black people and all raped women, whatever colour they are. Yet the perfect construction of *Disgrace*, its economy and lucidity, makes Coetzee's own monstrous ideologies, his misogyny and his calculating racism, all the more plausible.

11.
ON THE IMPOSSIBILITY OF MAKING WRITING

MRS ARBUTHNOT, MRS LEWES AND MRS WOOLF

Stevie Smith
Mrs Arbuthnot

Mrs Arbuthnot was a poet
A poet of high degree,
But her talent left her;
Now she lives at home by the sea.

In the morning she washes up,
In the afternoon she sleeps
Only in the evening sometimes
For her lost talent she weeps,

Crying: I should write a poem,
Can I look a wave in the face
If I did not write a poem about a sea-wave,
Putting the words in place.

Mrs Arbuthnot has died,
She has gone to heaven,
She is one with the heavenly combers now
And need not write about them.

Cry: She is a heavenly comber
She runs with a comb of fire,
Nobody writes or wishes to
Who is one with their desire.[1]

I want to speak about difficulty and the process of making writing. Mrs Arbuthnot encountered the most crippling difficulty that can ever beset a writer: the inability to write at all. Writer's block descends like a black curtain, however, upon different writers for different reasons. Mrs Arbuthnot was simply abandoned by her capricious and uncivil talent. It is something outside herself, beyond her control, free to stay and free to leave. Stevie Smith does use explicit Christian metaphors in her work, so that the word 'talent' is likely to have a Biblical echo. As the parable makes clear, we are morally required to use our 'talents'. We cannot simply report them as 'lost'. Please note that it is not 'inspiration' that is lacking, nor a subject, the eternally recurring waves are ever present. It is the actual ability to write. Yet Mrs Arbuthnot only mourns in the evenings. Housework and dozing take up the time in which she used to write. God knows what happened to Mr Arbuthnot. In any case, he is not, and clearly never has been, part of her writing life. Yet she is left with the nightmare obligation to use and develop her missing gift. She comes, empty handed, to face the eternal waves. It is not enough to enjoy the waves. She must write about them. Mrs Arbuthnot cannot rejoice in a reality that is not written. Thus, her identity as a writer, as a poet of high degree, becomes a torture to her. Her unhappiness at this separation from her talent could only be resolved by her death and subsequent apotheosis as a 'heavenly comber'. The only escape from the need to write is for the writer and her subject to become one.

> Cry: She is a heavenly comber,
> She runs with a comb of fire,
> Nobody writes or wishes to
> Who is one with their desire.

And here, in this ironic resolution, lies the secret difficulty of Mrs Arbuthnot's original wretchedness. The writing, that presents itself as difficult, or impossible to write is the writing that takes place in the space beween desire and its attainment. This is the writing, that occupies the gulf between the writer and the obscure object of her desire. Thus writing is a substitute for grief, absence, loss, longing. Writing becomes a kind of mourning, a coming to terms with bereavement. The moment of reunion, between the writer and the object of her desire, marks the end of writing.

What is peculiarly delightful about Stevie Smith's poet, whom she draws wearing a jaunty feathered cap and a string of pearls, is the tension between her ordinariness and banality and her extra-ordinary fate. The author and her perpetual dilemma are reinstated, with sinister simplicity. Mrs Arbuthnot never gives us a reason for her need to describe the waves; it is simply her destiny to do so.

I notice that we generally speak about writer's block, rarely, if at all about author's block. You can go on being an author, even if you do not write at all. Authorship is an identity. Writing is an activity. Mrs Arbuthnot was an author who had writer's block. But we should understand writer's block not simply as a blank wall upon which, for mysterious inner reasons, the writer is unable to scrawl their habitual graffiti through lack of inspiration, whatever we may think that is; we should also consider writer's block as the refusal to write, when writing involves the breaking of a taboo. Charlotte Brontë tried hard to stop herself writing because Southey told her not to. George Eliot, the self-styled Mrs Lewes, had to be protected from bad reviews in case she became discouraged in mid-novel. Her publisher wrote remorselessly encouraging letters. The danger was that she might stop writing. Elizabeth Barrett Browning worried that she was more famous than her husband. This anxiety affected her ability to write. Virginia Woolf suffered from overheated brains and often had to ration herself to one or two pages a day. She craved praise, yet suffered terribly waiting for each response to her writing. She noted that George Eliot had had the same problem. 'George Eliot would never read reviews, since talk of her books hampered her writing.' (Friday, 5 December 1919, Woolf 1972, p.21) There are many more circumstances than lack of inspiration, that prevent us from writing.

But the need to write is so consuming that many writers nurture several streams of writing in their lives. These private texts, diaries, journals, letters, from which writers' lives are made, are always of interest to us, not because writer's lives are generally action-packed—Mrs Arbuthnot appears to have lived very quietly—but because they are intimately related to other written texts. Writers' biographies and autobiographies, which are created out of these private texts, and their relation to the public texts, reflect the concerns not only of the writer, but also of the society that consumes both the life as text and the public, published work. Both are open to continual rewriting and reinterpretation.

Virginia Woolf's *A Writer's Diary*, both in Leonard Woolf's edited version and in the massive complete edifice, has assumed an iconic status as a monument to the writing process. It records the daily difficulty of writing, and of clearing space to write, but it also records the ways in which, for her, writing was a process of losing and re-gaining control over her own mind. She closed her *Diary* for 1897 on New Year's Day 1898, with the words: 'Here is a volume of fairly acute life (the first really *lived* year of my life) ended locked & put away.' (VW's emphasis, Woolf, 1992, p.134.) Here the young Mrs Woolf has something in common with Mrs Arbuthnot; the first really lived year of her life is the first written year. Writing became a method of possessing her world and protecting herself against loss. She could own her life, if it was written down. Woolf was writing, quite self-consciously, against the usual antagonists, Time and Death. This is not an uncommon gesture. Like prisoners in our cells, we all make marks upon the walls to record our presence and our passing. What was unusual about Woolf was that this was the central theme both in her *Diary* and in her major novels. When she had finished *To the Lighthouse*, she wrote, 'My brain is ferociously active. I want to have at my books as if I were conscious of the lapse of time; age and death' (Monday, 21 March 1927, Woolf, 1972, p.106). The *Diary* was her backbone, the central spine of her writing life. The writing was *in fact* continuous, what changed was the form, register, voice, as she made the transition from private argument to public statement. She remarked the pain of transition. 'How queer the change is from private writing to public writing. And how exhausting' (Friday, 26 January 1940, Woolf, 1972, p.324). But she kept it up.

The speed with which she could fling down her words in the *Diary* was crucial. She saw diary writing as a runaway carriage 'jerking almost intolerably over the cobbles', but she also took comfort from the fact that 'this diary writing does not count as writing', because,

if I stopped and took thought, it would never be written at

all; and the advantage of the method is that it sweeps up accidentally several stray matters which I should exclude if I
hesitated, but which are the diamonds of the dustheap.
(Monday, 20 January 1919, Woolf, 1972, p.24)

For Woolf the *Diary* was never an entirely private space. She always
imagined a reader. But it was an informal space, where she practised writing, tried out her ideas, chewed over the problems of
making writing and reached her decisions. And she knew that there
were diamonds in the dustheap. She frequently speculated about
subsequent publication: 'who's going to read all this scribble? I
think one day I may brew a tiny ingot out of it—in my memoirs'
(Monday, 19 February 1940, Woolf, 1972, p.327). There is no
writing that does not anticipate a reader.

The metaphors or indeed, the verbs, a writer uses to describe the
writing process are always revealing. Woolf sometimes described
her writing in terms of cooking, her idea 'bubbles' (1972, p.26) or
'brews' (1972, p.327), and, significantly, in terms of painting. When
she was retyping *Mrs Dalloway*, she describes the process as 'a good
method I believe, as thus one works with a wet brush over the
whole, and join parts separately composed and gone dry' (Saturday,
December 13th 1924, 1972, p.69). Recording the end of *Orlando*,
she wrote, 'the canvas is covered. There will be three months of
close work needed, imperatively, before it can be printed; for I have
scrambled and splashed and the canvas shows through in a thousand places' (Sunday, 18 March 1928, Woolf, 1972, p.124). Woolf
was at the centre of the modernist art movement in Britain. Her
sister Vanessa Bell was a painter. She was to write the first biography of the art critic, Roger Fry. That she should draw on painting
as a metaphor for her own work was hardly surprising. The
extended metaphor of writing and painting and the figure of the
artist, Lily Bristow in *To the Lighthouse*, are used to articulate a
complex argument concerning femininity and creativity. The significant players in *To the Lighthouse* are Mrs Ramsay and Lily Bristow.
Many writers produce at least one *Künstlerroman*, or somewhere
in their work include the figure of an artist. The significance of this
artist will not be constant, and the relationship this figure has to
the writer herself may well be mediated by other elements in the

composition. But the presence of this artist will always have a sinister and resounding echo, and reveal something important about the
writer's attitude to her art. They may not be performing imper-
sonators of the writer herself, but they are never innocent characters.

George Eliot's Herr Klesmer in *Daniel Deronda* is the only man
who takes art seriously enough to advise Gwendolen Harleth not
to waste her time trying to become an actress. Deronda's mother,
the lost diva, Alcharisi, marches into the book to deliver a torrent
of feminist invective, and then strides out again leaving the reader
and Deronda himself somewhat stunned. In fact, we should beware
of stage performers in Eliot's work. Eliot's publisher, John
Blackwood, and I share a fascinated admiration for what Blackwood
described as 'Lydgate's tremendous French adventure', an isolated
incident in the presentation of Lydgate early on in *Middlemarch*,
which, incidentally, explains his idiocy when it comes to women.
While pursuing his studies in France, he falls in love with a French
actress, Laure. She stabs her husband to death, on stage, in full view
of the entire audience. Her role requires her to do it, but as she
explains, in italics, to an appalled Lydgate, '*I meant to do it.*'

What distinguishes Deronda's mother and Laure from the other
women in their respective novels is their single-minded ruthlessness.
Eliot's performing heroines are never in the centre of her fictional
stage; that place is reserved for women obsessed with moral self-
sacrifice and an unselfish dedication to the good of all
humanity—with a silly, egotistical, supporting actress as her foil.
But they are still heroines: unsexed, exceptional and in every sense
deadlier than the male. I notice them, as one of Eliot's resisting readers, because they are curiously uninterpreted. Eliot always interferes
with the reader's perceptions of her characters. She takes up a great
deal of our time telling us what to think. But she doesn't do this
with the actress or the singer. They explain themselves in direct
speech, talking directly to the reader and to the men ready to adore
them. Eliot, for once, stands back and lets them have their say. Why?
Were they speaking for her? Were they saying the forbidden, selfish, opinionated things that women artists have, at least, to say to
themselves? Woolf's Lily Bristow is an altogether less dangerous
character. She has doubts, hesitations, is discouraged and haunted
by a wall of sexist negativity emanating from Mr Tansley: 'women

can't write, women can't paint.' But even she finishes her painting to her own satisfaction and has the last words in the book: 'Yes...I have had my vision.'

Lily takes decades to finish her picture. In this she was utterly unlike her creator. Woolf's ideal method of composition as a writer was to write at speed. She returns again and again to the metaphor of steeplechasing. Re-reading *The Voyage Out*, her first novel, and looking back at the young Virginia Woolf, she says admiringly, 'How gallantly she takes her fences' (1972, p.24). The horseracing metaphor reappears while she was writing *The Waves*, 'I must canter my wits if I can' (1972, p.156), and as she neared the end of the book she says, 'I have taken my fence' (ibid.). While reading Shakespeare she is left amazed at 'his stretch and speed' (1972, p.157). This passage is worth quoting at length because Woolf explains what she means by 'speed'.

> I felt [his power] utterly outpace and outrace my own, seeming to start equal and then I see him draw ahead and do things I could not in my wildest tumult and utmost press of mind imagine. Even the less well known plays are written at a speed that is quicker than anybody else's quickest; and the words drop so fast one can't pick them up. Look at this. 'Upon a gather'd lily almost wither'd'. (13 Sunday April 1930, 1972, p.157)

We don't actually know how rapidly Shakespeare wrote. Certainly, the extent of his work is enormous for a fairly brief professional career. Woolf is not, however, thinking of actual time, but written time, that is, textual time. This is the effect that Shakespeare has. The reader is confronted with a hurricane of words: condensed, rapid, packed, giant spaces covered with the tension of meanings. Woolf's example, 'Upon a gather'd lily almost wither'd', is in fact a phrase about time and decay, using the past participles of active verbs as adjectives. The action of the verbs—to gather, to wither— is compressed into description. But the action is not lost. It is still there, gnawing at the lily. It may, in fact, take years of actual working time to achieve the condensed speed of this textual time. Woolf herself spent day after day battling to achieve it. Her usual quota of first draft manuscript was just two pages a day. After reading Shakespeare, Woolf has the usual 'why bother?' reaction, that befalls every writer, except for George Bernard Shaw, who reads Shakespeare. She comments: 'Why then should anyone else attempt to write? This is not "writing" at all. Indeed, I could say that Shakespeare surpasses literature altogether, if I knew what I meant' (1972, p.157). Amen, amen.

And so Shakespeare gallops off into the distance, leaving Woolf to search for the rapidity that would give her what she desired most: the effect of a sketch in the finished composition. For her, successful writing was 'very quick and fierce' (1972, p.58), and she aims to 'skate rapidly' (1972, p.68), 'rush at it' (1972, p.89) and marvels when, writing *To the Lighthouse*, she is 'so flown with words and apparently free to do exactly what I like' (ibid.). Writing *The Years*, she says, 'I have never lived in such a race' (1972, p.190). This wonder at the miracle of lightness and speed, when it is achieved continues throughout the life of the *Diary*. She never lost confidence, even when she was writing criticism or journalism, that: 'One day, all of a rush, fiction will burst in' (1972, p.179).

The other artist in Woolf's work, who is given authority and control, is the novelist, Bernard, in *The Waves*. It is Bernard's voice that subsumes all the other voices in the text, who speaks for them. His voice is fairly close to that of the novelist herself. And it is Bernard's summing up which gives rise to Woolf's record in the *Diary* of a classic instance of what is commonly called inspiration. Here is Mrs Woolf, coming to the end of her encounter with her much desired 'comb of fire', the writing of *The Waves*. She has this to say:

Here in the few minutes that remain, I must record, heaven be praised, the end of *The Waves*. I wrote the words O Death fifteen minutes ago, having reeled across the last ten pages with some moments of such intensity and intoxication that I seemed only to stumble after my own voice, or almost after some sort of speaker (as when I was mad) I was almost afraid, remembering the voices that used to fly ahead. Anyhow, it is done; and I have been sitting these fifteen minutes in a state of glory, and calm, and some tears, thinking of Thoby and if I could

write Julian Thoby Stephen 1881–1906 on the first page. I
suppose not. How physical the sense of triumph and relief is!
Whether good or bad it's done; and as I certainly felt at the
end, not merely finished, but rounded off, completed, the
thing stated. (Saturday, 7 February 1931, Woolf, 1972, p.169)

'Inspiration' means to blow on to, or to breathe into something
or someone. In the western tradition we think of inspiration as a
form of possession, intoxication, even madness. Inspiration has
long been the property of genius and women have, on the whole,
been discouraged from claiming to be the latter and are therefore
unlikely to be possessed by the former. Christina Battersby, in her
study *Gender and Genius: Towards a Feminist Aesthetics* (1989),
suggests that the genitals of genius are firmly masculine. Satirical
accounts of inspiration, often written by women, describe the condition as the moment when the subject loses all grip on the rational,
the probable and the sensible, and becomes convinced that he is
possessed of infinite powers. What is especially interesting about
Woolf's record of 'inspiration', and her quite conventional compar-
ison with madness, is that she was in a position to know what she
was talking about. Woolf had no self-indulgent illusions about
madness. She knew what it was like to be mad, to lose control of
yourself, your mind and your life, and to lose all power over your
judgement and decisions. Judgement, that is, selection, is the basis
of all writing. At the end of *The Waves,* Woolf felt that she was no
longer producing the work herself, but that she was (at least) two
people, writing someone else's words: 'I seemed only to stumble after
my own voice, or almost after some sort of speaker (as when I was
mad).' In his study of inspiration and creativity, *The Theory of
Inspiration* (1997), Timothy Clark suggests (p.21) that what we call
inspiration is in fact a form of 'performance'.

> Although written composition is usually solitary, unlike the oral
> poet invoking the muse, it retains even in its privacy a minimal
> quality of ritual...The working-model of composition I propose
> is one of improvised performance, mediated by self-reading.

The writing 'I' is of course a separate, dramatized voice, a quite different entity from the 'I', who negotiates dailiness. What happens in the moment of inspired composition is that the usual balance of power between the two alters and shifts. The writing 'I' is ascendant, dictating the terms, and it is this loss of control that is at once so intoxicating and so disturbing. But the moment of possession, and finally of achievement, of surmounting difficulty and of making writing, also often resembles the record of satisfied, completed passionate physical love, the moment of union with that which you have most desired. It is an oddly genderless experience.

The writing, that presents itself as difficult, or impossible to write, is the writing that takes place in the space between desire and its attainment. This is the writing, which occupies the gulf between the writer and the obscure object of her desire. Inspiration is dramatic enactment of the union a writer achieves with the object of her desire. It is the moment of erotic possession.

The Waves was a lament, an elegy, a song of mourning for her lost brother. Woolf felt that she had 'netted that fin' that had appeared to her in the waste of water, while she was finishing *To the Lighthouse*. What she names as 'that fin' had been the sinister rising impulse for her next book. Now it was before her, possessed, stated. 'How physical the sense of triumph and relief is! Whether good or bad, it's done.' It was done, and done as she had 'meant to do it'.

George Eliot's actress calmly states, '*I meant to do it*'. Virginia Woolf did it. She did it as she meant to do it. But do we still care what a writer meant to do? The author's intentions died out as an area of critical interest some time before the author himself—and, somewhat belatedly, herself—was killed off. But to tell the truth, the author, even when records exist concerning the author in question, has always been regarded as a fleshly inconvenience, and something of an unnecessary diversion. To manifest a prurient interest in the author, in Mrs Arbuthnot, Mrs Lewes and Mrs Woolf, her existence, her intentions, and what she meant to do, is a sure sign of the amateur reader, the textual dilettante. Literary theorists, and even many a writer, have long been of the opinion that the writing is more reliable than its maker. The author should no longer be called upon to explain or justify her work or comment on its making. Whatever she has to say will be unreliable, egotistical, a trickle of excuses or downright lies. The author's life, behaviour, income, opinions, sexuality, even their gender can be discounted as pleasingly irrelevant. Nor, if we follow the logic of this argument through to its inevitable conclusion, can authors be held politically responsible for what they write. The text floats, across time, outside politics, beyond blame. Indeed, even if the author is still left clutching the legal copyright, and demanding hard cash for her work, the text now belongs to the reader.

Once upon a time the writer was the maker and the reader was the recipient of her gift—the text. For the writer, the other player in the game was the reader, the beloved reader, the reader to be entertained, convinced, harangued, cajoled, seduced, adored. And so far as the nether reaches of prose fiction were concerned women were often both the writers and the readers. We were an army of literary lovers, who never met. The relationship was that of the lover and the lady, whatever the sex of the participants, which made the process of making writing and the passion for reading a very queer game indeed. Reading, like writing, is a very intimate, private process. Which often takes place in bed. Suniti Namjoshi dedicated her book, *Building Babel*, to 'The Reader, that sweet Barbarian', and in the last section, 'The Reader's Text', she addresses the reader directly. 'We could rip off our masks. My own name is on the title page. And yours? We could meet, have a conversation, exchange messages. But the point, surely, is to exchange masks, not rip them off' (Namjoshi, 1996, p.182).

All writing is a game of masks and voices. The construction of a subjectivity, whether that of a character or the writing 'I', that is alien or simply quite different to your own is best undertaken as a gesture of sympathy, or identification. You, the writer, must be emotionally committed to the mask. There are good reasons for this. Even monsters must be imagined and portrayed with sympathetic intensity, or at least a good deal of energetic loathing. Otherwise they will not be interesting to read. And the reader's interest should be, always and in every word, the not so obscure object of desire. All writers imagine a reader. There is a reader for every text. Even Virginia Woolf imagined dressing up for the reader of her *Diary*. The writer's primary emotional commitment, no matter how much she loves her characters, must always be to her reader. The reader remains the other to be wooed, seduced, persuaded to turn the page, to stay with you, to read on. It does not matter whose subjectivity you construct or imagine, but how you do it. And there are consequences, damaging consequences, in writing badly, for the writer then, unknowingly, loses control of the text. It can all go horribly wrong.

For the reader's role is no longer as passively erotic or as humble as it sounds. Nor is the gallant courtesy Suniti Namjoshi assumes in her invitation to the reader to engage in the collaborative project of *Building Babel* always returned. 'The Reader's Text' comes at the end of her book. You've heard what I have to say, Namjoshi declares as she offers her book to the reader. Here are the publisher's home-page details on the Web. What have you got to say? Critics and theorists often describe themselves as readers. This kind of reader does not politely wait to be invited to add to the text, but demands the power to reinterpret, repossess, even rewrite the text. Perverse readings are positively acclaimed. A power struggle ensues. Reader and writer are locked in battle not only for the determination of meaning, but for possession of the text itself. The reader overwrites the page with her own meanings. Who cares what the writer meant to do? I only care to read what I want to read. Victory! The writer is vanquished and expelled from the body of the text.

Sometimes all this is very useful. I admit to having done it myself. I, too, have turned many a writer out of her text. Lesbian readers can decode the closet texts, finding homosexual passions in corners of the writing that the heterosexual critic, or even the supposedly heterosexual author, would rather not know about. Writers betray themselves. The writing hand can know things that the writing mind would rather not think. Sometimes the author is so opaque and mythic a presence in literary history, as is Shakespeare for example, that to bother playing games with his intentions and desires looks like highly speculative madness. It does, however, often produce very interesting criticism.[2]

The author's intention is something of a minefield partly because authors are notoriously unreliable, not to say dishonest, about their motives and methods. They seek revenge. They blame other people. They, or their craven publishers, routinely disclaim all resemblance between characters and people in real life, whatever that is. We all love to read books that have resulted in writs. The publicist at my own publishers told me outright that I should feel quite free to invent stories about my life and my writing. She argued that all the world is text, and truth was very overrated, especially if it is not that interesting. In fact, I agree. Neither biography, nor art is made of truth.

> *When my love swears that she is made of truth*
> *I do believe her, tho' I know she lies*

Shakespeare's attitude is a very wise one to take. Believe one thing, know another.

Within feminist writing the author's intention made something of a comeback. And so did the author. When the pen was firmly in the hands of men I was less inclined to champion the author's rights over the text. But when women's writing became a politicized battlefield, I became less certain that eliminating the author was a wise thing to do. Indeed, I had firmly persuaded myself that Anon, that prolific and powerful writer, was certainly a woman. Or perhaps a women's writing collective. Anon was to be the title of Virginia Woolf's last, desired, unwritten text. Besides, the dangers surrounding author-slaughter were self-evident. If the author was immaterial to the text, why not go on reading men's writing? Why not discover marvellous 'feminine' qualities in texts written by anatomically male writers? Thus preserving the genitals of genius. Why make a special case for women? Why publish women at all? So the author came galloping over the hill perched on the white charger of feminism. We had a text to write and an axe to grind. Initially, feminist writers and theorists operated with simplistic notions of authority and truth in their politics of representation. This was fuelled by a lot of healthy indignation. At last, woman would write woman and tell it how it is. But what is it like? Representation: to be presented as something, which you are not, to send a stand-in, a pseudo-presence. This is not a promising set of meanings. Especially to writers dedicated to the truth of experience. I think a writer needs to cultivate the traditional feminine qualities: duplicity and cunning. Feminist authors, myself included, have suffered from a surfeit of honesty.

The author has been sufficiently murdered over the past generation. I now wish to speak about writing and resurrection, the resurrection into language, into the bright light of words. Writing is a craft, with its own traditions, secrets and techniques. It is a mystery in the old sense, a trade that can be learnt, and in the more usual sense of an unfathomable puzzle. I began with Mrs Arbuthnot, abandoned by her disloyal talent and left, fruitlessly, to desire the waves. Desire is multiple and infinite. I have every faith in Mrs Arbuthnot. She should have turned from the vast eternity of the sea, abandoned the waves and learned to desire seaweed, scallops and jellyfish instead. Writers are heroes in the conquest of dailiness, boredom, the ordinary. In her final *Diary* entry before she set off towards the river, Woolf wrote heroically: 'I will go down with my colours flying' (Woolf, 1972, p.365), but she also got to grips with the dinner, by turning food into prose. 'I think it is true that one gains a certain hold on sausage and haddock by writing them down' (ibid.).

The end of each book was a dangerous moment for Woolf, because it reproduced the utter sense of loss and abandonment when a desire is achieved, yet withdrawn. Woolf could not deal with the absolute loss of closure. Mrs Lewes also pointed to this as a problem. She wrote: 'Conclusions are the weak point of most authors, but some of the fault lies in the very nature of a conclusion, which is at best a negation' (Eliot, 1994–5, 1978, vol. 2, p.234). Writing is infinite, continuous. For Woolf some part of the solution in the fight against closure lay in the open-endedness of the diary. Here writing need never end.

Does the author exist? Well, she too is multiple. She has many bodies and many heads. And yet she can be menaced, from without as well as from within. Woolf was finishing her last novel, *Between the Acts*, during the darkest part of the Second World War, when the invasion of Britain appeared to be a matter of weeks. The Woolfs knew that nothing but the concentration camp awaited Leonard, indeed, probably both of them, and had decided to commit suicide in the garage. The decision to die by her own hand had already been taken. But it had not been accepted. Woolf did not want to die. She says so.

What haunted Woolf in the last months, apart from the threat of invasion, was the loss of one of her selves, the writing 'I'. All writing desires the reader. And Woolf could no longer hear the reader's echo. In which case, the writing 'I' could no longer exist. Here is part of her *Diary* entry for Sunday, 9 June 1940.

> I don't want to go to bed at midday: this refers to the garage. What we dread (it's no exaggeration) is the news that the French government have left Paris. A kind of growl behind the cuckoos and t'other birds. A furnace behind the sky. It struck me that one curious feeling is, that the writing 'I' has vanished. No audience. No echo. That's part of one's death. Not altogether serious, for I correct Roger, [her biography of *Roger Fry*] send finally I hope tomorrow: and could finish P.H. [*Pointz Hall*, working title for *Between the Acts*] But it is a fact—this disparition of an echo. (Woolf, 1972, p.336)

Woolf's writing had been well received in her own lifetime. She was, at her death, a major literary figure, a best seller. She had readers, lots of them. Some writers never know that their readers exist, never hear the echo. But Woolf knew what she had lost and could no longer hear. Mrs Arbuthnot also lost her writing 'I', and with that her grip upon the waves. When a writer dies it is not the writing 'I' who is irrevocably lost, but the woman who lays her hands upon haddock and sausage. The writing 'I' vanishes with the reader. As Woolf says, 'That's part of one's death.'

Who calls the writer back to life? Well, I think that we, the readers, have the power to do precisely that. It is the reader, that sweet barbarian, who makes the writing live again. For there is no end to reading. The word is repeatable, eternal, infinite. And so is the reader's desire for the word.

1 2 .
WRITING ON THE WALL

I want to begin with a passage from my first novel, *Hallucinating Foucault*. It's an odd moment, which is never entirely explained in the text. But it does, in fact, illuminate the context within which I write. The reader, who is also the narrator of the tale, arrives at a lunatic asylum in Clermont-Ferrand. He is looking for a novelist, the man about whom he is writing his doctoral thesis: a madman named Paul Michel. He sees the cream walls of the asylum covered in writing. At this point he doesn't realize that the writing is by Paul Michel, but he stops to read the graffiti, the writing on the wall.

Then I saw, above a narrow door, a huge slogan written in giant black letters, curving like an arc over the entrance.
J'AI LEVE MA TETE ET J'AI VU PERSONNE
Beneath the words was a small bronze plaque, which said,
CMP Ste. MARIE
Service Docteur Michel
and beside the plaque stood the door, tight as an arrow slit. Beneath the bronze someone had written a poem on the wall. It was as if every official statement carried its own commentary.

Qui es tu point d'interrogation?
Je me pose souvent des questions
Dans ton habit de gala
Tu ressembles à un magistrat

Tu es le plus heureux des points
Car on te répond toi au moins.

I understood the French, but not the sense, not entirely.[1]

In my early drafts of the novel I didn't translate the French, so that
the text would remain as mysterious to the reader as it had first
been to me. What does it mean to write something that is unintelligible? Or unreadable? What is an unreadable text? Is it a code to
be cracked? Is an unreadable text, a text that conceals its meanings? Or is it a text, that resists the reader? Or is it a text that
chooses its own readers? Is it a text that is waiting, waiting for someone in some future time to decipher its meanings? The writing on
the wall in *Hallucinating Foucault* is about isolation, authority, the
right to ask questions and the longing for a reply. The writing articulates the longing for answers, for meanings. The writing itself
longs for the encounter with interpretation. The question mark
resembles a judge. He has the authority to ask questions. And he
at least can expect to be answered.

I liked the echo that is always there to those of us who have a
biblical education of the original writing on the wall. At Belshazzar's
Feast the hand of God appears upon the wall and writes, MENE,
MENE, TEKEL, UPHARSIN—Daniel the prophet, a literary inter-
preter of invincible authority, gives the meaning. MENE: God hath
numbered thy kingdom and finished it. TEKEL: Thou art weighed
in the balances and art found wanting. PERES: Thy kingdom is
divided and given to the Medes and Persians.[2] For Belshazzar the
writing is a threat, and the interpretation is a judgement. He was
murdered that same night. Interpretation foreshadows execution.
The writing on the wall was a death sentence.

Writing on the wall is not usually signed. It is not easily interpreted. It is not even instantly intelligible. The writing is
interrogatory, challenging, dangerous. You need a prophet to decode
its encrypted meanings.

Contemporary theorists of literature have assumed Daniel's role
as the prophet. But they have also attempted to grip God's hand.
Theory becomes writing rather than interpretation. Theory gener-
ates its own meanings, separate from the text. Or encases the text

in a silk cocoon of writing. I thought this reading Derrida's brilliant essay about, and for, Paul Celan, *Shibboleth*.[3] The essay, first delivered as a lecture in 1984, was dedicated to Celan. This is a subtle shift in critical emphasis. It is a love letter to the writing on the wall, Celan's compressed elliptical texts. Derrida stands before them. And describes them as a sort of non-writing.

> Ungeschriebenes, zu
> Sprache verhärtet
> (The unwritten,
> hardened into language)

Then he begins to write, clutching at each word, sucking its meanings, generating his own. When he published a revised version of this lecture (Paris: Galilée, 1986) Derrida wrote in the Preface, 'Despite certain revisions and some new developments, the plan of exposition, the rhythm, and the tone of the lecture have been preserved as far as possible.'[4] The lecture is described in terms of the poetry it explicates. It too has tone and rhythm.

But this is literary vanity. Derrida is still writing analytical and philosophical commentary, with Celan's gnomic text, 'das Unwiederholbare' (the unrepeatable), at the core. In dedicating his work to Celan, Derrida has taken a crucial step towards the writing edge. The work is personal, a letter to Celan. But *Shibboleth* is not a borderline text; that is, an interpretative, academic text on the edge of writing, the writing on the wall. It is still the prophet's text: exegesis and interpretation. We are not threatened by Derrida, but by Paul Celan.

More productive for me and for my own writing practice have been the hybrid texts by Roland Barthes, above all, the gender-bending love letters to the text, its writers and readers, in *Le Plaisir du texte* (1973). In this text Barthes occupies both crucial roles. He is both the reader and the writer. The text is the meeting point, the conjunction of desire and its satisfaction, the site of pleasure. Here is Barthes speaking as a writer.

> I must seek out this reader (must 'cruise' him) *without knowing* where he is. A site of bliss is then created. It is not the

reader's person that is necessary to me, it is this site; the possibility of a dialectics of desire, of an *unpredictability* of bliss:
the bets are not placed, there can still be a game.[5]

And as a reader, longing for the seduction of the text, he makes his
demand.

The text you write must prove to me *that it desires me*. This
proof exists: it is writing. Writing is: the science of the various blisses of language, its Karma Sutra (this science has but
one treatise; writing itself).[6]

Here is the borderline text. The text that addresses writing and,
beautiful and suggestive as it is, is itself writing.

I have always been an omnivorous reader. As soon as I could read
I began to wolf down books. And I read every kind of text: fiction,
biography, poetry and even military history. I adored spooky religious thrillers with elaborate plots where it was God who had
'dunnit' and there was no body for the detectives to discover. I can
even remember the titles: *The Footprints of Satan* and *We Would
See Jesus*. Writing was always linked to reading. I began writing
and reading at the same time. I wrote in the margins of my books.
I stuck extra pieces of paper between the pages. I was the reader
replying to my writer. It was as if the writer addressed me personally. Not to write back was at the very least bad manners, at worst,
a betrayal.

Hallucinating Foucault is a love story: a love story about a
writer and a reader. I began my work with the central section, set
in the lunatic asylum at Clermont-Ferrand. At first I had no idea
how complicated and strange the plot would be, but I saw two
characters, the mad writer and the reader who had set out to find
him. I wrote: 'The love between a writer and a reader is never celebrated. It cannot be proven to exist.' We seldom meet the writers
who have influenced or delighted us, or even changed our lives.
Yet we often talk about a writer we discovered, loved, read and
re-read with extraordinary intensity. Reading is intimate, silent,
solitary. We are accompanied only by writing and a distant mind,
locked in the text. We know that there is someone else on the

other side of writing. They are sometimes close, terrifyingly present. We listen hard, waiting for the writing to speak. It is an eerie, alien, intimate experience. But if we are readers this intimacy is our ruling passion. This was my central theme.

Reading seems to me to be an experience that is potentially genderless, and one that offers the possibility of sexual fluidity. We can fall in love with writing and the book, irrespective of the writer's sex, or our own. Reading enables us not only to escape our daily world but also to escape who we are. But the English student I had imagined in *Hallucinating Foucault* made the fatal step. He crossed the barrier of the text and set out to find the writer he loved. Now this really is a crazy thing to do. The writer does not exist outside the text. Reading is the act of deciphering the message that comes to you in a bottle. You find it, read it, dream. You can write back. But you can never know the writer. The reader's world is an imagined world. Yet we so want to believe that the reading world is not a dream world, a virtual projection of our own minds, and that our writer exists somewhere, touchable, knowable. The telephone number I gave in the text of *Hallucinating Foucault* for the mental hospital where Paul Michel is locked away is, in fact, a real one. All the locations in the book are real. I learnt that one of my readers, who had read the book in Paris, decided to ring the number. When he discovered that the hospital existed he went there himself to ask for Paul Michel. The puzzled doctor at reception said, 'You're the fifth person who's come looking for him.'

I was very alarmed and amused by this story. But I understood what had happened. Both my hero in the story and the reader in the world had found it impossible to accept that the textual world is the only world we have and that the book is the limit of our connection. The answer is to write a book yourself and to go on reading. There was one passage in *Hallucinating Foucault* that I wrote for all readers, and for the reader in myself:

This is my first and last letter to you. But I will never abandon you. I will go on being your reader. I will go on remembering you. I will go on writing within the original shapes you made for me. You said that the love between a writer and a reader is never celebrated, can never be proven to exist. That's not true. The more intimate relationship we had was the one you constructed when you were writing for me. I followed you, across page after page after page. I wrote back in the margins of your books, on the flyleaf, on the title page. You were never alone, never forgotten, never abandoned. I was here, waiting, reading.[7]

Writers need their readers. The lack of a substantial public audience is never a good thing for a writer. And a writer should be read alongside her contemporaries even, or, perhaps especially when she is a dissenter from every prevailing norm in the writing of her times. I would go so far as to say that a writer needs to read her contemporaries, even if she finds herself reading in a continuous rage. A coterie audience encourages self-indulgent obscurity and a fear of ordinary meanings. A writer who is caught in that trap may well produce the usual Comfort Clichés: I am a difficult writer and I demand more from my readers than other writers. Or more alarming still: my readers have yet to find me. I write for someone in some future time.

This has often been the case for women writers and especially for writers who are lesbian. We are the producers of texts that occupy extremity. Either we are cryptic, encoded, unreadable—Gertrude Stein is an example—or we are all too obvious. Of course this pattern, of the unreadable and the transparent, is evident in writing by men. Celan is an example of the cryptic. Genre fiction directed at a male readership, war stories, or fiction by contemporary popular writers, such as Patrick O'Brien, Thomas Harris and Bernard Cornwell, is not noted for its obscurity, or for its linguistic experimentation. But my point here is that the reasons for this division in women's writing are different. And women's work is read in radically different ways.[8] Let me explain.

The classic women's genre is the prose romance, easily dismissed as trivial, ephemeral, instantly consumed and rapidly obsolete. There are many classic women's texts that refuse to be difficult and insist on an instantly accessible surface. The form will be structured within easy clichés, the language will be undemanding. The text does all the work for the reader. Sometimes these texts vanish rapidly as soon as they have been produced and consumed. But sometimes they hover in an ambiguous critical limbo, categorized as 'women's interest' books, popular fiction, recuperable within the context of cultural studies, but not significant as art. The example that springs to my mind is Daphne du Maurier's novel *Rebecca* (1938). This suggestive, highly charged erotic novel presents no linguistic difficulties at all. It is a thundering good read, a romantic thriller with a strong plot. At the core of the novel's meanings is the absent body of the heroine, *Rebecca*. She still occupies all the interiors of Manderly and the gardens, the sea, the beach. Rebecca is at once invisible and present everywhere. Her nightgown still lies upon the bed, lovingly caressed by Mrs Danvers. The master text, the book behind the book, is of course, *Jane Eyre*. Du Maurier deliberately plays with the echoes but, significantly, chooses the first wife for her heroine, the other woman of the original text.

The lesbian theme in *Rebecca* is barely submerged. Danvers' passion for her mistress is explicit, but what is suggestive is the increasing fascination the narrator feels for her absent rival. She loses interest in the husband, the more she learns about the wife. She cannot take Rebecca's place without becoming her. Rebecca's body remains that obscure object of desire, the thing that is disputed, missing. And the fate of her body, the fact that it is both diseased and murdered, pushes the tale to its climax. The language, genre, events of *Rebecca* are not problematic. What is difficult to decode is the book's real meaning. Is this a lesbian rewriting of *Jane Eyre*?[9]

In some ways these two extremes in women's writing, the transparent and the unintelligible, signal a similar problem. The transparent texts in women's literary history are often just as strange and inexplicable, if not as unreadable as the gnomic texts. But I'd like to stick with the issue of the unreadable or unintelligible coded text for the moment and investigate a famous example: Emily Dickinson. Is Dickinson unintelligible? Why was she once more difficult to read than she is now? And if she was once more difficult to read, but has now yielded up all her secrets, what has changed? Or is she simply being read differently?

In 1862 when Dickinson asked Thomas Wentworth Higginson if her poetry was publishable he told her that her 'gait' (meter) was 'spasmodic' and that her writing was 'uncontrolled'.[10] Higginson was a champion of women's education and women's rights. He promoted women poets. But Dickinson was too odd. Her method was beyond him. Even the women who admired her poetry tended to see both the poems and the woman who wrote them as too ethereal to survive in the public world. Emily Fowler Ford, a former schoolmate of Dickinson, commented on her poems, 'They are beautiful, so concentrated, but they remind me of orchids, airplants that have no roots in earth'.[11] It was perfectly possible to be a woman poet in mid-nineteenth century America, but it was not possible to write as Dickinson did and be published.

The characteristic territory of Dickinson's poems is clear and not entirely alien to nineteenth-century women's writing: faith and doubt, identity, authority, the process of making writing and erotic passion. Her erotic poems are addressed, quite unmistakably, to both women and men. The fact her poems do not have titles ensures that we cannot use a title as a search engine to decode its significance. We read the poem itself to garner meaning. The absence of titles also ensures that we have to read all her poems, nearly two thousand of them, to see how she structures her patterns of meaning, and how her symbols and metaphors flicker and change across her texts.

One of her more startling metaphors is the volcano. Here is Poem 601.

> A still–Volcano–Life–
> That flickered in the night–
> When it was dark enough to do
> Without erasing sight–
>
> A quiet–Earthquake Style–
> Too subtle to suspect
> By natures this side Naples–
> The North cannot detect
>
> The Solemn–Torrid Symbol–
> The lips that never lie–
> Whose hissing Corals part–and shut–
> And Cities–ooze away–[10]

I am inclined to read this poem along with the other 'Volcano' poems, but also alongside Poem 271.

> A solemn thing–it was–I said–
> A woman–white–to be–

Both poems are about the small neglected life, a life ignored and belittled, which can swell like Horizons, prove to be infinite. Dickinson often addressed the illusions of safety and space. What seems small is infinite, what seems ordinary is amazing, what looks like a still volcano could erupt at any time. This poem works in terms of binary polarities, the quiet versus the earthquake, the North versus the South. That which is hidden is infinitely power-ful. The volcano can absorb all things. The drama of the poem is clear. It is perfectly readable. But what is its meaning?

Dickinson, it seems to me, is making claims for herself, her nature and her sexuality. The power that is in 'the lips that never lie' are the woman's hidden lips, the 'vagina dentata', her volcanic sex itself.

> The Solemn–Torrid Symbol–
> The lips that never lie–
> Whose hissing Corals part–and shut–
> And Cities–ooze away–[12]

The volcano absorbs and destroys all man-made things. These invocations of natural power are common in Dickinson. She will usually associate natural forces with herself or make use of objects in the natural world to act as a sequence of highly charged sexual metaphors.

Emily Dickinson is the ghost in the machine of *Hallucinating Foucault*. This is the link between my writing and the figure of Emily Dickinson. I first read her poems with some impatience when I was at school. Years later when I became a university teacher one of my students wrote an essay on her love poetry. I sat down to read the Letters for the first time and the poems once again.

I came across the 'Master' Letters.

The Master is one of the mysteries of Dickinson biography. Only three of them still exist, and these are drafts, carefully revised. They almost certainly indicate the existence of a much longer correspondence. When Dickinson died on 15 May 1886, Lavinia Dickinson said that she found a locked box containing 700 of her sister's poems. The Master letters may have been with these poems, because her sister, mindful of posterity, destroyed the correspondence. Mabel Loomis Todd, Dickinson's first editor, was unwilling to print the Master letters. They are too unsettling, too revealing.

At the core of *Hallucinating Foucault* is a sequence of letters addressed to a 'Master'—'Cher Maître'—presumed to be addressed to Michel Foucault. They were careful fair-copied drafts. Unsent. A letter is one of the most intimate forms of writing which links the writer and the reader. A letter claims kin, connection, relationship. Paul Michel's letters to Michel Foucault, if they were indeed to him, and Emily Dickinson's letters to her unknown 'Master' were love letters. Love letters will always tell you far more about the lover than the beloved. The beloved is a phantom, a spectre constructed out of desire. If the beloved is absent then the love letter operates like a charm, a glamour, a conjurer's trick to call up the beloved image. Love letters, especially if we are given only one side of the correspondence, are always narratives of speculation and demand. Dickinson's Master letters are texts of desire. They have been pored over and speculated about by generations of scholars. Their ultimate meanings remain unintelligible. They were addressed to one reader. We can never know if a version of these letters was ever sent. I have held facsimiles of them in my hands, knowing that I am not their intended reader. They are drafts: raw writing in the process of careful revision.

In the third letter Dickinson uses the metaphor of the Volcano.

> You say I do
> not tell you all–Daisy 'confessed
> and denied not'
> Vesuvius dont talk–Etna–dont–
>   2   1
> (They) said a syllable–one of them
> a thousand years ago, and
> Pompeii heard it, and hid

forever–She could'nt look the
world in the face, afterward–
I suppose–Bashful Pompeii![13]

The volcano, which is associated here with Dickinson's own voice
in her dramatic persona of Daisy, a name she uses elsewhere in her
poetry. The 'hissing Corals' utter a subtle, playful, sexual threat.
One syllable from me and my erotic force, and you, Sir, can hide
for ever. Notice that the Volcano is never shamed. It is the city that
hides its face—Cities ooze away. Notice also that the City is feminine.

Dickinson published few of her poems in her lifetime, but some
of them were in a fairly public domain. She sent them as letters.
They were shared texts. She chose her readers. Sometimes the fact
that they are not utterly private texts is what makes them startling,
even slightly shocking. Here is one of my favourite examples.
Dickinson sent this poem (Poem 334) as a letter to her cousin,
Eudocia Flynt, accompanied by a flower, very probably, given the
evidence of the poem, a red rose.

All the letters I could write,
Were not fair as this–
Syllables of Velvet–
Sentences of Plush–
Depths of Ruby, undrained–
Hid, Lip, for Thee,
Play it were a Humming Bird
And sipped just Me–[14]

Mrs Flynt's diary records her visit to Amherst and her receipt of
this letter on 21 July 1862: 'Had a letter from Emily Dickinson!!!!'
with four exclamation marks.

This poem is, I fear, all too readable. Dickinson suggests that she
can't write the meanings suggested by the flower, or, at least, not
so beautifully. Here are 'Syllables of Velvet, Sentences of Plush'. But
the sexual invitation, and to oral sex at that, is utterly explicit. The
Ruby Depths are not just an invitation to a kiss, but to the hidden
lips, which promises a far more intimate encounter. The Humming

Bird penetrates the flower and extracts the nectar. The flower is a sexual substitute for the speaker's body, just as flowers, especially the rose, always have represented a woman's sex. Remember that Dickinson was writing long before Freud. Remember that romantic friendships between women were encouraged in the nineteenth century. Remember that Dickinson sent the poem quite openly to her cousin. Remember too that in a society where sex is something that can only happen between a woman and a man you can get away with a good deal more explicit suggestion. Dickinson can be, and is, explicit, startling and unmistakably erotic. She can then retreat into playfulness, whimsy, a mere game of sex, not the real thing. Dickinson is playing the man, courting the lady, sending her flowers. But look at the poem again. This time in its original context as a letter:

> Dear Mrs Flint,
>   You and I, did'nt finish talking. Have you room for the sequel, in your Vase?
>   All the letters I could write,
>   Were not fair as this–
>   Syllables of Velvet–
>   Sentences of Plush–
>   Depths of Ruby, undrained–
>   Hid, Lip, for Thee,
>   Play it were a Humming Bird
>   And sipped just Me–
>
>   Emily.[15]

Dickinson has shifted effortlessly from speech to script. But the rose is also now doing the talking. The rose represents Dickinson's continued dialogue with Eudocia Flynt, and she suggests a little gender role reversal. Look! I am the rose of sex, my Depths of Ruby undrained, my hidden lips ready. You play at being the Humming Bird—sip me! No wonder that Mrs Flynt added a row of exclamation marks.

In the context of Dickinson's homoerotic poetry, the gender-bending propositions and the explicit sexual invitations are not unusual. Here is Poem 249.

Wild Nights–Wild Nights!
Were I with thee
Wild Nights should be
Our luxury!

Futile–the Winds–
To a Heart in Port–
Done with the Compass–
Done with the Chart!

Rowing in Eden–
Ah! the Sea!
Might I but moor–Tonight–
In Thee![16]

The beloved's body as the paradise Garden of Eden appears again in Poem 211 as do the Lips, a crucial element in Dickinson's erotic iconography.

Come slowly–Eden!
Lips unused to Thee–
Bashful—sip thy Jessamines–
As the fainting Bee–

Reaching late his flower,
Round her chamber hums–
Counts his nectars–
Enters– and is lost in Balms.[17]

The sexual imagery of bees and flowers plays with the heterosexual suggestiveness of penetration but feminize the bee, who is overcome by nectars and balms and, far from staying in control, is utterly lost. Dickinson not only plays with sexual roles, masks and masquerades, she luxuriates in the sheer pleasure of female sexuality, its violence and endlessness. Her symbols are Volcanoes, Pearls, the Sea and endless horticultural possibilities. She writes the desiring texts, which Barthes demanded. The text you write must prove to me *that it desires me*. This proof exists: it is writing.

Dickinson sets out to seduce her reader, sometimes quite literally and in the flesh. Her speciality is textual bliss, the sexual text.

We know what Dickinson thought about literary fame. She has told us (Poem 709):

> Publication–is the Auction
> Of the Mind of Man–[18]

But is this declaration ironic? scornful? defensive? Posthumous publication and generations of readers have transformed Dickinson into a canonical American poet who is legible, intelligible and celebrated. Over a hundred years have passed. Dickinson was the Sleeping Beauty of women's writing. She really did write for someone in some future time, a new generation of women writers and a new generation of feminists, who feel that she was writing for us. Dickinson's texts are a judgement on the society that offered a woman like her so restricted a vision and poetic register within which to write and no possibility of publishing her work. But Dickinson was neither a victim nor a prisoner of her time. She saw the world otherwise and wrote it down. She told all the Truth, but told it slant. She wrote to every reader who would listen to her letters, and she left her writing on the wall.

Dickinson has become increasingly significant for me, precisely because when I first read her work as a schoolgirl I didn't understand it. I thought that her writing was self-regarding, tiresome, wilfully obscure. But I didn't think that about William Blake, whose work now seems to be just as cryptic, encoded. I had the key to reading Blake, but not Dickinson. I had not yet learnt how to resist the 'man of noon': that structure of reading that serves the dominant order of things. Dickinson's understanding of gender and sexuality speaks to our time. She regarded sexuality as a slippery, fluid, powerful force, a playground full of infinite *jouissance*, and sex as definitely one of the performance arts.

But there is one thing that haunts me above all and that is Dickinson's life, read as a text. What was once regarded as eccentric behaviour is now perfectly intelligible. Is it eccentric and strange to insist on a room of your own and to lock yourself up in it, to write? Is it peculiar to remain unmarried? Is it selfish and perverse to refuse to have children or to shoulder most of the housework? Is it a manifestation of madness to prefer the company of other women? Is it arrogant to interrogate your faith and jettison whatever won't square with your conscience or reason? Is it vain to insist on writing in your own style, your own voice, and to refuse all compromise? I don't think so. To me, Dickinson's exploration of her identity in her writing and her iron insistence on her own right to live as she chose is perfectly intelligible, utterly readable and makes elegant sense. These are my conclusions:

Beware the unintelligible text.
Just because you can't read this text does not mean that it cannot read you.
You may have been weighed in the balances and found wanting.
You may have been judged.
You may only be able to read this text when it is too late.
There is no end to reading.
The writing on the wall awaits.

NOTES & REFERENCES

HUP: Harvard University Press
MUP: Manchester University Press
OUP: Oxford University Press
YUP: Yale University Press

KILLING DADDY

1. *Observer,* 29 April 2001, p.16. This is a very odd list. I note that it does not include V. S. Naipaul. See Theroux's account of their friendship and its ending, *Sir Vidia's Shadow: A Friendship across Five Continents* (1998, Harmondsworth: Penguin, 1999). Presumably Theroux could not resist putting the boot in again, by leaving him out.
2. One of my students, Cal Walters, wrote her MPhil thesis on Virginia Woolf and Anaïs Nin and their use of autobiographical forms. I persuaded her not to call it 'The Lady and the Tramp'.
3. Marilyn French, *The Women's Room* (New York: Jove Books, 1977), pp.289–90.
4. But see A. S. Byatt's careful redrafting of the map of post-war literary fiction, *On Histories and Stories: Selected Essays* (London: Chatto & Windus, 2000), in which she credits the rebellious realists with a perversity that is entirely to their credit. Writing deliberately against the contemporary grain is a powerful oppositional strategy to employ.
5. For my reading the most important among these are Alan Sinfield's *Faultlines: Cultural Materialism and the Politics of Dissident Reading* (OUP, 1992), *Cultural Politics-Queer Reading* (London: Routledge, 1994) and *Gay and After* (London: Serpent's Tail, 1998). Eve Kosofsky Sedgwick is the influential queen of queer studies and author of *Between Men: English Literature and Male Homosocial Desire*, (New York: Columbia University Press, 1985) the fascinating and impenetrable *Epistemology of the Closet* (Harvester Wheatsheaf, 1991) and the more personal and accessible collection of essays, *Tendencies* (London: Routledge, 1994). Another suggestive text is Kate Chedgzoy's *Shakespeare's Queer Children: Sexual Politics and Contemporary Culture* (MUP, 1995). But I am also grateful

to the lesbian critics of queer politics. Anyone who reads some or all of the above should also read *All the Rage: Reasserting Radical Lesbian Feminism*, ed., Lynne Harne and Elaine Miller (London: Women's Press, 1996). For my own views see ch. 9, 'Post Gender: Jurassic Feminism meets Queer Politics'.

6. For an eloquent example see Elaine Jordan, 'The Dangers of Angela Carter' in *New Feminist Discourses: Critical Essays on Theories and Texts*, ed., Isobel Armstrong (London: Routledge, 1992), pp.119–31. She assures us that Carter is safe for men to read and describes me as 'lesbian, woman identified'. I'm happy with both statements. To follow the debate read chs 5 and 6 of this book.

7. A. S. Byatt, *On Histories and Stories* (op.cit.), p.6.

1. READING GENESIS

PL—All references are to the following edition of *Paradise Lost: The Poems of John Milton*, ed., John Carey and Alastair Fowler (London: Longman, 1968).

1. Edmund Leach *Genesis as Myth and Other Essays* (Cape: London, 1969), p.7.

2. See J. M. Evans, *Paradise Lost and the Genesis Tradition* (Oxford: Clarendon Press, 1968), especially ch.1.

3. Christian commentators and Christian translators of the Bible often translate the tetragrammaton as 'Yahweh' or 'Jehovah'. This is tactless and often offensive to religious Jewish people because YHWH is the unpronounceable name of God, which cannot be spoken, nor translated.

4. See Christopher Hill, *Milton and the English Revolution* (London: Faber & Faber, 1977), pp.239ff.

5. See *Paradise Lost*, Book xii. 59–60: 'great laughter was in heaven'.

6. I am assuming that most queer people do not live in the rich western and European nations for, statistically, this must be the case. They live in Africa, the ex-USSR, China, India, South America. In many places outside the west the institutions of heterosexuality are more ruthlessly enforced.

7. Women have always contested the meanings men have given to the Scriptures. Priscilla Cotton's and Mary Cole's pamphlet *To the Priests and People of England* (1655) uses the Bible to argue against the limitations placed upon women's power and women's rights to speak within the religious community. The arguments—equating 'woman' with 'weakness', and therefore including men, who might well give way to 'weakness'—are far-fetched, but ingenious. See Elaine Hobby, *Virtue of Necessity: English Women's Writing, 1649–88* (London: Virago, 1988), p.43.

8. For further feminist thoughts on Adam, Eve, versions of Genesis and

the mystification of equal creation see Mary Nyquist, 'The Genesis of Gendered Subjectivity in the Divorce Tracts and in *Paradise Lost*', *Remembering Milton: Essays on the Texts and Traditions,* ed. Mary Nyquist and Margaret W. Ferguson (New York & London: Methuen, 1987), pp.99–127.

9. Cited in Edward Le Comte, *Milton and Sex* (London: Macmillan, 1978), pp.26–7.

10. See Roberta Hamilton, *The Liberation of Women: A Study of Patriarchy and Capitalism* (London: Allen and Unwin, 1978), p.56.

11. William Gouge not only argued that the husband's adultery was as bad as that of the wife, he also argued against wife-beating. See Christopher Hill's classic study *The World Turned Upside Down: Radical Ideas during the English Revolution* (1972), (Harmondsworth: Peregrine Books, 1985), p.308.

12. Hamilton, op. cit., p.58.

13. Ibid., p.67. See also Hill, *The World Turned Upside Down*, esp. ch. 7; and J. F. McGregor and B. Reay, ed. *Radical Religion in the English Revolution* (OUP, 1984), esp. ch.5, 'Seekers and Ranters'.

14. See Christopher Hill, *Milton and the English Revolution*, op. cit., pp.30–1.

15. *Paradise Lost,* ibid., pp.268–84.

16. Ibid., p.144.

17. In the following discussion of the Separation Scene in book ix I am indebted to Marilyn Frye's *The Politics of Reality: Essays in Feminist Theory* (Trumansburg: The Crossing Press, 1983), esp. her essay in that volume 'Some Reflections on Separatism and Power'.

18. 'Areopagitica: A Speech for the Liberty of Unlicenc'd Printing', in *Complete Prose Works of John Milton,* vol.2 (New Haven, YUP., 1959), p.511.

19. See Frye, op. cit., p.103.

20. Cited in David Aers and Bob Hodge, 'Rational Burning: Milton on Sex and Marriage', *Milton Studies*, vol.12, 1979, pp.3–33.

21. Michelene Wandor, *Gardens of Eden: Poems for Eve and Lilith,* (London: Journeyman/Playbooks, 1984).

22. *Gardens of Eden*, p. 37.

23. Ibid., p.60.

24. Monique Wittig and Sande Zeig, *Lesbian Peoples: Materials for a Dictionary* (London: Virago, 1980), p.52. This text was originally published in France as *Brouillon pour un Dictionnaire des Amantes* (Paris: Editions Grasset & Fasquelle, 1976).

25. Ibid., p.53.

26. *Complete Prose Works of John Milton*, vol. 6, ed., Maurice Kelley, (Newhaven and London: YUP, 1973).

2. THE SUGGESTIVE SPECTACLE

All textual references are to the Penguin edition of Sparks's texts and to the Penguin Popular Classics edition of *Villette* as these are the most easily available editions.

MJB = *The Prime of Miss Jean Brodie* (Harmondsworth: Penguin, 1961, 1965).

CV = *Curriculum Vitae: A Volume of Autobiography* (1992) (Harmondsworth: Penguin, 1993).

Villette = (1853) Penguin Popular Classics, (Harmondsworth: Penguin, 1994).

1. *The Essence of the Brontës: A Compilation with Essays* (1952) (new edn, Peter Owen, 1993). The first essay in the book is entitled 'The Brontës as Teachers'. Spark suggests that the pupils and colleagues of Charlotte Brontë deserved some sympathy for their fate in having to work with a woman consumed by frustration and rage.

2. Enid Blyton produced three major series of school stories: The Naughtiest Girl in the School, 1940, 1942, 1945; six books set at St Clare's between 1941–5, and the famous Malory Towers series 1946–51. The gorgeous Darrell Rivers is named after Blyton's second husband, Kenneth Darrell Waters. The supporting tomboy heroines never stop being tomboys. Blyton's books were written especially for girls. See Sheila Ray, *The Blyton Phenomenon: The Controversy Surrounding the World's Most Successful Children's Writer* (London: Deutsch, 1982). See also Mary Cadogan and Patricia Craig, *'You're a Brick, Angela!': The Girls' Story, 1839–1985* (2nd edn) (London: Gollanz, 1986).

3. Ann Radcliffe's *The Mysteries of Udolpho* (1794) is the novel that Henry Tilney praises in ch. 14 of Jane Austen's *Northanger Abbey* (1818) '*The Mysteries of Udolpho*, when I had once begun it, I could not lay down again—I remember finishing it in two days—my hair standing on end the whole time.'

   The deranged Sister Agnes, the Nun in *Udolpho*, is in fact the Lady Laurentini—nuns are never what they seem—and she serves as a warning to the heroine Emily, just as the Nun in *Villette* is a warning to Lucy Snowe. Sister Agnes suggests that unchecked irrational passion leads to madness: 'Sister! Beware of the first indulgence of the passions...their force if not checked then is uncontrollable—they lead us we know not whither.' General studies of the *Gothic* novel include: Fred Botting, *Gothic* (London: Routledge, 1996), Maggie Kilgour, *The Rise of the Gothic Novel* (London: Routledge, 1995), David Punter, *The Literature of Terror: A History of Gothic Fictions from 1765 to the Present Day* (London: Longman, 1980).

4. Cited in Lyndall Gordon, *Charlotte Brontë: A Passionate Life* (1st edn, 1994) (London: Vintage, 1995), p.283.
5. Gordon, op. cit., p.285.

3. FICTIONS AND HISTORIES

HAASSE, Helle S., *Een Nieuwer Testament* (1964) Eng. edn: *Threshold of Fire: A Novel of Fifth Century Rome*, transl. Anita Miller and Nini Blinstrub (Academy Chicago, 1993).
TOLSTOY, Leo War and Peace transl. Rosemary Edmonds (Harmondsworth: Penguin, 1957, 1982).

1. For a readable assault on the postmodernists see Richard J. Evans, *In Defence of History* (London: Granta, 1997).
2. See Pierre Macherey, *A Theory of Literary Production* (1966), English edn (London: Routledge & Kegan Paul, 1978), p.311. Lenin's articles on Tolstoy are reprinted in the Appendix.
3. Henri Troyat, *Tolstoy* (1965) transl. by Nancy Amphoux (New York: Harmony, 1980), p.315.
4. See Andrea Dworkin's *Intercourse* (London: Secker & Warburg, 1987), pp.4–20, for a radical analysis of Tolstoy's tale.
5. Terry Eagleton, *The Illusions of Postmodernism* (Oxford: Blackwell, 1996), p.51.

4. HOFFMANN'S UNCANNY REPLICANT

All textual references are to the following editions:
FREUD, Sigmund, *Art and Literature,* The Penguin Freud Library, vol. 14, ed. Albert Dickson (Harmondsworth: Penguin, 1985).
HOFFMANN, E. T. A., *The Golden Pot and Other Tales* ed. and transl. Ritchie Robertson, World's Classics, (OUP, 1992).
SHELLEY, Mary, *Frankenstein,* ed. M. K. Joseph (London: OUP, 1969). This text follows the 1831 edn.

1. 1831 Preface to the Bentley's Standard Novels edn, repr. in Shelley, p.9.
2. See Wordsworth and Coleridge, *Lyrical Ballads,* ed. R. L. Brett and A. R. Jones (London: Methuen, 1963), p.104. From 'Expostulation and Reply,'

   Nor less I deem that there are powers
   Which of themselves our minds impress,
   That we can feed this mind of ours
   In a wise passiveness.

2. The phenomenon of inspiration and the mental states in which it occurs is a central preoccupation of the Romantics and the subject of many poems. See Timothy Clark *The Theory of Inspiration: Composition as a Crisis of Subjectivity in Romantic and Post-Romantic Writing* (MUP, 1997). For duplicitous versions of the 'vision-dream' see Percy Bysshe Shelley's *Alastor*, written at the same time as *Frankenstein*.

3. *Blade Runner* (1982, Director's Cut, 1992) is a key film in the development of post-modern film theory and post-human cyborg theory. See Tim Woods, *Beginning Postmodernism* (MUP, 1999). See especially pp.214–55 for a brief introduction to post-modern film and a useful bibliography.

4. Roland Barthes, *The Pleasure of the Text* (1973), trans. Richard Miller (Oxford: Blackwell, 1990), p.47.

5. REIMAGINING THE FAIRY TALES

This essay was first delivered as a paper to the Modern Fiction Society in Oxford on 15 June 1982, where it raised a lot of male hackles and silenced the women completely. I wasn't happy about this. Since then it has been reprinted several times. Angela Carter now has a vast academic and university audience although a less certain acclaim among the general reading public. Carter died in 1992. There is nothing like dying before your time to generate a plethora of PhDs. She is a much studied writer. All her work is still in print. Andrea Dworkin, Carter's counterpoint in this essay, has continued her career as a polemicist, her latest book being an attack on the sexism inherent in the structures of the state of Israel. Both women are seriously preoccupied with the issues raised by pornography. Both women have written texts that have been described as pornographic. Dworkin appears in all the British newspapers at regular intervals, but is hardly ever cited as an authority in academic texts and articles. Most people, of all sexes and genders, don't like what she says. They like Angela Carter, but they don't like Andrea Dworkin. I have learned, over the last thirty years, that if nobody likes what you say you are on to something important.

All textual references unless otherwise stated are to the following editions:

CARTER, Angela *The Bloody Chamber and Other Stories* (1979, Harmondsworth: King Penguin, 1981).

CARTER, Angela *Fireworks: Nine Profane Pieces* (London: Quartet, 1974).

1. I have been much criticized for being rude about psychoanalysis in general and the unconscious in particular. People who are seized by the discourses of psychoanalysis often lose their grip on common sense. Imagine my delight at finding the following quotation in Jenny Diski's autobiographical quest, *Skating to Antarctica* (1997). Diski's monstrous mother disappeared from her life while she was doing her 'A' Levels. Diski was mightily relieved. And she had no desire to find

out where her mother was. Her entourage is disturbed: 'But what about attachment? How could this primary maternal connection have passed me by? Clearly, I was either fatally damaged, or I was in possession of the healthiest psyche since psychoanalytic annals began.' (London: Granta, 1998), p.30.

Is it mad to dislike and avoid people who do you harm whoever they happen to be? I would place my bets on the strength of Diski's psychic health. She is an extraordinary writer. Her novel *Nothing Natural* is discussed in ch.7.

2. Cited in Andrea Dworkin, *Our Blood: Prophecies and Discourses on Sexual Politics* (Women's Press: London, 1982), p.55.

3. Ibid.

4. See Roger Sale, *Fairy Tales and After* (Cambridge, Mass., & London: HUP, 1978), p.26.

5. Philip Ariès, *Centuries of Childhood* (1960); (London: Cape, 1962), p.41.

6. Peter Burke, *Popular Culture in Early Modern Europe* (London: Temple Smith, 1978), p.62.

7. See Jack Zipes, *Breaking the Magic Spell: Radical Theories of Folk and Fairy Tales* (London: Heinemann, 1979), pp.23ff.

8. See Zipes, op. cit., especially ch.3.

9. *Kinder und Hausmärchen* (1812–14).

10. I am indebted here to an essay by Michel Butor, 'On Fairy Tales', *European Literary Theory and Practice: From Existential Phenomenology to Structuralism*, ed., Vernon W. Gras (New York, 1973).

11. I am perfectly aware that some men loathe these discourses while others endorse them. The fact is that men have never organized themselves as men to challenge or dismantle the structures of sexist discourse.

12. *The Sadeian Woman* (London: Virago, 1979), pp.19–20. I must declare an interest here as I can certainly be accused of using pornographic material in my work. Most contemporary writers do. The difference between Carter and myself is simple. I don't accept 'the logic of a world of absolute sexual licence for all genders', although I'm delighted that she envisages genders in the plural.

13. *The Sadeian Woman*, op. cit., p.20.

14. Andrea Dworkin, *Our Blood: Prophecies and Discourses on Sexual Politics* (London: Women's Press, 1982), p. 62.

15. *The Fairy Tales of Charles Perrault*, transl. by Angela Carter (London: Gollanz, 1977), p.71.

16. *The Fairy Tales of Charles Perrault*, p. 41.

17. See Iona and Peter Opie, *The Classic Fairy Tales* (London: OUP, 1974).

18. Andrea Dworkin, *Pornography: Men Possessing Women* (1981, London: Women's Press, 1982), p. 109.

19. See Rosika Parker, 'Images of Men', *Spare Rib*, 99, Nov. 1980, pp.5–8.
20. I first became interested in this theme when I accompanied Patricia
    Beer to Haworth in June 1981. She gave a quite extraordinary lecture
    on Clothes and Transvestism in the Brontë's novels for the annual
    meeting of the Brontë Society. She wrote a poem on the subject,
    'Transvestism in the Novels of Charlotte Brontë', published in her
    collection *The Lie of the Land* (London: Hutchinson, 1983). I wrote
    ch. 2 of this book, which investigates the sexual enigmas of Lucy
    Snowe and Miss Jean Brodie.
21. Since I wrote this essay women writers have gone on to do this. Interfering
    with the traditional structures of myths and tales has been something of
    an obsession in the last few decades. The fairy tales are reworked in impor-
    tant ways in Jeanette Winterson's novels, especially *Oranges Are Not the
    Only Fruit* and *Sexing the Cherry*. Two collections that have been espe-
    cially successful are Emma Donoghue's *Kissing the Witch* (London: Hamish
    Hamilton, 1997) and A. S. Byatt's *Elementals: Tales of Fire and Ice* (London:
    Chatto & Windus, 1998). But Carter's tales were pathbreakers. She cleared
    the ground for other women's work.

6. QUEER GOTHIC

All textual references are to the following editions:
CARTER, Angela, *Black Venus* (1985) (London: Picador, 1986).
LEWIS, M. G., *The Monk* (1796), ed., H. Anderson (London: OUP, 1973),
    p.41.
RADCLIFFE, Ann, *The Mysteries of Udolpho* (1794) (London: Dent,
    1969) 2 vols.
— *The Italian* (1797), ed., F. Garber (London: OUP, 1968).

1. Many of the Gothic novels of the late eighteenth and the early nine-
   teenth century immediately became very successful stage plays. Ann
   Radcliffe's work reappeared in both dramatic and operatic versions:
   The Mysteries of the Castle: an Opera by Miles Peter Andrews (Covent
   Garden, 1 January 1795) and *The Italian Monk*: a Play in Three Acts
   by James Boaden (Theatre Royal, Haymarket, 15 August 1797) with
   Charles Kemble playing the romantic hero, Vivaldi. The stage versions
   were also very popular in revolutionary France. There were three
   French versions of *Udolpho-Le Testament, ou Les Mystères d'Udolphe*,
   A Drama in five acts by Lamartelière (June 1798) and *Montoni, ou
   le Château d' Udolphe*: a Drama in five acts by Alexandre Duval also
   performed in 1798. A third version *Le Château des Apennins ou le
   Fantôme Vivant* , *drame en cinq actes* was performed in December
   1799. Even the second generation of Gothic writers received the same

treatment. There were two rival productions of *Frankenstein* running on the London stage in 1823. A Romantic Melodrama, *Frankenstein, or The Demon of Switzerland* by H. M. Milner, opened at the Coburg Theatre, 18 July 1823, and *Presumption or The Fate of Frankenstein*: a melodrama in three acts by Richard Brinsley Peake, opened at the Lyceum Monday, 18 July 1823. Both versions continued to be performed throughout the nineteenth century. Walter Scott records seeing one of them in 1827. Milner's play was revived in Edinburgh between 1856 and 1859 with Henry Irving in the star role. See Montague Summers, *A Gothic Bibliography* (London: Fortune, 1940), pp.141–2 and pp. 330–1. This bibliography should be treated with some caution as it is often inaccurate.

2. *Monthly Review*, no.22 (March 1797), p.283.
3. Literary Hours (1798) 3rd edn (London, 1804), 3 vols, i, pp.361–2.
4. Transl. as 'Reflections on the Novel', *The 120 Days of Sodom and other Writings,* comp. & Transl. by Austryn Wainhouse and Richard Seaver (New York: Grove, 1966), p.109.
5. *Critical Review*, xix (Feb. 1797), p.197.
6. *Critical Review*, op. cit. p.198.
7. See Judith Butler, *Gender Trouble: Feminism and the Subversion of Identity* (London: Routledge, 1990), esp. pp.137–41 on gender and drag. Her more philosophical text, *Bodies that Matter: On the Discursive Limits of Sex* (London: Routledge, 1993) is fascinating in small doses. Even more influential on my thinking here has been queer theorist Eve Kosofsky Sedgwick. See esp. *The Epistemology of the Closet* (Hemel Hempstead: Harvester Wheatsheaf, 1991) and her essay 'Queer and Now' in her collection *Tendencies* (London: Routledge, 1994), pp.1–20.
8. Paula Bennett 'Gender as Performance: Shakespearian Ambiguity and the Lesbian Reader' in *Sexual Practice, Textual Theory: Lesbian Cultural Criticism,* ed., Susan J. Wolfe and Julia Penelope (Oxford: Blackwell, 1993), pp.94–109, 100.
9. Michelle Massé, *In The Name of Love: Women Masochism and the Gothic* (Ithaca, New York: Cornell UP, 1992), p.2.
10. Angela Carter, *Nights at the Circus* (London: Chatto & Windus, 1984), p.172.
11. See George Eliot, *Middlemarch* (1871–2), ch.15. I am obsessed with Eliot's Laure and return to her in ch.11 of this book.
12. Charlotte Brontë, *Jane Eyre* (1847), ch.12.
13. Especially wild animals, tigers, cats and wolves. See her tales of metamorphosis in *The Bloody Chamber and Other Stories* (1979) and the tigers in *Nights at the Circus* (London: Chatto & Windus, 1984): 'It came out of the corridor like orange quicksilver, or a rarer liquid metal, a quickgold. It did not so much run as flow, a questing sluice

of brown and yellow, a hot and molten death' (p.111). This particular tiger, like Blake's, is both metal and flesh, beautiful and deadly.

14. James Robson, 'Bestiality in Greek Myth', unpublished paper delivered at 'Violence and Power: An International Symposium on Rape in Antiquity', University of Wales, College of Cardiff, 19 November, 1994. Most stories about bestiality are also rape stories. Robson pointed out that the only myth which involves homosexual bestiality is the rape of Ganymede by Zeus. This is a late myth, that dates from the fourth century. See also Dominique Fernandez, *Le Rapt de Ganymède* (Paris: Bernard Grasset, 1989), a meditation on gay history that appropriates the myth.

15. These were the buzzwords at the conference 'Fireworks: Angela Carter and the Futures of Writing', University of York, 30 September–2 October 1994. One of the papers was entitled "Unexpected Geometries: Transgressive Symbolism and the Transgressive Subject in Angela Carter's *The Passion of New Eve*', given by Heather Johnson. I presented a version of this essay at that conference and was therefore also guilty of talking about transgression.

16. Elizabeth Wilson, 'Is Transgression Transgressive?' in *Activating Theory: Lesbian, Gay and Bisexual Politics*, ed., Joseph Bristow and Angela R. Wilson (London: Lawrence & Wishart, 1993), pp.107–17, esp. p.113.

17. Lorna Sage, *Women in the House of Fiction: Post-war Women Novelists* (London: Macmillan, 1992), p.168.

18. Angela Carter, *The Passion of New Eve* (London: Gollanz, 1977), pp.128–9.

19. Start with the crucial essay Joan Riviere, 'Womanliness as a Masquerade', first published in *The International Journal of Psychoanalysis*, vol. 8 (1927), republished in *Formations of Fantasy*, ed. Victor Burgin, James Donald and Cora Kaplan (London: Methuen, 1986), pp.35–44.

20. From *The Supplement to the Onania* (*c.*?1710), cited in Emma Donoghue *Passions Between Women : British Lesbian Culture: 1668–1807* (London: Scarlet, 1993), p.41.

7. HETEROSEXUALITY: FICTIONAL AGENDAS

All textual references are to the following editions:
ATWOOD, Margaret, *The Edible Woman* (1969, London: Virago, 1980).
— *Life Before Man* (1979) (London: Virago, 1982).
— *The Handmaid's Tale* (1985) (London: Virago, 1987).
— *Cat's Eye* (1988) (London: Virago, 1990).
DISKI, Jenny, *Nothing Natural* (1986) (London: Minerva, 1990).
GOLDING, William, *Rites of Passage* (London: Faber & Faber, 1980).

JEFFREYS, Sheila, *Anticlimax: A Feminist Perspective on the Sexual Revolution* (London: Women's Press, 1990).

1. The Toronto ravines are also used to sinister effect in her novel *Cat's Eye* (1988). I have only visited Toronto once and was very anxious to see these gulfs of green, precipices in the midst of the city. They are very alarming. They also appear in Jane Urquhart's historical novel *The Stone Carvers* (London: Bloomsbury, 2001). Interestingly, the focus in Atwood's more recent novels, *The Robber Bride* (1993), *Alias Grace* (1996) and her Booker prize-winning novel *The Blind Assassin* (2000), is more closely upon relationships and connections between women.
2. Here I find myself in agreement with Sheila Jeffreys in her book about the sexual revolution, *Anticlimax*. See especially her utopian Ch.6, 'Creating the sexual future'.

8. 'THE LONG LINE OF BLOOD/AND FAMILY TIES'

All textual references are to the following editions:

BENGHIAT, Norma, *Traditional Jamaican Cookery* (Harmondsworth: Penguin, 1985).

BERRY, James, *Fractured Circles* (London: New Beacon, 1979).

BOYCE DAVIES, Carole, *Black Women, Writing and Identity. Migrations of the Subject* (London: Routledge, 1994).

BRENNAN, Timothy, *Salman Rushdie and the Third World: Myths of the Nation* (London: Macmillan, 1989).

BURFORD, Barbara; Pearse, Gabriela, Nichols, Grace, and Kay, Jackie, *A Dangerous Knowing* (London: Sheba,1984).

COBHAM, Rhonda, and Collins, Merle, ed. Watchers and Seekers: Creative Writing by Black Women (London: Women's Press,1987).

EASTON, Alison, '"The Body as History" and "Writing the Body": The Example of Grace Nichols', *Journal of Gender Studies,* vol.3, no.1 (1994), pp.55–67.

MORRISON, Toni, *Beloved* (London: Chatto & Windus, 1987)

NASTA, Susheila, ed. (1991) *Motherlands: Black Women's Writing from Africa, the Caribbean and South Asia* (London: Women's Press, 1991).

NGCOBO, Lauretta, *Let it Be Told, Black Women Writers in Britain* (London: Pluto, 1987).

NICHOLS, Grace, *i is a long-memoried woman* (London: Karnak House, 1983).

— *The Fat Black Woman's Poems* (London: Virago,1984).

— *Whole of a Morning Sky* (London: Virago, 1986).

— *Lazy Thoughts of a Lazy Woman and other Poems* (London: Virago, 1989).

— *Sunris* (London: Virago, 1996).

OWUSU, Kwese, ed., *Storms of the Heart: An Anthology of Black Arts and Culture* (London: Camden Press, 1988).

PHILIP, M. Nourbese, *she tries her tongue, her silence softly breaks* (London: Women's Press, 1983).

RENAN, Ernest, 'What is a nation?' (Lecture delivered at the Sorbonne in 1882), republished in Homi K. Bhabha, *Nation and Narration* (London: Routledge, 1990).

SULTER, Maud, ed., *Passion: Discourses on Blackwomen's Creativity* (Hebden Bridge, West Yorks: Urban Fox, 1990).

Walker, Alice, *In Search of Our Mothers' Gardens: Womanist Prose* (London: Women's Press, 1984).

WALL, Cheryl A., ed., *Changing Our Own Words: Essays on Criticism, Theory and Writing by Black Women* (London: Routledge, 1990).

WHITE, Antonia, *Frost in May* (1933, London: Virago, 1978).

WISKER, Gina, *Black Women Writing* (London: Macmillan, 1993). This collection includes an important article by Gabrielle Griffin, '"Writing the Body": Reading Joan Riley, Grace Nichols and Ntozake Shange'.

1. The notion of 'unbelonging' derives from Joan Riley's first novel, *The Unbelonging* (1985), which deals with alienation and identity. See also Carole Boyce Davies, *Black Women, Writing and Identity: Migrations of the Subject* (London: Routledge, 1994), esp. pp.100–107 on 'unbelongingness' in Black British women's writing.

2. Benedict Anderson, *Imagined Communities, Reflections on the Origins and Spread of Nationalism* (1983) Revised edition (London: Verso, 1991), see especially ch.8.

3. Alice Walker entitled her first collection of essays, *In Search of Our Mother's Gardens* (London: Women's Press, 1984). Nichols entitles one of her poems with a quotation from this collection: 'There is no centre of the Universe' (*Lazy Thoughts*, p.33) and addresses other poems to black women writers, Ntozake Shange and Jean Binta Breeze. These writers share common themes of identity, community, roots, nation. In her most recent collection, *Sunris*, Nichols suggests that Caribbean writers should spend less time worrying about their 'roots', which will usually entail looking backwards, into the past and into history, and concentrate on their 'wings'. See her poem 'Wings'.

4. Many women poets, both lesbian and heterosexual, write about oral sex. Christina Rossetti (*Goblin Market*) and Emily Dickinson are two nineteenth-century examples. The motif reoccurs in Nichols' work. See ch.12 of this book for more on Emily Dickinson and lesbian oral sex.

9. POST GENDER

1. Noël Burch, the translator of Michelle Coquillat's *La Poétique du Mâle* (1982), has this to say about the erasure of most French feminists from the canon of Anglophone feminist theory.

   'French feminism' is an American invention...the hermetic writings of Irigaray, Cixous, Kristeva et al. are not representative of today's feminist scholarship in France which on the whole is quite unsympathetic to their politics, although their opaque theorising has earned them academic prestige under the modernist canon. Unfortunately this distorted perspective has completely obfuscated for English language readers the writings of Christine Delphy, Geneviève Fraisse, Françoise Gaspard, Marcelle Marini, Michelle Perrot, Christine Guillemin, Michèle Le Doeuff, Anne-Lise Maugue, Christine Planté, Eliane Viennot, to name only a few.

   See 'A Male Poetics', *Women: A Cultural Review,* vol.11, no.3 (Winter 2000), pp. 223–37.
2. Stevi Jackson, 'Gender and Heterosexuality: A Materialist Feminist Analysis' *(Hetero)sexual Politics*, ed. Mary Maynard and Jane Purvis (London: Taylor and Francis, 1995), pp.11–26, 13.
3. Monique Wittig, 'The Straight Mind' (1980), *The Straight Mind and Other Essays* (Hemel Hempstead: Harvester Wheatsheaf, 1992), p.32.
4. Radicalesbians, 'The Woman Identified Woman' (1970), *For Lesbians Only: A Separatist Anthology,* ed., Julia Penelope and Sarah Lucia Hoagland (London: Onlywomen, 1988), p.17.
5. See Patricia Duncker, 'Bonne Excitation: Orgasme Assuré: The Representation of Lesbianism in Contemporary French Pornography', *Journal of Gender Studies,* vol.4, no.1, 1995, pp.5–15.
6. Gender is never simple or undisputed in Shakespeare's work and in fact *A Midsummer Night's Dream* does have its queer moments. The object of Titania and Oberon's quarrel is a beautiful Indian boy. They both want him. What for, one wonders. But then, Shakespeare is a complicated case. For more on *A Midsummer Night's Dream* and Angela Carter's not quite so queer version see ch.6 of this book.
7. Adrienne Rich's classic essay, 'Compulsory Heterosexuality and Lesbian Existence', *Blood, Bread, and Poetry: Selected Prose, 1979–1985* (New York: Norton, 1986), pp.23–75.
8. Andrew Sullivan, *Virtually Normal: An Argument about Homosexuality* (London: Picador, 1995).
9. See Adrienne Rich 'Women and Honor: Notes on Lying' (1975), republished in *On Lies, Secrets and Silence: Selected Prose, 1966–1978* (New York: Norton, 1979), pp.185–94.
10. See Marjorie Garber, *Vested Interests: Cross-dressing and Cultural Anxiety* (New York & London: Routledge, 1992), and Emma

Donoghue, *Passions Between Women: British Lesbian Culture, 1668–1801* (London: Scarlet, 1993), esp. ch.3.

11. Cherry Smyth, *Lesbians Talk Queer Notions* (London: Scarlet, 1992), p.26.

12. Ibid., p.27.

13. Kate Bornstein, *Gender Outlaw: On Men, Women and the Rest of Us* (London & New York: Routledge, 1994), p.143–4.

14. Ibid., p.234.

15. Janice Raymond, *The Transsexual Empire* (London: Women's Press, 1980), p.106.

16. One of the most imaginative in the period of Jurassic Feminism was Marge Piercy's *Woman on the Edge of Time* (1976). Piercy imagined a society in which he and she did not exist, but we were all referred to as 'per'. Technology took care of reproduction and the role of mothering was undertaken by women and men alike. Piercy was trying to imagine the abolition of the gender hierarchy, rather than proposing a multiplicity of genders, as Bornstein does.

17. Stevi Jackson, 'Gender and Heterosexuality: A Materialist Feminist Analysis', *(Hetero) sexual Politics*, op. cit., p.18.

18. I am indebted to Jonathan Dollimore for this expression, and I was much influenced by his essay 'Bisexuality, heterosexuality, and Wishful Theory', *Textual Practice*, 10 (3), 1996, pp.523–39.

19. This saying is attributed to Rabbi Hillel, but I first came across it as the title to Primo Levi's novel of Jewish resistance and survival: *Se Non Ora, Quando?* (1982), first published in English in 1986 under the title *If Not Now, When?* (London: Abacus, 1987).

10. ON NARRATIVE STRUCTURES IN CONTEMPORARY FICTION

All textual references are to the following editions:
COETZEE, J. M., *Disgrace* (London: Secker, 1999)
MELVILLE, Pauline, *The Ventriloquist's Tale* (1997) (London: Vintage, 1998).

1. Aristotle 'On the Art of Poetry' in *Classical Literary Criticism*, transl. by T. S. Dorsch (Harmondsworth: Penguin, 1965), pp.35–40.

2. Peter Brooks, *Reading for the Plot: Design & Intention in Narrative* (1984) new edn (Cambridge, Mass: HUP, 2000), pp.5, 13.

3. I am more than happy with any writer who *rewrites* the Bible. See my arguments with Milton's rewriting of Genesis in chapter 1 of this book. Other contemporary feminist rewriters of Genesis are Michèle Roberts and Sara Maitland.

4. *Disgrace* was highly praised by the British literary establishment and won the Booker Prize 1999. For a sympathetic defence of the novel and a careful placing of the book in the context of Coetzee's earlier work see a long review article by Elizabeth Lowry, 'Like a Dog', *London Review of Books*, 14 October 1999, pp.12–14. Even more interesting, because *Disgrace* is compared to a tale by Alice Walker, which also deals with a black man raping a white woman, is Mary Eagleton's article 'Ethical Reading: 'Advancing Luna-and Ida B. Wells' and J. M. Coetzee's *Disgrace*', *Feminist Theory*, vol.2, no.2 (August 2001), pp.189–203. Her reading of Coetzee is also sympathetic, but partial in all senses. She starts from the assertion that he is 'a deeply serious writer who confronts with feeling and terrible honesty the problems of apartheid and post-apartheid South Africa' (p.189). I don't share her views. Eagleton is especially interesting on the issue of rape and silence. My point is that Lucy's silence has a parallel in the book. The blacks don't explain themselves either. But they are not powerless as she is, they are the rising class. It is the combination of these two silences, that renders the race and gender politics of the book sinister, but intelligible.

11. THE IMPOSSIBILITY OF MAKING WRITING

All textual references are to the following editions:
BATTERSBY, Christine, *Gender and Genius: Towards a Feminist Aesthetics* (London: Women's Press, 1989).
CLARK, Timothy, *The Theory of Inspiration: Composition as a Crisis of Subjectivity in Romantic and Post-Romantic Writing* (Manchester and New York: MUP, 1997).
ELIOT, George, *The George Eliot Letters,* ed., Gordon S. Haight, 9 vols (Connecticut, USA: New Haven, 1954–55, 1978).
NAMJOSHI, Suniti, *Building Babel* (Melbourne, Australia: Spinifex, 1996).
WOOLF, Virginia, *A Writer's Diary*, ed. Leonard Woolf (1953, London: Hogarth Press, 1972).
—*A Passionate Apprentice: The Early Journals, 1987–1909* (London: Hogarth,1992).

1. Repr. from *The Collected Poems of Stevie Smith* (Harmondsworth, Penguin Twentieth Century Classics) by kind permission of Mr James MacGibbon.
2. See Jonathan Bate, *The Genius of Shakespeare* (London: Picador, 1997), for lengthy, elegant critical speculation.

12. WRITING ON THE WALL

1. *Hallucinating Foucault* (London: Serpent's Tail, 1996), p.88.
2. See *Daniel* V: 24–8.

3. Jacques Derrida, *Acts of Literature,* ed. Derek Attridge (London: Routledge, 1992), pp.370–413.

4. Ibid., p.372.

5. Roland Barthes, *The Pleasure of the Text,* trans. Richard Miller (Oxford: Blackwell, 1990), p.4.

6. Ibid., p.6.

7. *Hallucinating Foucault* (London: Serpent's Tail, 1996), p.171. I have altered this quotation a little from the published text. I can do this. This writing is mine. The question of ownership is strange, intriguing, fraught. And too broad to investigate here.

8. See Jane Spencer, *The Rise of the Woman Novelist* (Oxford: Blackwell, 1986), p.ix.

   'We need to be careful here. I do not claim that in any respect, thematic or stylistic, women's writing is essentially different from men's: indeed the most crucial insight afforded by feminism is in my opinion the deconstruction of the opposition masculine-feminine as essential categories. But if women writers exhibit no essential 'femininity' they are still working within a patriarchal society that defines and judges them according to its notions of what femininity is. They may internalize their society's standards of femininity and reflect this in their writing. Or they may write in opposition to those standards. In short women writers are in a special position because of society's attitude to their sex; and their work is likely to be affected by their response to that position (even when the response is an attempt to ignore a situation which might be debilitating if acknowledged). Women having been oppressed as women, it is not only reasonable but necessary to consider women as forming a group with significant interests in common.'

9. See Daphne du Maurier, *Rebecca* (1938) (London: Arrow, 1992). See esp. ch. 14 where Mrs Danvers forces the new Mrs de Winter to fondle Rebecca's most intimate clothing.

10. See Paula Bennett, *Emily Dickinson: Woman Poet* (Hemel Hempstead: Harvester Wheatsheaf, 1990), p.24.

11. Ibid., p.10.

12. Emily Dickinson, *The Complete Poems,* ed. Thomas H. Johnson (London: Faber & Faber, 1970, 1982), p.295.

13. Emily Dickinson, *The Master Letters of Emily Dickinson,* ed. R. W. Franklin (Amherst College Press, 1986), p.39.

14. *The Letters of Emily Dickinson,* ed. Thomas H. Johnson (HUP, 1986), p.414.

15. Ibid.

16. *Complete Poems,* op. cit., p.114.

17. Ibid., p.98.

18. Ibid., p.348.

INDEX

Ackee
  saltfish and ackee, 119
  toxicity, 120
Adam
  Eve as property of, 14
  Eve, relationship with, 18
  Fall, fault as to, 19
  sin of, 23
Advertising
  gender constructions, 105, 106
Anderson, Benedict, 133
Aristotle
  Poetics, 159
Atwood, Margaret
  Edible Woman, The, 103–7, 110
  Handmaid's Tale, The, 112, 113
  Life Before Man, 103–111
  literary psychoanalysis, 108
  nature of writing, 104, 105
  studies of, 101, 103

Barthes, Roland
  hybrid texts, 189
  Pleasure of the Text, The, 63,
    189, 190
Battersby, Christina
  *Gender and Genius: Towards a
    Feminist Aesthetics*, 180
Belshazzar's feast
  writing on the wall, 188
Berry, James, 121, 122

Bible
  narrative, as, 161
  patriarchy, as book of, 3
  women, use against, 20
Black Writers workshop, 122
Blade Runner, 61–3
Bluebeard, 79–82
Borden, Lizzie, 93, 94, 96
Bornstein, Kate
  Gender Outlaw, 152–4
Brent Black Music Workshop,
  122, 123
Brontë, Charlotte
  love life, 29, 30
  tranvestism in novels, 81
  Villette. See Villette
  writing, trying to stop, 174
Brontë, Emily
  Wuthering Heights, 165, 166
Brooks, Peter, 160
Butler, Judith, 89

Caribbean
  people, ancestry of, 121
  psychic space, as, 121
Caribbean language
  Creole, 126
  literary, 123
  Nichols, views of, 125, 126
  political implications, 120
  political tensions, 125

source of, 121
Caribbean literature
  Britain, writers in, 120, 121
  construction of, 120
  displacement and alienation,
    fictions of, 131
  music, basis of, 122
  oral cultures and traditions, 122
Carter, Angela
  Black Venus, 92–6
  Bloody Chamber, The, 67, 72–83
  economics of sex, view of, 92,
    93
  episodic writing, 95
  'Erl-King, The', 72
  female characters, 99, 100
  Fireworks, 67
  Gothic, interest in, 84
  identity in flux, presentation of,
    95
  literary territory, 91
  Passion of New Eve, The, 67
  Perrault's fairy tales, translation
    of, 67
  radical feminist inheritance, 92
  Sadeian Woman, The, 67, 75
  short narratives of, 82, 83
  'Snow Child, The', 74, 75
  tales of, 68, 69
  'Tiger's Bride, The', 73
  transgressive writing, 97
  transvestite mysteries, 98
Catholicism
  nationality, as, 133
Clark, Timothy
  Theory of Inspiration, The, 180
Classrooms, revolution in, 27
Coetzee, J. M.
  Disgrace, 157, 161, 163, 167–71
Comorre the Cursed, 79

d'Aulnoy, Countess, 71
de Beauvoir, Simone, 143
de Rais, Gilles, 79
de Sade, Marquis, 91
Derrida, Jacques

Shibboleth, 189
Dickinson, Emily,
  biographies, 195, 196
  homoerotic poetry, 198, 199
  intelligibility, 193
  letters, 197, 198
  life of, 200, 201
  literary fame, view of, 200
  poems, 194–200
  sexuality, claims for, 195
Diodati, Charles, 16
Diski, Jenny
  Nothing Natural, 113–17
Divorce
  Milton, writings of, 10
Drake, Nathan, 87
du Maurier, Daphne
  Rebecca, 193
Duncker, Patricia
  Hallucinating Foucault, 187,
    188, 190, 191, 195, 196
Dworkin, Andrea, 68, 69, 76

Education
  classical notion of, 69
  Renaissance, in, 70
*Een Nieuwer Testament
    (Threshold of Fire)*
  characters, 45
  description in, 47, 48
  female characters, 48, 49
  gaps in knowledge, explaining,
    50, 51
  Hadrian, character of, 49
  literal meaning, 39
  period of, 45
  recognisable parts of, 49, 50
  recreation of sources, 46, 47
  Roman monuments, description
    of, 47, 48
Eliot, George, 158
  bad reviews, protection from,
    174
  Daniel Deronda, 177
  Middlemarch, 177
  Mill on the Floss, The, 165, 166

Essences
  opposites, division into, 3
Eve
  Adam's power over, 19
  Adam's property, as, 14
  Adam, response to, 16
  creation of, 4, 5
  first person seen by, 15
  inferior sex, of, 9
  Lilith, and, 21, 22
  serpent, confronting, 17
  temptation, 18

Fairy tales
  boys, addressed to, 77
  Carter, reworking by, 67–9,
    72–83
  childhood, as property of, 71
  fantastic nature of, 72
  girls, metaphors for, 77
  infernal trap in, 73
  inverted world of, 71
  Märchen, 69
  original folk tales, 70, 71
  sexual politics of, 82
  Sleeping Beauty, 77–9
  Volksmärchen and
    Kunstmärchen, 70
Femininity
  heterosexual construction of,
    143, 147
  lesbians, and, 144, 145
  masculinity, opposition to, 151
  mother, taught by, 149
Feminism
  break with, 155
  Jurassic, 143, 151, 153–6
  lesbianism, separation from,
    150, 151
  revolutionary movement, as part
    of, 150
  1960s critique, 146, 147
Fiction
  women, by, 49
Frankenstein
  date of, 53

dissenting text, as, 63
Facts of Life, search for, 55, 56
genesis of, 52, 54
good fathers of, 58
ideological pole, 64
letters and documents, key role
  of, 54
Monster, character of, 59, 60
Paradise Lost, references to, 58
Sandman compared, 53–64
sister figure, woman as, 58, 59
stage play, as, 53
text, afterlife of, 53
textual reader, 158
Victor, effect of death of wife,
  60
women characters, 60
women, voice of, 55
Freud, Sigmund
  Christoph Haizmann, fascina-
    tion with, 57
  Creative Writers and Day-
    Dreaming, 55
  Sandman, key text of, 56, 57
Seventeenth Century
    Demonological Neurosis, 57

Gender
  literature, as concern of, 102
  system, 146
  violent political system, as, 152
Genesis
  creation stories, 4
  Eden story, 3–4, 7
  Milton's reading of, 17
  Priestly Narrative, 4, 8
Gordimer, Nadine
  Conservationist, The, 170
Gothic
  Coleridge, denunciation by, 88
  female characters, 86
  gender confusion in, 89, 90
  iconography, 84
  male characters, 85, 86
  melodrama, 85
  mother, absence of, 87

queer writing, 85, 96
romance form, as, 84
transformations in, 85
Ur-plot, 91
voyeur, motif of, 86
woman writers, 84
Gouge, William, 11, 12
Grimm, Brothers, 70, 71

Haasse, Hella
Een Nieuwer Testament. See Een Nieuwer Testament (Threshold of Fire)
Haizmann, Christoph, 57
Hermaphrodites
sex of, 98, 99
Heteropatriachy
women, view of, 145
Heterosexuality
Eden story, analysis using, 3
femininity, construction of, 143, 147
fictional representations of, 102, 103
foundation myth, 10
grammar of, 3
institution manipulated by state, as, 113, 117
lesbian concern about, 111–13
male and female, differentiating, 115
patriarchal religions, endorsed by, 147
script, fact of, 114
structures, interpretation of, 7
texts, margins and gaps in, 7
women, infantilising, 148
Higginson, Thomas Wentworth, 193
Historical fiction
contemporary problem, concerning, 38
cyclical nature, 38
gaps in knowledge, explaining, 50
history, relation to, 51

homosexual, 37
Jolly Heritage version, 38, 39
seasonal nature of, 37, 38
serious purpose, use for, 37
sources, overdependence on, 46
women, by, 44, 45
writers choosing to write, 36, 37
Hoffmann, E. T. A.
Sandman, The. See Sandman, The.
Homer
epics, narrative of, 161, 162
Homosexuality
English literature, in, 102
narcissism, accusation of, 116
Homosexuals
heterosexual structures of relationships, 147
lies, living, speaking and writing, 7
Human
words and concepts deriving from, 53

Jackson, Stevi, 144, 155
Judaism
nationality, as, 133

Kay, Christina, 24, 26, 27
King Lear
fairy tale mould, in, 75

Language
Caribbean. *See* Caribbean language
Otherness, 133
Lesbians
choosing to be, 149
femininity, and, 144, 145
gene, 149
heterosexuality, concern about, 111–13
institution, changing, 112
lies, living, speaking and writing, 7
radical, 146

revolutionary movement, as part of, 150
sex, representation of, 114, 115, 145
sex, subversive nature of, 151
slogans, 143–5, 149
warrior women, as, 146
women, not, 146
writers, as, 192
1970s, choosing to be during, 111
Lewis, M. G.,
Monk, The, 85, 87–91
Love
courtly, traditions of, 148
social construction of, 147

Marriage
adultery, threat posed by, 13
Gouge, terms of, 11, 12
metaphor of, 16
Milton, writings of, 10
Puritan, 12, 13
Melville, Pauline
Ventriloquist's Tale, The, 158, 159, 163–7, 171
Milton, John
Areopagitica, 18
Ars Logica, 5
contempt of women, 17
creation of woman, story of, 8
daughters, 16, 17
De Doctrine Christiana, 22
divorce, views on, 10
eternal inequality, statement of, 8
first love, 16
Genesis, reading of, 17
God, version of, 21
justification of ways of God to man, 5
justification of ways of God to woman, 6
marriage, view of, 10
misogyny, 14, 15, 19, 20
Paradise Lost. See Paradise Lost

revolutionary, as, 10
solitary pillar of righteousness, as, 22
wives, 10, 11
YHWH, problematic nature of, 6
Mythologies
essences, division into opposites, 3

Namjoshi, Suniti
Building Babel, 182, 183
Narrative
Bible, the, 161
chain, 158
definition, 159, 160
Homeric epics, 161, 162
master, 161
plot, 160, 161
queer, 162, 163
quest, 162
siege, 162
voice, 157
Narrators
implied author, and, 158
reader, relationship with, 157
Nation
ancestral memory, as, 137
belonging to, 138
choice of, 134, 138
Jewish, 133, 134
meaning, 132, 133
National character
nature of, 133
Nichols, Grace
black female sexuality, version of, 139–140
'Configurations', 138, 139
Fat Black Woman's Poems, The, 127–30
i is a long-memoried woman, 126–8
language, view on, 123, 125
Lazy Thoughts of a Lazy Woman, 137
music, working with, 123

nation, defining, 136–7
poems, structure of, 136, 137
'Praise Song for My Mother',
135, 136
psychic narrative technique, 126
Sunris, 121
unbelonging, addressing, 134
'We New World Blacks', 134,
135
Whole of a Morning Sky, 131,
132
Nourbese Philip, Marlene
*Discourse on the Logic of
Language*, 123–5
Novels
first, nature of, 163, 164

Paradise Lost
Eve, creation of, 8, 9
first creation, story of, 5, 6
first publication, 5
Frankenstein, references in, 58
God's Creating Word, story of, 7
lust, view of, 13, 14
theological basis for, 22
Perrault, Charles, 67, 71, 77–80
Poetry
incarnation, art of, 7
Politics
queer, politics of, 155, 156
Pornography
language of, 74
lesbian sex, representation of,
114, 115
moral, possibilities of, 76
Prescod, Marsha, 122
Prime of Miss Jean Brodie, The
Brodie, basis of, 26, 27
love triangle, 28
Sandy Stranger, character of,
28–30, 33, 34
sexual knowledge, intrigue of,
25
sexual substitution theme, 33,
34
Sister Helena, 28, 29

spirit of heroines, narrative
reflecting, 35
spying, 28
themes of, 24, 25
women breaking rules, about, 32
Protestantism
women, view of, 11

Radcliffe, Ann, 84, 86–8, 92
Raymond, Janice
Transsexual Empire, The, 151–3
Readers
identities of, 158, 159
lesbian, decoding text, 183
narrator, relationship with. 157
recipient of text, as, 182
role of, 183
writers needing, 192
Reverie, state of, 52

Saltfish and ackee, 119
Sandman, The
blinding, link with castration
and fear of the father, 63
Clara, character of, 55
Coppelius, identity of, 56
date of, 53
dissenting text, as, 63
father substitutes in, 58
Frankenstein compared, 53–64
Freud, as key text for, 56, 57
hero, dreams and premonitions
of, 52, 54
ideological pole, 64
letters and documents, key role
of, 54
Olimpia, character of, 59
opera and ballet, as part of, 53
sister figure, woman as, 58, 59
text, afterlife of, 53
women characters, 60, 61
women, voice of, 55
Science fiction
women, by, 49
Sexuality
fluidity of, 149

Shakespeare. *See* Woolf, Virginia
Shelley, Mary
  Frankenstein. See Frankenstein
Shreiner, Olive
  Story of an African Farm, The,
    170
Slogans
  lesbian, 143–5, 149
  types of, 143
Smith, Stevie
  'Mrs Arbuthnot', 172–4
Spark, Muriel
  Brontë letters, compilation of,
    24
  Prime of Miss Jean Brodie. See
    Prime of Miss Jean Brodie, The
Stein, Gertrude, 192

Text
  unreadable, 188
  writer existing within, 191
Threshold of Fire. See Een
  Nieuwer Testament (Threshold
  of Fire)
Tolstoy, Leo
  critics, 43
  history, method of making, 45
  War and Peace. See War and
    Peace
Transsexuals
  recreation of women as, 20

Villette
  gallery scene, 33
  Ginevra Fanshawe, character of,
    30, 31
  love triangle, 28
  Lucy Snowe, character of, 30–32
  Lucy, teaching by, 27
  nun, pedigree of, 29
  school play scene, 32
  sexual knowledge, intrigue of, 25
  spirit of heroines, narrative
    reflecting, 35
  spying, 28
  themes of, 24, 25

women breaking rules, about, 32

Wagner, Richard
  Tristan and Isolde, 115, 116
War and Peace
  central characters, 42
  Cossack, interrogation by
    Napoleon, 43, 44
  critics, 43
  hero of, 40, 41
  Kutuzov, character of, 40–42, 50
  narrator, 40
  period of, 39
  publication of, 39
  women, role of, 44
Whately, William, 12
White, Antonia, 133
Wittig, Monique, 144
Women-only institutions
  stories set in, 25
Woolf, Virginia
  end of books, dangerous
    moment of, 185
  loss of writing, 185, 186
  To The Lighthouse, 160, 176–9
  Voyage Out, The, 178
  Waves, The, 179–81
  Writer's Diary, A, 175, 176
  writing, Shakespeare's speed of,
    178, 179
Writing
  desire and attainment, between,
    181
  feminist, intention of writer, 184
  intention of author, 183, 184
  masks and voices, as game of, 182
  narrative. *See* Narrative
  need for, 174, 175
  process, description of, 176
  resurrection, and, 185
  voice of, 181
  women's genre, 192
Writing on the wall
  Belshazzar's feast, at, 188
  unsigned, 188